In the case of social collectivities, precisely as distinguished from organisms, we are in a position to go beyond merely demonstrating functional relationships and uniformities. We can accomplish something which is never attainable in the natural sciences, namely the subjective understanding of the action of the component individuals. . . . This additional achievement of explanation by interpretive understanding, as distinguished from external observation, is of course attained only at a price—the more hypothetical and fragmentary character of its results. Nevertheless, subjective understanding is the specific characteristic of sociological knowledge.

Max Weber
*The Theory of Social and Economic Organization* (c. 1919/1947)

To My Father

# Foreword

America's basic industries need self-examination and renewal to respond effectively to the economic challenges and opportunities of global competition. Even languid, relatively isolated domestic businesses are noticing crossties and interdependencies with many and sundry elements which are pulling them into participation with groups with which they had little connection in the past. Intricate networks, composed of regulators, competitors, supporters, customers, and owners, often form patterns that reach across nations and around the world.

Analytic skill in decomposing these networks, in understanding their structures and potential uses, is of great importance to both working managers and theorists of organizations. For working managers, flexibility and strategic confidence can come from applying network connections to obtain business advantages. For organizational theorists, power relationships among firms are clearer when a systematic network analysis is used. The premise of this study is that a hard look at a single industry's interorganizational network and its responses to international challenge will provide insights and examples helpful to other industries and to the refinement of organizational theory. The interconnectedness of the world has arguably not increased so rapidly as has the general perception by many participants of our interconnectedness. A network framework can provide a systematic way of looking at interorganizational relationships that is equally applicable to placid as to dynamic industries.

# Acknowledgments

It would not have been possible to complete this study without the cooperation I received from many members of the U.S. coal industry, particularly executives at the firm where I worked for seventeen months. That they are not identified here by name is in deference to their desire that this study not identify a specific firm. I am indebted to the candor they showed toward me and to their patience in answering my questions. I was continually impressed by the energy and "quick-study" grasp that many of these individuals displayed in what was a difficult and challenging situation for them. My particular debt to the Director of Planning at the firm where I worked must go unacknowledged here.

Others have also contributed to the work presented here. My academic advisor, Walter Nord, was, throughout my graduate work at Washington University, a stalwart supporter, fine critical reader, and friend. I have learned much about the art of getting the best out of people through nondirective management from his interactions with me. During the evolution of this project, which began as my Ph.D. dissertation, he was patient with my frustrations and at the same time helpful in getting me to clarify my thoughts.

My thesis committee, James W. Davis from political science, David Gillespie from sociology, and Gary Natriello from educational sociology, provided encouragement and consistently good advice in keeping the study on track and in assuring me that I had an interesting story to tell. At a later stage the manuscript benefited from a generous reading by Professor Charles Perrow of Yale University.

I would like also to acknowledge the help of Michael Aiken and his students in a seminar on organizational theory I attended during 1982–83. These sessions helped me bring my ideas into focus and clarified the relationship of my data to the social action perspective of Crozier, Friedberg, and Karpik.

It would be impossible to acknowledge adequately the patience and good cheer of my family over the course of this long project. My children, Alice and David, have hardly known a time when I was not poking out parts of this study on a typewriter. My mother and parents-in-law gave financial and moral support when we most needed it. My husband, Winslow, has been, as always my greatest source of strength, for his unfailing goodheartedness, his keen attention to critical details, and for his remembering to bring me a sandwich when I forgot. Finally, Beverly Stroup made her way patiently through many revisions and tight deadlines on this manuscript. She turned my scratchings into beautifully typed pages. I thank them all. The errors here of judgment or fact are, of course, entirely mine. I want to dedicate the study to my father who was the first to teach me how to combine factual details with complicated arguments. His careful attention to both lives on, I hope, in me.

# Contents

xi

# List of Tables and Figures

## TABLES

## FIGURES

# List of Acronyms

| | |
|---|---|
| AAPA | American Association of Port Authorities |
| AMC | American Mining Congress |
| CEA | Coal Exporters Association of the United States |
| CEO | chief executive officer |
| CIAB | Coal Industry Advisory Board |
| CRS | Congressional Research Service |
| DOC | U.S. Department of Commerce |
| DOE | U.S. Department of Energy |
| DRI | Data Resources, Inc. |
| EEC | European Economic Community |
| ICC | Interstate Commerce Commission |
| ICE | Interagency Coal Exports Task Force |
| ICG | Illinois Central and Gulf Railroad |
| ICR | *International Coal Report* |
| IEA | International Energy Agency |
| IMCO | Intergovernmental Maritime Consultative Organization |
| MARC | Mining and Reclamation Council of America |
| NCA | National Coal Association |
| NERCO | Northwestern Energy Resources Company |
| OECD | Organization for Economic Cooperation and Development |
| USCOE | U.S. Army Corps of Engineers |
| WESTPO | Western Governors Policy Office |
| WOCOL | *World Coal Report* |
| | |
| mtce | metric tons of coal equivalent |
| dwt | dead weight tons |
| | |
| Chessie | Chesapeake and Ohio, Baltimore and Ohio, and Western Md Railroad |
| N & W | Norfolk and Western Railroad |

# 1  *Overview*

This is the story of how the coal industry in the United States responded to changes in a dramatically growing sector of its market—the demand for exports—from 1980 to 1982. The study examines how the industry's responses to this market reoriented its relationships with other groups.

I was originally drawn to these events because, from November 1980 through May 1982, I participated first as a planning intern and then as a consultant to a major U.S. coal firm. In this position I saw that the challenge represented by export trade was unprecedented. Very little information, prior warning, or supporting services were available to help industry participants evaluate emerging factors or advance their aspirations. Also, involvement with exporting coal was bringing U.S. coal producers into direct proximity with the goals of United States foreign policy as never before. A case study of the emerging situation, which was straining normal modes of operation and which had the potential to change the outlook of U.S. coal firms from domestic to more international concerns, seemed an exciting opportunity to examine organization-environment relationships in a dynamic, real-world context.

## Audience

The study is aimed at three audiences: management scientists, institutional sociologists, and government-business policymakers. I feel that these groups are not fully aware of their overlapping concerns. This study attempts to bring together issues which concern all three groups and to examine them in the light of a complex, contextual situation. Although the study is apt to be read somewhat differently by each group of readers, I hope that it will begin to build a bridge between these fields.

*Management scientists.* Formal organizational theorists attempt to derive from empirical studies predictive models for the relationships between organizations and their environments. This approach has usually relied on abstractly defining the characteristic attributes of environmental types and then empirically deriving the characteristics of organizations whose management structures make them suited (best adapted) to cope in a particular setting. Environments are assumed to cause certain management responses to occur. Management scientists have advanced many theoretical explanations for how environments shape organizations. Comparatively little work has focused on how organizations shape their environments. Indeed, for some theorists, this seems to be a definitional impossibility (see Appendix).

Network theorists focus on *inter*organizational relationships. This is an advance over the organization-environment approach, because it implicitly acknowledges that the environment is composed of many interacting organizations. However, network theory has been disappointing in its reliance on single modes and channels of exchange. It has not yet provided a dynamic model of the multiple layers of interaction and their modifications that take place daily. The theories of management scientists are particularly unsatisfying when environments or networks are undergoing fundamental change. Many researchers call for more work in this area, but so far management theories have had trouble predicting the course of business adaptations when change originates in social values or political events beyond the field of normal business operations. Too often management scientists fall back on the uncertainty of a loosely-described "turbulent" environment to explain fundamental managerial and interorganizational changes. Yet, unpredictable political and social factors touch business more and more directly in modern times, and they require the most strategic thinking and planning within organizations. It is essential to advancing managerial theory to pin down what responses to expect from a turbulent environment and to specify how adaptation to it takes place.

This study takes the model prepared by management scientists seriously, but it attempts to provide a different explanation than the correspondence between environmental types and managerial coping mechanisms for how organizations respond to challenges. Rather than focusing on the causal forces in the environment, this study focuses on how organizational actors perceive their environment: how they interpret what they see and what they choose to do about it. There is no such thing as objectively defined turbulence using this approach.

In reading this study, management scientists will be most concerned with the revised interpretation I have offered of organization network relationships and the causal views of the environment I have offered. I argue that patterned relationships in the network can be explained more convincingly as originating in perceptions about the uncertainty the environment presents than in objective, external environmental types. For those readers Chapters 1 and 2—especially those sections dealing with the social action perspective—Chapter 10, Conclusion, and the background presented in the Theoretical Appendix will be most useful.

*Institutional sociologists* have been drawn to the examination of large, whole industries by their importance in modern society and by the desire of these writers to draw out the embeddedness of social trends and historical values in cultural institutions. Until quite recently the contributions of these scholars have been neglected by most mainstream organizational researchers. Writers such as Selznick, Touraine, Goldthorpe, Hirsch, Lindblom, and Wallerstein examine how worldwide trends are played out and how large questions are addressed in specific institutional settings. They follow the comparative historical tradition practiced by Max Weber. Thus, in Philip Selznick's classic study of TVA (1949) the tension between planning and constituency-building stood for the larger question of whether comprehensive, regional planning was possible in a democracy; and Paul Hirsch's examination of the recording and pharmaceuticals industries (Hirsch, 1972, 1975b) provided insights about collusion and oligopoly in free market versus controlled-market industries. The studies prepared in this tradition have emphasized detailed case examinations. They are closely paralleled by the work of the Marxists, who also emphasize historical methods and economic interpretations based on their reconstructions of the motivations and perspectives of organizational actors from contemporary documents. The main implication of the institutional sociologists' approach is that strategic action is decided upon and implemented by interrelated individuals who nevertheless act within the limits of an historical setting, a set of values, and access to fixed, physical resources. These constraints essentially determine their actions.

This study also has adopted a case study approach. It takes seriously the warning of the institutional sociologists to consider historical conditions and political and social contexts as the background for decisions. However, it does not find history and resource constraints in the environment to be automatic determiners of action. Organizational actors exhibited quite varied interpretations of the environment, and they implemented many kinds of strategies in response to the same historical conditions and events. External events were mediated through the interpretations of individuals and led to many different action alternatives. The final outcome of the rearrangements within the industry could not be predicted from the setting itself; it fundamentally depended upon how actors viewed the uncertainty to which they were responding.

Institutional sociologists reading this study will be interested in my findings that realignments in the coal industry's network are favoring large over small firms. Outside ownership is also shown to have important consequences for the network patterns now emerging. The development of the U.S. coal industry from a domestic, parochial industry into an industry with international aspirations, connections, and scope is another finding that this group of readers will be interested in. These themes are traced in the chapters dealing with the historical context and the case study of the coal industry (Chapters 3–9). My interpretation of macropolitics in the U.S. coal industry and the ideas of the French sociologist Lucien Karpik may also be of interest to this group of readers. Karpik's ideas are touched on in Chapter 2 and explained more thoroughly in the Appendix.

*Government-business policymakers* is the third group to which this study is addressed. Government regulators and policy analysts are aware that business today exists in a complex and dynamic political economy. The relationships between government and business and business and society are more and more crucial to the operation of a successful enterprise and thus to the concerns of long-range strategic planners.

The fields of business policy and government regulation have focused on how executives should mobilize their resources given these new contingencies. In many cases, however, these fields have concentrated on prescriptive organizational designs and data-gathering techniques and have neglected the equally important task of developing proactive approaches, a menu of potential strategies, that the firm can use to respond to these new areas of business exposure. Less emphasis has been placed on understanding goal development and choices and on how the environment can be shaped to enhance organizational ends, than on how to assess trends and gather data. Secondly, the relationships between government and business are often not treated with enough sensitivity to the multiple ways in which these groups interact.

Regardless of the degree to which the U.S. coal industry self-consciously and successfully shaped its environment from 1980 to 1982, the general techniques used by industry participants to respond to uncertainty and to shape it to their ends could be applied by managers in other settings. The coal industry's responses offer a diverse menu of interorganizational strategic actions with different interactive implications. The contribution that I hope the study will make to managers is that the environment—particularly the political environment—need not be considered a fixed set of facts and resources. Its leverage on a firm or an industry can be rearranged, deflected, or heightened depending on a variety of strategic options which might be undertaken individually or with members of the interorganizational network. There are lessons here for many other industries entering the international arena.

Government-business policymakers and policy analysts will be most interested in the close analysis I have provided of U.S. energy policy and the increasingly amicable interactions between the coal industry and the U.S. government. These readers may see parallels between coal industry export activities and other business-public policy situations, such as agriculture, strategic weapons, and steel. U.S. coal policy has been inconsistent and often inarticulate. If it were more unified in promoting overseas coal trade, the industry changes I observed would be even more forceful and obvious. This industry's relationships with government are still emerging, and the amount of negotiating space is relatively large. There is still plenty of space for strategic activities by canny managers to shape industry-government interactions.

Government-business policymakers will probably have the most interest in those chapters which focus on current business-government interactions. These issues are treated primarily in Chapters 6–9, although the section on foreign joint ventures in Chapter 5 also has implications for business-government relations. These chapters and their documentation provide background for the relationships between coal industry policy and the public policies adopted toward related industries.

## Problem

The basic problem addressed by this study is: How can we conceptualize the interorganizational relationships that occur in response to a rapidly changing, so-called turbulent setting, and how can we explain or causally model the types of behavior and structural effects that accompany these relationships? Operationally, this question translated into three related questions. What kinds of new interorganizational patterns occurred in the U.S. coal industry as it entered a challenging new market for exporting steam coal? How can we explain the origins of these interorganizational patterns in terms of current interorganizational theory? Finally, what effects did new patterns of interaction have on distributions of power among U.S. coal firms, and what might be socially significant about this reorganization?

## Importance of the Coal Industry

Over half of the world's electrical power is generated from coal, although it provides only 22 percent of the world's total energy (down from 50 percent in 1960). With dwindling supplies of available oil and natural gas and the inherent health risks and political unacceptability of nuclear power, coal is expected again to increase its share of utility, industrial, and commercial energy markets in coming decades, at least until nondepletable and/or renewable energy sources such as solar power, geothermal power, and hydropower can be perfected for large-scale use. Control of coal, the world's most abundant fossil energy resource, will be critical to our future.

From early 1980 and continuously through to the end of 1982, U.S. steam coal was shipped abroad at a rate unprecedented in history.[1] Overseas exports increased from 2.5 million tons in 1979 to 33 million tons in 1981. They dropped to about 25 million tons in 1982.[2] This surge in U.S. steam coal export demand was widely believed to be the beginning of a worldwide increase in steam coal trade which would extend for the next twenty years. Planners predicted that overall world coal use would double or even triple by the end of the decade. To support this increase, world steam coal trade would need to increase tenfold!

The opportunity to export steam coal represented a magnificent growth prospect for the typically slow-growth coal industry.

Before 1980, overseas sales of U.S. coal (which were mainly of metallurgical quality) had been considered by large coal firms an insignificant part of total industry sales. This market sector had become largely the province of small, east coast, Southern Appalachian firms. With the 1979 oil crisis and the subsequent expansion of world steam coal demand, the largest American coal firms began to take an interest in world steam coal trade. In 1980, when expanded demand for overseas steam coal sales was first felt in the United States, the large firms took major, proactive steps and used a diversity of strategies to shape the export environment and its delivery structure to their needs and away from those of the small producers.

## Importance of the Study

As I have said, most conventional literature on organizations and environments gives causal power to the environment in determining the structural relationships between organizations. Successful managerial strategies and interorganizational patterns are interpreted by organizational theorists as evidence that firms have correctly decoded the uncertainty presented by an external situation and have adapted the organization to explicit environmental demands.[3] Both management scientists and institutional sociologists argue that environments exert obdurate, causal influences on the decision-making structures of organizations as well as on their relationships with one another. As I observed what was happening in the coal industry from 1980 to 1982 I say that these traditional explanations of the relationship between the industry and the environment were inadequate to explain interorganizational patterns and changes in interindustry power. Rather than a single pattern of adaptation to the powerful external force of a turbulent environment, I saw a series of simultaneously overlaid patterns of interorganizational relationships.

These patterns did not seem to originate in some powerful shaping mechanism contained in the environment outside the set of organizations I was observing, but rather emanated from the strategies of firms (and groups of firms) in light of what they wanted to accomplish. Perceptions about the problems and opportunities that the new market offered lay behind the strategies and hence behind the characteristic patterns of interorganizational interaction which were occurring.

There was no objectively definable "turbulence" which was forcing the industry to adopt new interorganizational patterns. Instead, different groups and firms in the industry were perceiving the demands of the new market for steam coal exports in different ways and were making different and often multiple strategic responses to it.

Portraying the linkages between interorganizational relationships which form the texture of macrostructure and the strategic perspectives or institutional logics behind them had not yet been addressed in an interorganizational study of a large-scale industry. This study attempts to get close to institutional perceptions and to examine them for their effects on interorganizational behavior and power relationships. It extends the definition of a functional interorganizational network to include continuous processes of exchange and strategic realignments among interacting organizations. It employs the concept "realignments" to stand for patterns in the ongoing process of strategies and operational tactics firms employ within their historically bound settings. As such, I am hopeful that it will provide a more adequate model for describing the processual complexity of interorganizational networks and will help us reconceptualize the causality of organization-environment relationships.

## Themes: Five Types of Realignments

I observed five layered patterns of interorganizational realignment in the U.S. coal industry. They are closely related to what other researchers have associated with responses to different environmental types. The difference is that I observed these patterns occurring simultaneously and in response to one environmental situation. I therefore concluded that they were not indicators of singular types of *environments* but of the variable *perceptions* or interpretations that arise in response to complex and confusing historical reality.

In this study, perceptions which the dictionary defines as insights, observations, or mental images interpreted in the light of experience, refer to institutionally-shared understandings rather than to psychologically interior motives and reflections. An intermediate level of data and interpretation is employed: Between macroinfluences from a determinate environment on one hand and the private reflections of individuals on the other. Activities and statements by corporate actors embody the institutional logic and perceptions about uncertainty that an organized group is attempting to address. Such data display even better than private musings how structural patterns in an interorganizational network originate and become rearranged through organizational strategic choices.

Five levels of alignments emerged in the coal industry's interorganizational network from 1980 to 1982. Each type of realignment included responses to the environment which were directed at trying to control a specific area of uncertainty peculiar to the coal export market and new to many steam coal operating firms. The types of realignments were:

1. Entrepreneurial activities—competition for sales
2. Use and organization of new sources of information
3. Transindustry and intraindustry coalitions
4. Supraorganizational activities
5. Macrocooperation in policymaking

In the following summary, the area of uncertainty is highlighted within the discussion of each type of realignment.

*Entrepreneurial activities.* New entrepreneurial activities were directed at the uncertainty of *effective participation* (survival) in the expanding export market. Firms did their best to respond to unprecedented demand by developing new marketing activities.

Announcements of new coal terminals, foreign joint ventures, innovative contracting procedures, new delivery systems and equipment were all tried to respond to competitive market challenge.

*New sources of information.* The use and organization of information and the availability of expertise gained significance in the new market. New information was needed to specialize and to document and predict the market changes which were occurring. The challenge posed by insufficient and untried *technical knowledge* about how to export steam coal was met by new reliance on conferences, journals, statistical summaries, and consultants. The need for new knowledge formed a layer of industry supporting groups. Many of these sources provided political and economic intelligence about foriegn markets which had been unimportant to major coal companies in the past. Companies tended to cluster around these new information-providers.

*Transindustry and intraindustry coalitions.* Political coalitions and ad hoc groups organized around specific legislative and policy issues. These groups tried to confront the uncertainty of the eventual *distribution of sales and profits* for particular groups of firms. Coalitions were particularly active in areas like port development policy and midwestern and western trade promotion, where the market share among firms would be influenced by government policy considerations (such as railroad ratemaking, inland waterway fees, and harbor taxes). Coalitions generally developed around areas in which firms felt vulnerable and knew the least. Coalition participants tried to retain control of critical issues and resources by pooling their knowledge and energies for individually selfish ends. In coalitions they could use their combined strength to obtain concessions from others. The ability to set the terms of an issue and create conflicts when convenient is an important tool for use of coalitional tactics. Coalitions, brokering, bargaining, and factional power are not new to the U.S. coal industry nor to its interorganizational network (see Ackerman and Hassler, 1981). However, steam coal export issues elicited powerful and dramatic new alliances with the potential to transform the industry.

*Emergence and reorganization of supraorganizations.* Federative-style trade organizations, formed to standardize and regulate export activities and to speak officially and collectively for the industry, confronted the uncertainty posed by *potential regulators* of the emerging market. The Coal Exporters Association was enlarged and reorganized to represent better the interests of larger coal firms in the emerging steam coal export market. Another group emerged to head off interference by international government regulators. The supraorganizations offered self-regulation, standardization of the new market, and centralized negotiation with outside groups. The image the industry tried to create was of responsible coordination and consensus.

*Macrocooperation with policymakers at the national and international level.* In these relationships, coal firms were drawn into cooperative planning relationships with U.S. government representatives, with foreign coal industries, with potential world buyers, and with each other; these new relations reoriented traditional patterns. The essential uncertainty confronted in such groups was coal's *social acceptability.* Important issues bearing on this type of uncertainty were U.S. national security, environmental protection, competing fuel economies, and labor issues; international economic growth; expansion of world electricity demand; the capacity and desirability of mining industries within individual nation-states. These issues involved policy and economic considerations at the very highest levels of world politics.

Coal firms drawn into macrocooperative groups could be expected to attain high stature, both in the U.S. industry and abroad, through their acquired advisory and agenda-setting roles, and to achieve an influential, leadership position within the coal export market.

**TABLE 1.1.   Five Types of Perceived Uncertainty
and Corresponding Network Realignments**

| *Sources of Perceived Uncertainty* | | *Realignments in the Network* |
|---|---|---|
| 1. Market participation | → | 1. Entrepreneurial activities |
| 2. Technical knowledge | → | 2. Organization of information |
| 3. Market distribution, market share, and profits | → | 3. Coalitions |
| 4. Regulation | → | 4. Supraorganizations |
| 5. Social values agenda | → | 5. Macrocooperation |

## Conceptual Model of Network Realignments

Table 1.1 summarizes five types of perceived uncertainty and shows how each type is linked to the particular network realignments I have just described. The realignments are not mutually exclusive; also they do not encompass all that was going on in this situation. I wish merely to provide a framework for showing that network realignments were not the result of the smooth

workings of universal laws of interorganizational network formation which proceeded from the necessities of external events. They
proceeded, instead, from particular institutional views about problems the environment presented. These views will be more fully
discussed in the next chapter.

The overlaid patterns of interorganizational relationships I have
identified can be compared to colored theatrical lighting gels or to
the textbook transparencies used to illustrate three-dimensional interactive systems (such as the human body). Together they create a
complex picture of interactivity. Individually they illustrate levels or
layers of linked similar systems and subsystems.

Many researchers have had trouble finding a way to represent
the complexity of interorganizational networks. Some have solved
the problem by relying on arbitrary definitional boundaries (Aldrich
and Whetten, 1981), or by positing an infinite regress (Scott, 1979).
Charles Perrow (1979) uses an analogy with nested boxes to describe
the way an organization relates in sequence to a larger and larger
network of interrelationships. Each box is constrained by larger
and smaller ones in the series. I prefer the analogy to design
transparencies, because each design or gel contributes a particular
element to the composite effect. Designs can be superimposed in
series and some elements may even appear to interact with one
another, forming new designs, but the particular order of gels is not
critical to the final effect created. When light passes through the
whole set, a total design is revealed. Yet each design or gel can also
be removed and considered separately.

*Organization of the study.* I have organized this study around
my desire to explain the emergence and importance of new relationships in a crucial U.S. industry and my desire to link my observations and explanations to a new understanding of organization-
environment relationships.

This chapter has presented an overview of the themes of the
study. Chapter 2 discusses my theoretical paradigm (the "social action perspective") and my approach and method. (A fuller discussion
of previous literature and of the network model developed here is in
the Appendix.) Chapter 3 provides the historical/structural
background prior to 1980 against which the interorganizational
changes I observed took place. It outlines both the economic structure of the U.S. coal industry prior to 1980 and a history of world coal
exports. Chapter 4 describes the external events, the economic and
historical constraints and opportunities, which entered the relevant
environment of the U.S. industry from 1980 to 1982. It was on the
basis of their perceptions of these events that organizational actors
formed the strategies which altered their interorganizational

relationships. Chapters 5 through 9 describe each of five types of realignments which emerged in the U.S. coal industry's interorganizational network during the time I observed it. and the implications of each type of realignment for power redistribution among firms in the industry. In these five chapters I argue that each type of realignment brought about (in different ways) dominance by the largest U.S. coal firms over the export market, a market they had largely ignored before 1980. Chapter 9 suggests a possible causal explanation for why the export market is being dominated by large steam coal firms. It speculates on the implications of realignments in the coal industry for the larger society. Chapter 10 summarizes the patterns of network realignment I describe and reconnects my interpretive scheme to earlier research on organizational environments.

## NOTES

1. Steam coal is the predominant grade of world coal. It is bituminous coal used to produce heat for industrial boilers and electrical utility turbines. Roughly 80 percent of the coal used worldwide is bituminous steam coal (Lapedes, 1976). Steam coal is different in its essential heating qualities and availability from metallurgical (met) coal which is used in steelmaking. However, both steam and "met" coal are bituminous products.
2. An oil glut and price decline took hold in 1982. The lowered price of oil may cause world coal export growth to stagnate through 1985. Most resource economists agree, however, that the absolute limit on world oil resources means that any "glut" can be only a temporary phenomenon (Barnet, 1980; Bartlett, 1979).
3. My interpretation of the organization-environment dynamic is stated more fully in the Appendix.

# 2 Approach and Method: The Social Action Perspective

## DEFINITIONS

### Definition of the Industry

This study focuses on the U.S. coal industry by which I mean the U.S. producers of bituminous metallurgical and steam coal[1] and their relationships with one another. This is a definition of convenience.

Operationally the coal industry I will describe is a flexible and unspecified group of U.S. coal firms. It can be divided roughly into major producers representing 20 to 50 of the largest firms. These firms are usually active members of trade associations,[2] engage in lobbying activities and public relations campaigns, and often identify themselves as "the coal industry" before national groups. They all produced more than 2 million tons of coal per year. The remaining 3,000 firms in the U.S. coal industry could be called small firms. Their sizes range from 5,000 or 10,000 tons-per-year, family-owned mines to firms producing about 1 million tons. Many metallurgical export mines are among these small firms.

The term industry is not strictly defined in economics (Pearce, 1981). Here it is meant to convey more than a group of competitive producers of an economically substitutable product. Producers of coal in the United States are united by history and common definitions of themselves. They are particularly united by their past relationships with government.

An industry, or at least the dominant coalition of leaders in the critical mass of firms, often promotes homogeneous values and pursues similar functional ends. Through trade associations, internal communications, and public relations activities an industry may even develop a "sense of itself," or at least a sense of the official self its leaders are promoting. These are the images of the industry I will discuss.

The scope of interaction which defines an industry or an interorganizational network is ultimately a set of relationships among people who are exercising conscious personal and political preferences about what activities are relevant to them. They are constantly assessing various strategic options for interaction or noninteraction. Therefore, defining the precise boundaries of a particular industry and network cannot, strictly speaking, be done *a priori*. For convenience I have limited the use of the term industry to a set of coal producers. The interorganizational network is the broader, empirically defined group of organizations with which these producers are involved.

## Definition of the Coal Industry's Network

Equipment companies, railroads, barge companies, ports, terminal operators, banks, oil companies, and engineering firms, which are affiliated with the U.S. coal industry in a variety of roles (such as suppliers, subsidiaries, customers, owners, and service providers) are considered parts of the coal industry's interorganizational network. This conceptualization of an interorganizational network parallels the central chain and supporting groups imagery developed by Brian Scott (1979), who studied the international sugar industry. It is also similar to Perrow's idea of a task environment (1979).

Figure 2.1 is a rendering of the U.S. coal industry's network as adapted from Perrow's diagram of an imaginary community health service network (1979: 222). The industry, the network, and environment are inclusive of one another. As Lucien Karpik (1978) has said, the organization (here an industry) and the environment are not analytically separable, but exist in a mutually defined realm of politically negotiated interrelationships.

Perrow's network diagram represents an ideal mapping not of empirical reality but of the critical associations among functional institutions. Figure 2.1 is divided into four parts. The center is a constellation of tightly coupled, interaction units representing coal producing companies. This is what I have called the coal industry. On the right are the major customers and support groups which feed into or receive supplies from producers. On the top left and center are the service providers (infrastructure) which make it possible for the industry to finance, produce, and deliver its product. These groups are not all closely tied to one another, and each represents a special

**FIG. 2.1. Pictorial Model of the Coal Industry's Network**

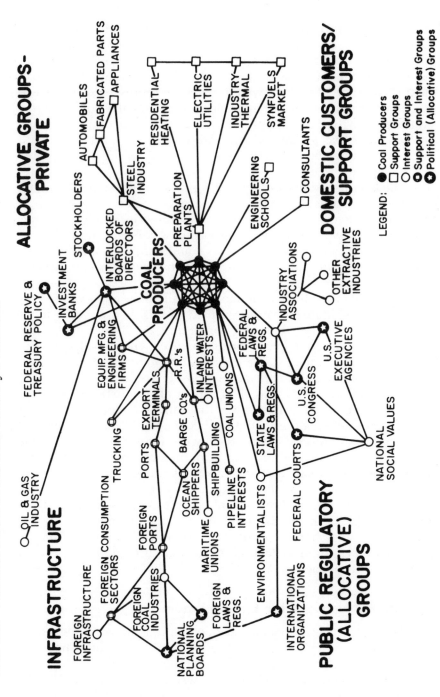

INFRASTRUCTURE

ALLOCATIVE GROUPS—PRIVATE

DOMESTIC CUSTOMERS/SUPPORT GROUPS

PUBLIC REGULATORY (ALLOCATIVE) GROUPS

OIL & GAS INDUSTRY

FEDERAL RESERVE & TREASURY POLICY

FOREIGN INFRASTRUCTURE

FOREIGN CONSUMPTION SECTORS

TRUCKING

PORTS

EXPORT TERMINALS

FOREIGN PORTS

BARGE CO's

OCEAN SHIPPERS

MARITIME UNIONS

SHIPBUILDING

PIPELINE INTERESTS

FOREIGN COAL INDUSTRIES

FOREIGN LAWS & REGS.

NATIONAL PLANNING BOARDS

ENVIRONMENTALISTS

INTERNATIONAL ORGANIZATIONS

FEDERAL COURTS

NATIONAL SOCIAL VALUES

STATE LAWS & REGS.

U.S. CONGRESS

U.S. EXECUTIVE AGENCIES

FEDERAL LAWS & REGS.

INDUSTRY ASSOCIATIONS

OTHER EXTRACTIVE INDUSTRIES

COAL UNIONS

INLAND WATER INTERESTS

R.R.'s

EQUIP. MFG. & ENGINEERING FIRMS

INVESTMENT BANKS

STOCKHOLDERS

INTERLOCKED BOARDS OF DIRECTORS

COAL PRODUCERS

PREPARATION PLANTS

STEEL INDUSTRY

AUTOMOBILES

FABRICATED PARTS

APPLIANCES

RESIDENTIAL HEATING

ELECTRIC UTILITIES

INDUSTRY THERMAL

SYNFUELS MARKET

ENGINEERING SCHOOLS

CONSULTANTS

LEGEND:
● Coal Producers
□ Support Groups
○ Interest Groups
◉ Support and Interest Groups
✪ Political (Allocative) Groups

15

interest or point of view. For example, railroad haulers and barge companies may be competitive or successive haulers of coal. Their interests are very different, and they represent, in most cases, antagonistic points of view. On the lower left of the diagram, government regulatory and allocative interests are represented. These are groups whose access to and influence on the industry (and vice versa) are primarily through political rather than economic channels. Private allocative groups which determine policies and allocate resources within the industry are represented on the upper center of the diagram.

The lengths of lines in Figure 2.1 give an intuitive sense of how closely tied the organizational groups are to each other. Of course, a functional network like this can be elaborated infinitely. It would soon outgrow two-dimensional representation. For example, barge, port, and railroad interests serve as equally important infrastructures for the grain industry. Hence, the coal industry is indirectly linked to grain.

Coal is also one linked commodity chain in the energy industry. The oil and gas industry is represented in this diagram only in its ownership role, rather than as a competitor for similar customers or as another user of delivery infrastructures. The consultants who provide technical advice to the industry are often the same ones advising government and financial interests. It would be impossible to represent the complete network of this or any industry. It is better to think of each intersection in the diagram as a potential starting point for building another complex linked chain. Perrow's image is of a complex molecular structure with tight and weak bonds holding the atoms together. The structure can be disturbed and recomposed by a change in the forces of attraction or by the introduction of new elements. Social systems are in this way analogous to the three-dimensional complex chains found in DNA molecules. They can be analyzed from various beginning points.

On the other hand, the diagram shows that not *everything* is linked to everything else. Parts of the network are relatively isolated or buffered from each other.

## Operational Network for Export Trade

The interorganizational network of the coal industry relevant to U.S. export trade cuts across many of the relationships shown in Figure 2.1. The technical tasks which support coal exports are conceptually the same as those for the whole industry, because the domestic industry's network is simply extended by infrastructure, government policy, and regulation at the import end. Thus Figure 2.1

gives a fairly good representation of the U.S. coal industry's export network. Yet it should be remembered that in this study only issues and relationships relevant to exports will be considered. A great many relationships relevant to the coal industry as a whole will be entirely omitted. Only those which bear on the conduct of overseas export trade will be discussed.

The basic tasks which support U.S. coal exports are very straightforward. They include all the interindustry and industry-government connections needed to bring coal from a mine to its final consumption in a foreign country. This involves coal preparation, inland transportation, transshipment and storage, government regulation, insurance and financing, labor, port facilities, ocean shipping, tariffs, fees and taxes, and domestic competing markets. However, defining these tasks does not describe how the various elements fit together, whether barges or railroads wield more power, whether ports or labor unions are more critical allies for achieving an expanded export market. These relationships can be understood only through direct observation.

In this way the interorganizational relationships in the industry's network are not fixed. The network diagram is a static construction of dynamic relationships. Relationships between interacting groups are constantly being renegotiated and changed.

## APPROACH

### The Social Action Perspective

The approach I have used in this study is based on the social action perspective, which is a practical sociological method and explanatory approach currently being developed by the French organizational sociologists, Michael Crozier, Erhard Friedberg, and Lucien Karpik. Its roots are in the strategic decisions school of organizational studies as practiced, among others, by Barnard, Chandler, Child, Selznick, and Perrow.

Crozier and Friedberg in their book *Actors and Systems* (1980) propose a network model which is based on constant renegotiation of interorganizational relationships depending upon how individual actors (persons or firms) assess their own resource positions and the stakes involved in certain activities. Crozier and Friedberg remind us that organizations are, by definition, *social constructions*. They are set among a collection of other organizations (also social entities) which pose specific problems which each organizational actor has to solve. Organizational actors strategically (i.e., in the context of the opportunities and constraints presented to them and with particular goals in mind) enter into relationships of power and exchange with other actors to solve particular problems. This reciprocal process of exchange and influence defines the relevant environmental stimuli (the relevant network) for that organization. Organizations continually seek to control and to dominate external sources of uncertainty by developing strategies and elaborating permanent procedures to handle their exchanges. They seek interaction modes which will allow them the greatest freedom and autonomy and which will reduce their risks. Organizations (and individuals) do not seek interdependence in a network; they try to avoid it. The continually negotiated set of exchanges in which actors involve themselves can give us insights into the problems organizations are attempting to solve. However, patterns and arrangements of power in a network cannot be derived logically. They must be discerned empirically (Crozier and Friedberg, 1980, Chapter 5).

Crozier and Friedberg emphasize that the network (or relevant environment or interorganizational field) is nonabstract. It can be known only through direct observation of contingency relationships to discover what in an environment is most salient for a particular organization. Although fairly stable patterns of association and interaction of an organization with its surroundings are often enduring (as they serve to normalize frequent exchanges), they are maintained not because they are necessary or rational, but because they are congruent with the goals and mutual strategies of interacting parties. Routines are thus strategies maintained over time.

It is this sense of the interorganizational network as a set of structured, but not fixed, relationships in a prevailing, but not permanent, contingency equilibrium that I wish to convey in this study. The network usually involves a mapable set of suppliers, clients, subcontractors, delivery systems, regulators, and financiers. The precise relationships of these elements to one another can change from day to day or even from minute to minute, depending upon the goals and stakes which exist between them and their abilities to satisfy one another.

I have called the process of emergence of new structural patterns which upset any prevailing equilibrium a realignment in the interorganizational network. Of course, exactly when a new relationship has endured long enough to constitute a new pattern is a matter of judgment and is to some extent irrelevant. The concept I want to put forth is that the alignments in the network are constantly in motion, in that they are continually being negotiated either through their continued formalized use or through minute (or drastic) modifications which take place as the goals and strategies of various parties change.

The major analytic assumption at the basis of this study is that historical constraints and opportunities, acting as stimuli, set up a context which brings about a continuous process of network realignments as responses. These responses are, however, determinately modified, shaped, manipulated, and directed by a set of intervening variables: the personal decisions, strategies, goals, and assumptions of individuals who act based on their views of the environment. Figure 2.2 depicts this key causal relationship.

## Methodological Implications of the Social Action Perspective

The methodological implications of the social action perspective as stated by Crozier, Friedberg, and Karpik are that organizational studies should be conducted in institutional contexts informed by rich descriptions, and explanations unique to the particular setting. The formulation of universal laws is put aside.

The definitions of settings as seen by those involved should not be assumed, but should be the subject of inquiry. Strategies, goals, and assumptions of individuals, how they see the environment, and the rules of the "game" they are playing are then analytically reconstructed from observable events. Thus the primary sources of data are formal statements, documents, and interpretive interviews with organizational actors. In the social action perspective, attitudes are not signs primarily of personality, but of the strategies

**Fig. 2.2. Causal Model: Contingency Model of Network Realignments**

Context:

Historical /
Situational
Stimuli

Responses:

Strategies:
Network
Realignments

Mediation
by Perceptions, Strategies
and Decisions of
Individuals
Based on their "views" of the
Environment

individuals have adopted. By analyzing contextual data in this way—by placing oneself apart as a neutral observer—the sociologist can hope to explicate the situation and can see the kinds of power relationships which exist among organizational and extraorganizational actors.

In the interorganizational situations I observed, network realignments were the concrete illustrations that strategic decisions had been and were being made. By analyzing network realignments it was often possible to infer the specific strategies and sources of uncertainty on which they were based. This is what followers of the social action perspective call reconstructing goals, strategies, and perspectives from observable relationships.

## Views of the Environment Shaped Strategies Firms Employed

Firms, which were the main actors that I observed, exhibited institutional perspectives (influenced by their resource positions, analytic capacities, and data-gathering processes) about what kind of problematic uncertainty the organization should address. They shaped their strategies and operational tactics to fit that uncertainty.

In the previous chapter I identified five types of perceived uncertainty (market participation, technical knowledge, market share and profit, external regulators, and social values agenda) that lay behind new interorganizational patterns in the coal industry's responses to export trade. New interorganizational alignments were formed, based on the strategies and tactics of individual firms. Each type of realignment resulted from simultaneous approaches adopted by a number of firms to deal with that corresponding type of uncertainty. The environment was not perceived as requiring a unified and homogeneous response, but as fragmentary, fluctuating, ambiguous, and even contradictory. Requirements were not imposed on firms *by* the environment, but instead organizations chose to acknowledge certain external constraints (or opportunities) when they invested in strategies to overcome (or enhance) them. When they did so, they created new interorganizational patterns.

One view of the environment did not preclude simultaneous retention of other views and the pursuit of multiple strategies. Groups within firms often disagreed about how to evaluate what the salient characteristics of economic and historical conditions were and which ones should receive priority. Rather than choose, they adopted a menu of approaches. New interorganizational relationships were overlaid simultaneous patterns of interaction in a complex, continually negotiated process of network realignments.

Each of the five views I identified in the 1980–82 export situation with its implied strategy, operational tactic, and interorganizational goal is highlighted in the discussions below. Table 2.1 summarizes the linked relationships.

The model presented in Table 2.1 is, of course, greatly simplified. It helps to show, however, that patterns of interorganizational interaction—not all having the same structural characteristics

**TABLE 2.1. Contingency Relationships Between Sources of Uncertainty and Types of Realignments**

| *Source of Perceived Uncertainty* | *Implied Nonobservable Assumptions* | | *Type of Realignment* |
|---|---|---|---|
| Market participation | view: | environment is simple | Entrepreneurial activities |
| | goal: | survival in market | |
| | strategy: | trial and error | |
| Technical knowledge | view: | environment is differentiated, complex | New sources of information |
| | goal: | meritocracy among firms | |
| | strategy: | specialization | |
| Market share, profits | view: | environment is restricted | Coalitions |
| | goal: | oligopoly | |
| | strategy: | zero-sum operations | |
| External regulators | view: | environment is adversarial | Supraorganizations |
| | goal: | protection of industry interests | |
| | strategy: | coordination among similar interests | |
| Social values | view: | environment is interconnected | Macrocooperation |
| | goal: | institutionalization of industry values | |
| | strategy: | cooperation among dissimilar interests | |

or proceeding toward the same goals—may be ongoing in a network simultaneously. Nonmutually exclusive thematic sources of uncertainty are identified by organizational actors from the stimuli presented by the historical world. These sources of uncertainty are organized by actors into implicit environmental views and are then translated into strategies of interorganizational action. Strategic actions, intended to solve certain kinds of problems (such as survival, information availability, industry protection, etc.) continuously realign interorganizational networks. The sum of ongoing views of problematic uncertainty—sometimes called institutional logics or rules of action—held by organizational participants forms the relevant environment of any organization. (Not all of these logics are identified here; for example, uncertainties of labor relations, capital markets, and technologies of production are barely touched on.) The kinds of strategies or realignments operationalized in a network reveal the stakes or "games" that organizational actors are playing and the relative distribution of power among firms. Perceptions about uncertainly and patterns of interorganizational realignment (and the assumptions which they imply) overlap, but this in no way alters the critique they imply of conventional organization-environment theory. The central causal agent for network realignments in this model of network interaction remains the freedom of organizational actors to make decisions, rather than the force of the external circumstances surrounding them.

1. *First view*. Viewing the environment as a *simple market* implied the strategy of *trial and error competition* among similar firms and innovative *entrepreneurial activities* as an operational tactic to capture business. Scrambling by coal firms to make sales was based upon a view that the environment held grand opportunities for a multitude of capable firms competing equally on the basis of price for new business. The major strategies involved were trial and error marketing and direct price-competition with other coal producers. Emphasis was placed on doing "one's best" in each particular case. Firms tried to provide guaranteed quality, services, accessibility, delivery efficiency, prices, or whatever the customer might desire to assure sales. Profitable participation and *survival* in the new market—if only gaining a foothold—were the goals. Hence, all firms to the extent that they were dominated by this thinking were scouting for the best business partners to guarantee their future sales and were promising the most desirable terms to potential buyers. There was no central decision-making mechanism or common goal in this interorganizational network pattern. Survival seemed to be based on luck as much as on expertise or services.

2. *Second view.* A view of the environment as *differentiated and complex* implied operational or product specialization. The emphasis shifted to quality rather than mere performance. Since coal is a relatively undifferentiated, unbranded product, but with many quality gradations, the tactical shift was to the *use and organization of information and expertise.* Those firms which could command specialized knowledge or sophisticated "intelligence" judged that they could possibly obtain an extra edge in sales. Many firms invested in *specialization* by attending conferences, subscribing to journals, and engaging consultants. Some formed new sales or international departments. Some firms specialized quickly in a focused market area such as France, Spain, Germany, or Japan. Others exploited their knowledge of barge-shipping or pipeline technology, or their experience with previous foreign sales to offer customers specialized services. Firms scrambled to master complex information quickly. The implied goal of this view is to rise to the top of a *meritocracy* by obtaining the best expertise or providing the best service in a particular focused area. Competition remained the prevailing mode of interaction, but clusters of supporting groups formed.

3. *Third view. Coalitions* as an operational tactic were based on the perception (or fear) that the market for coal exports would be *demand-limited* and would soon become a relatively stable, normalized system to be divided among only a few participants. The capabilities of firms and/or the demand for coal were viewed as capped-off. This view implied an eventually *oligopolistic* market. Each organization improved its own chances of dominance and success by hindering those of others and by judiciously playing off its position against the calculated reactions of competing interests. The strategy which influenced organizational activities was *zero-sum operations,* to obtain the most favorable position for oneself. Since the terms or stakes kept changing, coalitions were generally short-lived, ad hoc groups which had limited focus and high issue consensus. In the coal export environment coalitions quickly grew up around passage of a Coal Port Development Bill. The implied goal of this jockeying for position was a power oligarchy in which a group of firms with the swiftest comprehension in determining the stakes of a particular issue (the fastest footwork in obtaining concessions, alliances, and managing the opposition) were able to control the terms of the market to their advantage. Decision making in this type of network pattern was by bargaining. Leadership came to those who could gain practical concessions and results.

4. *Fourth view. Supraorganizations* emerge generally in response to an adversarial view of the environment. Firms seek

safety in numbers. They consolidate their efforts and band together to withstand threats they perceive from the outside. However, individual firms pursue such strategies for two somewhat different reasons. Officially and ostensibly they seek *industry coordination* as a protection from external regulation, through egalitarian representation of a number of equally participating firms. Joining together in supraorganizations thus implies a strategy of buffering the vulnerability of individual firms by presenting a united front. To borrow a phrase from Burton Clark (1965) confederation is chosen as a way of "concerting action without bureaucracy" (p. 233). Supraorganizations can take actions on the part of an entire industry which serve to protect and represent it. Two examples of this representative supraorganizational activity were the development of a task force to address problems in transporting large quantities of steam coal (the "Hot Coal" Task Force) and testimony by the National Coal Association before congressional committees. Decision making in this network pattern was usually based on voting. Industry power was assigned to a federation.

In practice, supraorganizations nearly always draw their power from a combination of the autonomy they achieve above and beyond their individual members and from their frequent cooptation by powerful voices from within their membership, which they represent more fully than others. Supraorganizations often are able to achieve a status of institutional legitimation which assumes that they speak consensually about the needs of a particular group, when in actuality their positions are merely those of their most powerful members clothed in institutional garb. To the extent that supraorganizations are manipulated by powerful firms, supraorganizations do not reflect merely a common refuge from external regulators but also an oligopolistic strategy on the part of individual firms. The supraorganization itself can become one more zero-sum tactic employed by powerful firms to obtain a favorable position in an unpredictable situation. Both representative and oligopolistic supraorganization activity occurred during 1980–82. Decision making in the oligopolistic supraorganization was orchestrated by dominant firms.

From the outside, supraorganizations want to be seen as a representative voice for their constituency—an institution for focus and coordination which provides an official point of reference and *legitimation* for industry views. The network pattern which emerges is one of shieldlike *unity and consolidation* against outside threats.

5. *Fifth view.* When firms act as though their fortunes are tied to a variety of disparate, formerly conflicting, interests and events, they display a view that the environmment is *interconnected*. A

multiplicity of cross-linkages seem to connect a vast array of previously opposed interests. The view is of deepening interdependence, increased interaction of economic organizations with legislation and public policy, and heightened unpredictability caused by newly emerging values in a widened environmental field. *Macrocooperation* becomes a tactic when industry, government, clients, and supporting industries work together to modify a values crisis or to forecast and plan toward an uncertain future. Strategies to achieve stability, given the premises of this environmental view, involve *cooperative relationships among dissimilar organizations* whose fates are becoming positively correlated. Network decision making is often consensual. National and international advisory groups and cooperatively developed policy recommendations are examples of macrocooperative mechanisms in the coal export network.

Organizations which view the environment as interconnected use their individual interests and expertise to support a far-reaching policy agenda favorable to all cooperating parties. They may even develop a sense of *noblesse oblige* toward weaker members. Their goal is the *institutionalization of group values*. The result of macrocooperation can be collusion, in which monolithic power is asserted over the social agenda, or macrocooperation may lead to a broad transformation of social values and centralized national planning. When new values become indigenous to a cultural situation and are in the interests of an array of cooperating organizations, their goals interfuse. Among the changes that occur from the interfusion of business and political goals and social values is that "the executive becomes a statesman" (Selznick, 1957: 154). Business and public policy are united. The U.S. coal industry was becoming involved in the strategic designs of world governments and of multinational corporations. Whether the resulting fusion is viewed as a humanistic transformation bringing enhanced ability to solve complex problems (Metcalfe, 1978), or as an example of the imperialistic hegemony of capitalism (Karpik, 1978; Weiss, 1981; Barnet and Muller, 1974) may be less determined by the actual events than by approval or disapproval by a particular observer of the values represented in any particular social transformation and the faith we have in the possibility of a future based on consensual rather than conflictual social relations. In other words, consolidation of values in pervasive political and economic institutions could promote social conformity, economic subservience, and political tyranny, or might lead us to a fuller, more enlightened world.

Coal is a fundamental energy source. The many ties of this industry to the essential operation of world industrial life mean that any major change in its market or delivery structure might have repercussions that could augur a social values transformation. Whether this will be a positive or a threatening development is examined here.

## METHOD

### Empirical Indicators of Network Realignments

Table 2.2 identifies the empirical indicators which illustrated each type of realignment I identified in the 1980–82 coal export

**TABLE 2.2. Types of Realignments Occurring in the Coal Industry's Interorganizational Network and Their Observable Indicators, 1980–82**

| Type of Realignment | Network Indicators |
|---|---|
| Entrepreneurial Activities | coal terminal announcements<br>foreign joint ventures<br>new export delivery systems<br>procedural changes |
| Sources of Information | trade data<br>journals<br>consultants<br>government reports<br>conferences |
| Coalitional Activities | interindustry alliances<br>conflict creation<br>ad hoc industry groups<br>lobbying executive departments and Congress |
| Supraorganizations | new and reorganized trade associations<br>industry task forces<br>official testimony |
| Macrocooperation | industry-government panels<br>executive and congressional policy statements<br>official documents of international groups |

industry and from which the particular strategies, goals, and tactics of firms and their views of the environment were reconstructed.

The layers of interaction I have identified revealed that the largest steam coal firms were increasing their dominance and hold over the export market in 1980–82.

## Data Sources

The primary data for this study were gathered during the course of work I did for a major coal firm from November 1980 through May 1982. During this time I spent approximately twenty hours per week at the corporate headquarters of the firm. I reported to the Senior Vice-President for Legal and Public Affairs, and I worked closely with the Director of Corporate Planning and the Vice President of Government Affairs of the firm. Much of my work centered on the company's response to demand for steam coal exports.

My role with respect to this research was that of participant-as-observer. Many of the events affecting coal exports were ones in which I had some advisory or participatory role. I did not conceal my interest in observing the course of events and in analyzing how the industry was responding to them. Top executives in my firm were aware that I wished to turn these observations into a formal study. But I did not conduct formal interviews or identify myself in a primarily research role. My observations are based on roughly 1,300 hours of direct involvement in one firm.

My involvement within one firm afforded me access on a daily basis to current industry publications on the rapidly changing export situation as it was actually occurring. It also allowed me to observe the attitudes of coal executives who were engaged in export trade. My participation in the industry also made available to me internal memos, records of interorganizational events, and data which provided insights into overall industry relationships, positions, and strategies. Examples are memos from NCA and AMC to their affiliate members which outlined the industry's legislative positions, and information about the decisions made at NCA board meetings. I have purposely filtered out those events and perspectives peculiar to the firm in which I was working, and I have tried instead to present a picture of the whole coal industry. Although my position within one firm was a priviledged position which could potentially bias my analysis of the industry as a whole, this inside perspective has been invaluable in helping me disentangle the informal (nonpublic) assumptions and institutional perspectives behind actions.

During my participation in the coal industry I continuously reviewed trade periodicals and read government reports on coal exports. I collected the available documents I could find on emerging coal trade. I attended internal policy-making meetings with the top executives of my firm on legislative and public relations issues. I made recommendations for this firm's export strategies. I also met with members of other firms and with members of the National Coal Association to discuss legislative issues. I prepared testimony for and attended several public hearings. I kept detailed reading notes of the documents and memos I read and extensive conversation notes of the meetings I attended. In addition, I kept written records of conversations I had with individuals on the telephone, and brief notes of personal interactions. Because the firm where I worked was an industry leader and active in export trade, these written records provided a rich running account of how key individuals in the industry, in Congress, in related industries, and in government were responding to the export situation during 1980–82.

Nevertheless, I have tried to rely on publicly available archival and documentary data sources to reconstruct industry strategies and to draw my conclusions. This has both preserved the privacy of the firm where I worked and increased the validity of my generalizaions about the whole industry. It is also more in keeping with my purpose of describing the effects of institutional perspectives on interorganizational structural patterns rather than relying on personalized and private comments.

One major source that has been helpful here are the fifteen volumes of congressional hearings on coal exports at which many industry officials spoke and which had made their way to library shelves by the time of this writing. These volumes provided a wealth of anecdotal and technical information on industry activities and attitudes which extended beyond my own firm. Much of this evidence confirmed observations I had made originally in one setting. In writing up my observations I have tried to choose from the public record the most succinct and dramatic examples of industry opinions to illustrate my points. The same points could have been made with many other examples from other public and nonpublic sources.

Focusing on the industry as a whole, rather than on one firm, has proved challenging. At a minimum it has meant that I must explain the changes I observed in the context of both the historical development of the U.S. coal industry and of world coal trade. After I left the coal firm, I expanded my knowledge of the U.S. coal industry with wide reading about the history and economics of the

U.S. coal industry and—to the extent possible given the dearth of available sources—about world coal trade. For this phase of my work I drew on both contemporary and historical secondary sources and news articles.

## Data Limitations

The limitations of the study are obvious. I was involved in the coal industry for only a short time. I had no previous knowledge of it. I was performing a dual role as both an advisor and participant in one firm and as an observer of a complicated ongoing situation affecting the whole industry. I was located in one firm and one office within that firm and information was filtered to me in that role.

The situation demanded a hybrid use of research methods. Obviously, time and resources would not permit me to interview all major industry participants, even if my affiliation in one firm had not already made that ethically questionable. Instead, my observations in one firm provided a hub which I used to check insights and to fill out my knowledge from other sources. My direct observations helped me to see where to look for interesting data or to see where problems might arise. For the most part, perceptions and institutional rules of action have been reconstructed from public statements and reconfirmed in my single-institution observations. My period of observation, fortunately, was long enough to allow for modifications and subtleties.

There were severe limits in the industry's own record keeping and available data base about coal exports at this time which made getting a handle on the export situation difficult. It took me many months after leaving, for example, to reconstruct from available information the world trade picture for exported coal. Some of these data limitations were important influences on the responses the industry was making to the uncertainty of the export situation, and they are discussed in Chapter 6 on sources of information. The absence of information was an important source of data to me and an important reason for many industry realignments.

Another limitation was caused by my entry on the scene in November 1980, which was after the first effects of the 1980 export boom had begun. I was thrust into the midst of the industry's confusion over the meaning of its new export market. I have had to reconstruct the beginnings of this boom and its origins from documents and from the remembrances of participants in order to construct a baseline for the study. Of course, this reconstruction lacks the immediacy that observation at this earlier stage would have offered.

I have taken practical and theoretical steps to counteract these limitations. Charles Perrow has said that operative goals are best judged by the actions organizations take. Lucien Karpik enjoins students or organizations to examine the institutional "logics of action" of firms as they are revealed in the statements and actions of top executives. These, he says, can be analyzed by a neutral observer to reveal the structural links between powerful organizations and society. Examining behavior of organizations and statements of leaders is the logic that my study has followed to link perceptions about uncertainty to strategies and interorganizational realignments. I have assumed that public statements of leaders and time and resources committed to policies were valid indicators of the goals that large organizations were trying to pursue.

Practically, I have made a conscientious effort to be sure that the information I received and from which I generalized about the entire industry was available to others, and that it reflected a fair sampling of what was being published, discussed and done about coal exports at this time.

Being located in one firm is a potential source of bias, but it is difficult to imagine how another researcher could have gotten the richness, depth of understanding, and immediacy that my position offered without an inside industry position such as I had. One can regret that the observation period did not exactly coincide with the export boom, but there are unforeseen limits to all longitudinal and observational studies. I was located in a firm that was well recognized in the industry. I was in the office of that firm which was involved in making interorganizational decisions about export trade. The information routinely available to me would have been prohibitively expensive for a researcher to amass from outside a coal firm, because most of it was from small-circulation periodicals available only in a few widely-scattered libraries. The opportunity to judge unobtrusively the assumptions of working industry executives as they went about the job of responding to a new challenge would have been impossible to obtain in any other way.

## NOTES

1. Lignite and anthracite producers and exports are not considered in this study. Lignite does not travel in international trade. U.S. anthracite exports average about 1.2–2 million tons per year. They are not expected to increase.

2. The coal industry's major trade associations are the National Coal Association (NCA), the Mining and Reclamation Council of America (MARC), and the American Mining Congress (AMC). There are also sundry state associations and other trade groups.

# 3    *Historical Constraints and Opportunities to 1979*

U.S. coal trade and changes in the industry's interorganizational network from 1980–82 are intimately tied to the organizational structures of foreign coal industries and of world coal commerce.

Coal mining is an old industry, and coal is a widely distributed resource. Mineral economists estimate that currently known coal reserves could supply world energy needs for 200 years. But European coal seams are becoming depleted and there are virtually no coal resources in Japan. Thus, increased coal trade will be needed to sustain or to increase current coal use.

## WORLD COAL TRADE

### Coal Industries Abroad

Coal industries are under national control in all countries except the United States, Canada, Australia, South Africa, and West Germany. (Most German production is state-owned.) Because of its wide availability and predominantly local consumption, mining and coal trade have never become cartelized on a world scale. Unlike the international "families" which facilitate grain trade, and the favored contractors that distribute weapons, governments usually conduct coal trade without middlemen. No coordinated, international coal trading system exists. Even within the European Economic Community (EEC), national governments plan production and trade goals for their coal industries (the United Kingdom and West Germany as well as France and Belgium) without consulting each other. Import quotas, price subsidies, and carefully monitored production goals emphasize the fact that in most foreign nations coal industries are carefully protected to preserve national economic security and jobs. Coal policy holds great importance in the domestic politics of these countries, decisions are frequently based on political concerns rather than on economic criteria. This embedding of foreign coal industries within the national political consciousness of nation-states has many implications: For example, foreign coal executives are frequently accorded high status and are drawn from a socially prominent and politically adept elite comparable to the U.S. foreign service corps. These backgrounds contrast sharply with the scrappy, self-made owners of many U.S. firms.

In every country of the world except the United States, energy use (not just coal) is closely supervised. Electricity supply boards and national energy planning commissions determine annually the purchase amounts and mix of primary energy fuels in their economies: how much will be domestically produced; how much imported; how much coal, nuclear energy, or oil will be used. National governments are often the primary negotiators for imports. Fuel is allocated to various economic sectors by government bureaucracy.

## World Coal Trade to 1979

When I began studying U.S. coal exports, it was dismaying to discover how little information was available about world coal trade. The information that existed did not distinguish metallurgical from steam coal volumes. I had a great deal of trouble piecing together a picture of U.S. trade and the world market through 1979 which would provide some baseline against which to compare the 1980–82 U.S. surge. Accurate, officially recognized information about pre-1979 trade was simply not available. I put together best-guess estimates and compared information from scattered sources, such as the U.S. Department of Commerce, U.S. State Department, United Nations, and European Coal and Steel Community. The magazine *World Coal* was also helpful. The estimates presented here are therefore best guesses, although they are probably as accurate as any that were being used by industry and government at the time.

The major exporters of coal in the world market in 1979 were the United States, Poland, Australia, South Africa, Canada, West Germany, and the United Kingdom.[1] Total world trade in coal up to 1979 was about 200 million tons. It may have reached 230 million tons in 1979 (*World Coal*, 1980: 30). International coal movements were about 70 percent metallurgical coal, i.e. 140–160 million tons and 30 percent steam coal. Table 3.1 shows the approximate total trade volumes of coal shipped by exporting countries from 1977 to 1980.

Most analysts estimate that only 50–60 million tons of steam coal was traded annually through 1979 (WOCOL, 1980; The Energy Bureau, 1980; ICF, Inc., 9/80 1–3). George Markon, an international trade analyst, has some evidence that steam coal might have jumped to as much as 82 million tons in 1979 (*World Coal*, 1980: 37), but this cannot be confirmed.

It is certain that much of the steam coal traded in world commerce in 1979 traveled only short distances, such as from the United States to Canada (11 million tons) or from Poland to the Soviet Union and to Western Europe (about 30 million tons). Thus, perhaps as little as 25 million tons of steam coal was being delivered long distances by oceangoing ships (see Table 3.2).

**TABLE 3.1.  Major World Coal Exporters:**
**Total Coal Shipped 1977–1980**
**(million metric tons)**

| *Exporting Country* | *1977* | *1978* | *1979* | *1980* |
|---|---|---|---|---|
| United States | 49 | 37 | 60 | 83 |
| Poland | 39 | 40 | 41 | 31 |
| Australia | 38 | 39 | 40 | 43 |
| U.S.S.R. | 28 | 29 | 26 | 25[c] |
| South Africa | 13 | 15 | 23 | 28 |
| Canada | 12 | 14 | 14 | 14 |
| China, P.R.[b] | 0.5 | 0.8 | 1.5 | 6 |
| West Germany | 15 | 19 | 16 | 13 |
| Czechoslovakia | 3 | 4 | 4 | 4[c] |
| United Kingdom | 2 | 2 | 2 | 1 |
| France | 0.6 | 0.5 | 0.5 | 0.5 |
| Netherlands | 0.4 | 0.4 | 0.9 | 1.5 |
| Belgium/Luxembourg | 0.3 | 0.3 | 0.3 | 0.6 |
| Other | 2 | 1 | 1 | 1.6 |
| Total[a] | 203 | 201 | 231 | 252 |

[a]Totals may not add due to rounding.
[b]Excludes trade with N. Korea.
[c]Estimated.
*Source*: Markon, *World Coal*, November 1981, p. 44.

**Table 3.2. Major Shippers and Receivers
of Steam Coal in 1979 (million metric tons)**

| Exporting Country | Tonnage Shipped | Long Distance Ocean Tonnage[a] | Importing Countries | Amount Received |
|---|---|---|---|---|
| Poland | 30[b] | 3[c] | Western Europe[d] | 19 |
| | | | CPE countries | 11 |
| | | | U.S. | 0.5 |
| South Africa | 19[e] | 17 | EEC countries[e] | 16 |
| | | | U.S. | 0.5 |
| | | | Japan | 0.4 |
| | | | Other Asia | 0.1 |
| United States | 13[f] | 2 | Canada[f] | 11 |
| | | | Western Europe | 1.5 |
| | | | Asia | 0.4 |
| Australia | 6[g] | 6 | Western Europe | 4.5 |
| | | | Japan | 1.6 |
| Other[h] | 2 | 0 | Intra-EEC | 2 |
| U.S.S.R. | 11[i] | unknown[j] | CPE countries[i] | 10? |
| | | | Finland, Denmark | 1? |
| Total | 70–80 | 25–35? | | |

[a]Author's estimates of long distance trade.

[b]Markon, *World Coal*, Nov. 1978, p. 21. Proportion of steam coal estimated from totals.

[c]Only about 1 million tons of Polish coal travels long distances by sea to Greece, the United Kingdom, and the United States. The remainder which is seaborne goes short distances to Baltic Sea ports, perhaps 7 million tons.

[d]Estimated based on data from Markon, Nov. 1980.

[e]Markon, *World Coal*, Nov. 1980.

[f]U.S. Bureau of Mines, export data, received from NCA (converted to metric tons).

[g]NCA, *International Coal Review*, May 12, 1982.

[h]Primarily from West Germany.

[i]Reported by Doerell, *World Coal*, Dec. 1979 for 1978 Soviet trade.

[j]Most Soviet shipments of steam coal probably travel by rail to CPE destinations.

## Assessment of Major U.S. Competitors for Steam Coal Trade

Among the major competitors for U.S. steam coal trade, in reverse order of importance, West Germany and the United Kingdom export primarily within the European Economic Community. Both have occasionally been net importers in recent years. West Germany exports primarily metallurgical coal to its EEC neighbors and it imports steam coal. The United Kingdom enters and leaves the export market according to decisions of its

National Coal Board. In 1979, the United Kingdom had a net balance of 1 million tons of exports. Both the United Kingdom and West Germany are deliberately scaling down their coal industries.

Canada has a small coal industry primarily in the western provinces. During the 1970s Canada sent 10 million tons of metallurgical coal per year to Japan. Canada may have the potential to enter the steam coal market, if it can develop rail infrastructure to its west coast ports. However, Canada is not likely to become a major steam coal exporter. WOCOL (1980) projected that Canada would probably export only 24 million tons of steam coal by 2000.

Poland is a major steam coal supplier. Poland divides its coal exports between European communist (CPE) countries, primarily the U.S.S.R., and the EEC. Polish exports are normally about 40 million tons per year. Of this about 30 million tons is steam coal. Poland's coal production is drawn from seams which are becoming worked out. Labor unrest is likely to be a continuing problem. Poland's industry is expected to decline or at best remain at current production levels in the coming years.

Australia and South Africa are relative newcomers to world coal trade. Each has a developing coal industry with potential for rapid expansion. Australia entered international coal trade in the early 1970s when large American investments began to spur mine development to supply metallurgical coal to Japan. Currently, Australia exports roughly half of its total production. Exports in 1979 were 40 million tons. However, steam coal exports were only 6 million tons (NCA *International Coal Review,* 5/12/82). Steam coal mines are being developed, and exports could grow to 75 million tons by the year 2000 according to WOCOL (Vol. 2, cited by ICF, Inc., 8/80). Australia is likely to be a major competitor for U.S. trade to Asian countries.

South Africa is primarily a coal fueled economy. It expanded its steam coal shipments to Europe following the first oil embargo in 1973. South African mines were developed with British, Dutch , and French investments. Ninety percent of South African exports are steam quality. Exports increased each year after 1973, from just 2 million tons in 1975 to 23 million tons in 1979 (*World Coal,* 1981; 1980). South African exports accounted for the slight expansion in world steam coal trade from 1973 to 1979. They made up for domestic production declines in France and West Germany. By 1979, 21 percent of South Africa's production of coal was entering world trade. South African exports will probably continue to expand. The country has opened a major port at Richards Bay and is planning two major phases of port expansion. WOCOL estimated that South African exports would probably reach 55–75 million tons by 2000. However, the South African government officially places limits on export tonnage to protect its policy of energy self-sufficiency. This policy could restrict the amount of South African coal allowed to enter the world market. Nevertheless, the government projects an export level of 55 million tons by 2000. South African coal is low in price and in sulfur content. It is a major competitor for U.S. steam coal trade to Europe.

This profile of factors relevant to international coal trade in 1979 set the stage for changes which began to be felt by the U.S. coal industry in 1980. What is important to remember is that prior to 1980 world steam coal trade was miniscule. The coal mining industries in other countries were carefully protected national interests with significant domestic importance and official involvement in national politics. Among the coal industries competing with the United States for export sales, all exhibited greater reliance on coal exports and greater interfusion of goals with their national governments than did the coal industry in the United States. Thus, the leaders of these industries were more accustomed to diplomatic policy-making than were U.S. coal leaders.

To some extent any involvement in sales of an export commodity places U.S. industry in a special relationship with its own and with foreign governments. However, the fact that this commodity was considered crucial to economic health and industrial survival by customers, was embedded in the official governmental structures of consuming nations and of competitive selling countries, and the fact that U.S. coal producers had little experience with this type of trade placed new expectations and strains on the U.S. coal industry.

## THE U.S. COAL INDUSTRY

### Geographic Context

The U.S. coal industry has the world's largest production capacity. Contrary to mining industries abroad, it includes many competing firms. Currently, the U.S. coal industry includes over 3,000 coal producing companies, most of which own only one or two mines.

The coal industry is concentrated in three regions of the United States:

1. The Appalachian states of Kentucky, West Virginia, Pennsylvania, Virginia, and Maryland.
2. The midwest, especially Illinois and Ohio (and to a lesser extent Indiana, Western Kentucky, and Missouri).
3. The west, Montana, Wyoming, Colorado, and Utah.

In the east, mining firms are usually small. Underground mining methods predominate. The midwest has medium and larger firms which use both underground and surface methods to remove coal.In the west, enormous reserves are being developed by very large coal companies and by oil companies using surface mining methods.

The majority of industry production is still located in the east. However, U.S. coal production is moving from east to west. Wyoming, Montana, and Illinois are expected soon to produce over half of U.S. coal. The U.S. Energy Department predicts that by 1995, 47 percent of U.S. coal will come from west of the Mississippi River (Congressional Quarterly, 1981: 69).

## Economic Issues

The economic history of the coal industry has been one of alternating periods of boom and bust. During periods of high demand many small companies expand their production to full time. But because of the high sunk-cost of opening new mines, firms are slow to leave the market during slack times. This leads to price cutting.

The coal industry characteristically has low profit margins compared to other basic industries (Chakravarthy, 1981). There is some evidence that companies more heavily reliant on export sales realize higher profits than primarily domestic firms (Moyer, 1975), but whether this is due to differential pricing for exported coal (primarily metallurgical quality) or to other factors is hard to say. There is certainly less public oversight of U.S. coal prices in foreign markets than in domestic sales.

*Size of firms.* Risser (1958) and Moyer (1964) showed that U.S. coal firms tend to be either very large or extremely small. Either larger companies have swallowed up the medium-sized firms, or the medium-sized companies have disappeared. Thus, below the top fifty major producers with average annual productions of at least 2 million tons, the average size of firms drops off quickly to less than 100,000 tons yearly. Over a thousand firms produce much less than 100,000 tons of coal each.

The top fifty firms in the industry can be considered major companies. The top fifteen to twenty which have average annual productions of about 20 million tons, I consider very large. Yet, even the largest companies in the U.S. industry are not especially big by the standards of other industries. The largest coal firm, Peabody Coal Company produces 60–70 million tons of coal. It had $1.2 billion in sales in 1983, which was just 8 percent of the annual U.S. coal market (*Million Dollar Directory*, 1983). Consolidation Coal, the second largest company, produces about 50 million tons of coal per year. Firms below the top fifty producers are for purposes of this study small firms. (See Table 3.3 for size of producers, 1976, 1980.)

Small mining firms are often so small that it is difficult to find out much about them. The 10,000–50,000 tons-per-year mines might employ 5–25 people, all of whom are direct mine workers. Obviously, there is little central administrative staff or planning in such firms. Many of these companies do not participate in trade groups or associations. Their contact with the market is through independent coal brokers, the sales departments of larger coal firms,and through the railroads which haul their product to market. Virtually all small coal companies are located in the older coal mining regions in the eastern United States. This is also where all U.S. metallurgical coal reserves are found.

Small producers have been particularly active in the export market where "spot" sales offer them flexibility and good prices. They do not usually hold long-term contracts. Two-thirds to three-quarters of U.S. export sales through 1980 were handled by small and medium-sized firms, according to coal industry spokesmen, although the exact sizes of these firms is often unclear.[2]

*National market concentration.* During the 1950s the coal industry became the primary supplier of fuel to the electric utility and steel industries—these being coal's only nondeclining markets (Gordon, 1975). Many coal companies merged. Traditionally major firms in the industry consolidated their power. Peabody Coal Company acquired 10 firms; Consolidation Coal got 8; Island Creek 7; Pittston 6. By 1968, the fifty major firms controlled about 70 percent of total production. The U.S. government became alarmed about the growing concentration of American coal sales. Kennecott Copper was eventually forced to divest its holdings of Peabody Coal (Loomis, *Fortune*, 1977). Since 1977, industry concentration levels have remained steady. Roughly two-thirds of U.S. production is held by the top fifty firms.

In spite of the government's concern, economists now agree that the period of mergers was essentially a survival tactic for the industry (Newcomb, 1978). The low cost of oil, with its tax credits for foreign exploration, and the beginning of nuclear power research meant that coal was having a hard time competing with other energy sources. Mergers were an effort to control excess coal supply.

After a series of investigations, the Federal Trade Commission (1978) concluded that oligopoly in its strict economic definition did not prevail in the U.S. coal industry. (The top four producers produced less than 50 percent of total production.) In fact, the U.S. coal

**TABLE 3.3.** Concentration of Production in the U.S. Coal Industry, 1976, 1980

| | 1976 | | | 1980 | | |
|---|---|---|---|---|---|---|
| | tonnage (10⁶ short tons) | percent tonnage | average firm production (10⁶ short tons) | tonnage (10⁶ short tons) | percent tonnage | average firm production (10⁶ short tons) |
| Top 15 firms | 302.8 | 44.6 | 20.2 | 336.8 | 40.5 | 21.9 |
| Firms 16–50 | 126.6 | 18.6 | 3.6 | 200.7 | 24.1 | 5.7 |
| Firms 51–3,000 | 249.3 | 36.8 | .1 | 194.5 | 35.5 | .1 |
| Total | 678.7 | 100.0 | .1 | 832.0 | 100.0 | .1 |

Source: Keystone Coal Industry Manual, 1980.

39

industry was not nearly as concentrated as other U.S. industries such as electric light bulbs, breakfast cereals, cigarettes, automobiles, and soap. Four to eight dominant firms account for 70–100 percent of the total sales in these industries (Samuelson, 1973: 116).

In the U.S. coal industry the top fifteen coal firms hold just 40 percent of the total coal market, the top four firms only 20 percent. However, there are reasons to believe that the coal industry may become more highly concentrated over the next two decades. As eastern coal seams are depleted and production shifts to the west a few large firms may become more dominant in national coal production. Regional markets were already showing signs of high concentration by 1974. In the midwest, four firms accounted for 56 percent of total sales, eight firms accounted for 73 percent. In the West in 1974 four firms controlled 34 percent of sales, eight firms 51 percent (FTC Report, 1978). The coal industry continues to be carefully monitored by federal regulation.

*Regional market competition.* Sales competition in the coal industry is primarily regional. The interdependence of electric utilities and coal is so close that a new utility will often locate near an existing mine or will seek equity participation in the development of a new mine to assure itself of available fuel and reserves. Opening a new mine can take from three to five years of planning with tens of millions of dollars of up-front investment. Because public utilities are overseen by quasi-public state regulatory commissions, coal companies develop their ties with state legislatures and utility commissions which are often more important than national politicians for advancing their sales goals.

Sales are most often based on long-term commitments of dedicated production and reserves. Output is, in effect, presold. Boilers are usually designed and sited to burn the coal at a particular mine most efficiently.

In the 1960s large steam coal firms initiated policies that would buffer them from the effects of their declining markets. They initiated long-term contraction policies which extended fifteen, twenty, or even thirty years: often the life of a particular power plant. They improved handling procedures by purchasing their own hopper cars and barge companies and instituting unit train deliveries of large volumes of coal (Duchesneau, 1975). These business procedures and relationships with state government officials made for an extremely stable, buffered, and conservative orientation among major firms. Spot sales were virtually squeezed out of domestic coal purchasing.[3]

The industry's relationships with public utilities also mean that the coal industry is accustomed to significant interaction with and oversight by government at all levels of its operations. Its interactions with policymakers are generally easier on the state and local than on the national level. Nationally, coal has often meant pollution, ravaged land, and labor unrest. But in the thirty states where it is mined, coal also represents jobs in local economies and significant contributions to state tax coffers.

Working to offset its declining demand, the coal industry developed strong, regionally isolated markets. Coals from different regions normally do not compete with one another.[4]

The opening of an export market for steam coal is complex, because there is opportunity for much more interregion competition among firms than typically prevails in domestic steam coal sales. Buyers may solicit sales from any coal producing region. Considerable choice can be exercised about barge or rail shipment and the port of embarkation. This is in many ways upsetting the ways companies have previously conducted their business.

## Political Issues

*The coal industry and the federal government.* Compared to other U.S. industries, coal has never enjoyed a favored relationship with the federal government. Nationally, coal has not shaken its image as a trust, an exploiter of labor, and a polluter of industrial towns (Corcoran, *Coal Industry News*, 6/30/80). Even before the turn of the twentieth century, coal was being investigated by Congress for price fixing and other abuses (Johnson, 1979). The industry has been the continuous object of congressional investigations. U.S. producers have not been perceived as deserving protection by the federal government. Even when its markets and overall production underwent rapid decline, the coal industry did not receive special concessions. It was allowed to wither and to lose its dominant position in the fuel market to oil and gas, whose prices were kept artificially low. Rather than becoming the partner of the federal government, the coal industry was often the testing ground for the growing power of social legislation to intervene in industrial relations. First labor conditions; then safety regulations; then environmental protection of air, water, and noise; then land reclamation became subject to federal regulatory controls. All these regulations added to the expense of mining coal. Coal executives have a long history of distrust and enmity toward federal officials.

Coal is still not generally considered a national resource which needs protection by the federal government. Coal is not preserved from wasteful or subversive exploitation. Unlike mining industries in Europe, miners' jobs are not preserved as essential to U.S. economic strength and self-sufficiency.

I do not want to imply that the regulatory measures taken by the federal government have been unnecessary. I merely want to suggest that unlike many industrial establishments within the United States and unlike the history of coal development abroad, relationships between the coal industry and the U.S. federal government have been marked by mutual suspicion and wariness. These attitudes formed the background against which post-1979 efforts at joint industry-government planning and cooperation for export trade took place.

*The influence of outside owners.* It is ironic that the U.S. coal industry's national political power and prestige improved significantly after it became the target for takeovers by cash-rich oil and high technology companies in the late 1960s and early 1980s. Beginning with Gulf Oil's purchase of Pittsburgh and Midway Coal in 1963, a constellation of outside owners began investing in the coal industry. Continental Oil purchased Consolidated Coal in 1966. Occidental Petroleum bought Island Creek in 1968. By 1976, all but three of the top forty firms were subsidiaries of noncoal corporations. Among the top forty producers in 1976, twelve were owned by gas or oil companies, eight by steel, six by electric utilities, four by minerals, metals, or construction, two by electronics, and five by other groups or manufacturing interests (Vietor, 1980, Table D-1). Fourteen firms were captives. That is, their entire output was sold to their electric utility or steel owner.

Gas and oil companies were particularly strong investors in coal companies and reserve lands. By 1976, forty-eight oil-gas-energy corporations had bought coal lands; thirty-four oil land gas companies owned coal producing subsidiaries (Vietor, 1980, Table D-3). Virtually all major oil companies became owners of coal assets. Between 1976 and 1980 at least thirteen more coal companies were acquired by oil interests (*Business Week*, 9/24/79).

The result has been a growing interfuel coalition of technical, financial, and industrial power interested in coal at the national level. Vietor (1980) says that seven industries (coal, steel, oil and gas, utilities, equipment manufacturing, railroads, and commercial banks) have formed a "unified political purpose and interlinked organizational system [which] led to relatively concerted and sustained political behavior by a very large sector of American industry" (p. 231).

While my findings do not entirely confirm the unity of elite industrial power that Vietor found, financial and institutional underpinnings must be continuously considered when analyzing the coal industry's activities in relation to the export market. For example, a high coal executive in the firm where I worked reported back to headquarters on the chances of a bill favored by coal in Congress. "The oil and gas interests aren't going to give us any trouble on this one, because they *are* us," (Legislative meeting notes, 1/16/81).

Outside ownership has changed the profile of the coal industry by opening western lands for coal development. Oil and gas companies had no prior involvement with the coal industry until they began to buy coal lands. Since then many have formed huge western coal-producing firms. Originally drawn to coal investments by the possibility of developing synfuels, these companies began mining coal for direct sales after the Clean Air Act of 1970 increased the demand for low sulfur western coal in midwest and eastern markets. The west represented a blank field for expansion by big coal companies and their outside owners. Dominance by the old, eastern, underground producers could be challenged. Western lands were not partitioned among hundreds of competing companies, the resource was not depleted; labor was as yet relatively unorganized and not subject to the long history of labor-management enmity which marked the eastern mines. Outside ownership has allowed the U.S. coal industry to revitalize its marketing and management styles and its public image. Lawrence and Dyer (1983) claim that the industry is being refreshed by these new owners.

By 1979, the coal industry had changed enormously from the faded, divided, archaic industry it had been in 1960. The export market for steam coal was another possible outlet capable of reorienting the industry's old-fashioned ways.

*Interfuel connections: Continued government oversight.* Outside owners of coal became a concern of Congress in the early 1970s. Investigations considered the need for price regulation and "horizontal divestiture" by competing energy fuels. Concerns heightened when coal prices doubled between 1973 and 1974 (Chakravarthy, 1981), but Congress could not trace price increases to collusion by oil companies (Charles River Associates, 1976; Horizontal Divestiture joint hearing 6/28/78). Increased safety and environmental regulations and drops in labor productivity seemed to have more effect on coal prices than did the price of oil. There was no evidence of illegal restraint of trade. However, an undeniable coalescence of economic power was clearly revealed (CRS, *A Congressional Handbook*, 1981).

The 1973 oil crisis introduced the possibility—at least to oil companies and other sophisticated investors—that increased demand for exported steam coal would come about. It did not. World coal use actually declined between 1973 and 1979 (Kohl, 1982). Investors in coal assets were becoming poised, however, to enter this trade when it did arrive.

## Implications of the Domestic History of the U.S. Coal Industry for Exports

The U.S. coal industry's conservative marketing orientation and its position as a weak industry throughout the 1960s carried over into a conservative outlook among many coal managers and a distrust of federal government intervention. These attitudes continued to be a prevalent logic of action through 1980–82. The U.S. coal industry was not accustomed to looking at itself in a nationally competitive market. Since 1970, the movement of coal production to the west and ownership of coal reserves by oil companies and by other multinational investors have become important features of modern coal industry structure. These investors are bringing a new orientation to the marketing and management of coal firms. They are also endowing the coal industry with increased national political power. Economic factors such as the efficiencies of larger-sized mining units and mergers to survive declining markets have significance for the export market which began to emerge in 1980–82 because they parallel the political trends and strategic interorganizational decisions that were moving in the same directions: toward greater economic concentration of the industry among larger, more nationally-oriented, and multinationally-owned steam coal producers, and the concomitant decline in importance of the vast numerical majority of small, eastern mining companies which until the 1950s had dominated the U.S. industry.

## History of U.S. Coal Exports

U.S. coal has been sent abroad since 1897 (*Keystone Manual*, 1980: 194). Overseas exports [5] are only 5–7 percent of U.S. national production. Overseas exports of bituminous coal since the early 1960s have been almost exclusively metallurgical coal. This has concentrated sales among eastern coal producers and sales organizations. Throughout the 1960s steam coal exports probably amounted to only 2–4 million tons of trade per year. Total overseas trade was about 35 million tons. Consequently, most steam coal producers ignored the export market.[6]

European coal miners demanded and received import restrictions and subsidies to protect them from U.S. coal competition in the late 1950s. European coal demand was declining in favor of imported oil, and European coal was not cost competitive with oil or with other world coals (Gordon, 1970). Trade restrictions lasted well into the 1970s, and many were not removed until after 1979. During this time the United States allowed much of its port handling infrastructure for coal to deteriorate, as European and domestic coastwise trade declined.

Japan became a significant buyer in the U.S. export market in the 1970s as it sought high quality metallurgical coal for its steel industry. While exports to Europe continued to fall (even after the 1973 oil crisis), Japan became the United States' major customer. Japan took half of overseas U.S. exports in the late 1970s. But again none of it was steam coal. U.S. overseas trade was 40–50 million tons per year. The United States had become the world's largest coal exporter.

The 1973 oil crisis had no effect on U.S. coal sales. After 1973, many countries took fresh inventory of their coal reserves and issued energy policies calling for conservation, development of coal and other domestic energy sources, and an increase in coal imports. However, there was no big move to coal. Overseas U.S. steam coal trade remained unimportant. World trade in steam coal increased only slightly.[7] The U.S. coal industry stood in anticipation after 1973, but the call never came. By 1979, steam coal exports overseas had gone nowhere (see Table 3.4). In 1979, U.S. steam coal exports were just 2.5 million tons.

U.S. coal export sales were conducted on a spot sales market for immediate delivery to foreign customers. This pattern contrasted with the stable, long-term contracts typical of the domestic coal market. Wide yearly swings in U.S. volume tended to confirm that the United States was a supplier of last resort.

Most exported coal was shipped by members of the Coal Exporters Association of the United States (CEA), a small, closely-knit group of brokers, sales groups, and a few companies. CEA, housed within the National Coal Association, represented a nucleus of contacts, information, and experience with foreign trade within the U.S. coal industry. But after 1979 this group's experience would seem highly specialized and inapplicable to the growing interest in a broad market for exported steam coal. The paradox of the post-1979 period was that firms with the greatest experience and brokers with great confidence in negotiating foreign trade agreements and making infrastructure arrangements for complex deliveries of coal to foreign destinations were not necessarily the most likely to receive future growth in foreign sales.

Throughout their experience with export trade, according to *Fortune* magazine (12/62), U.S. coal producers avoided deep

**TABLE 3.4. U.S. Steam Coal Overseas Exports, 1971–82 (million short tons)**

| Year | Overseas Exports | Overseas Steam Coal |
|------|------------------|---------------------|
| 1971 | 39.0 | 5.0 |
| 1972 | 37.8 | 4.3 |
| 1973 | 36.6 | 1.7 |
| 1974 | 46.2 | 2.0 |
| 1975 | 48.9 | 5.2 |
| 1976 | 42.9 | 2.4 |
| 1977 | 36.5 | 1.1 |
| 1978 | 24.3 | 0.1 |
| 1979 | 43.1 | 2.5 |
| 1980 | 72.8 | 16.0 |
| 1981 | 92.4 | 33.0 |
| 1982 | 110.0* | 35.0* |

*These were the estimates being used during my observation of the coal industry. The actual totals shipped during 1982 at year's end were 105 million tons of overseas exports and 27 million tons of steam coal sent overseas (*Keystone News Bulletin*, 12/27/84: 4).

Source: 1971–79: unpublished export data U.S. Bureau of Mines; 1980, 1981: *NCA International Coal Review*, 1/12/82; 1982: estimate by NCA Economics Committee, 5/82.

involvement with this sector of their business. They did little to develop a foreign market. U.S. coal owners left the export business in the hands of brokers, developed few personal contacts with consumers, and (contrary to oil companies) made no attempt to vertically integrate the task of exporting coal by establishing sole source mines, buying coal ships, or establishing their own marketing outlets abroad.

With the coming of the export market in 1980–82, companies became more interested in these possible means of providing service to foreign customers.

In contrast to the major steam coal producers who dominated and continue to dominate sales and marketing techniques in other sectors of the industry, the U.S. coal export market has mainly been dominated by small Southern Appalachian coal mining firms of 10,000 to 1 million tons of coal production per year. These small and medium-sized producers, some of whom enter and leave the market according to annual coal export demand, contact foreign buyers through an array of reputable and not-so-reputable coal trading companies, sales companies from larger firms, and independent brokers. These dealers contract for the coal at minesite and arrange for its transshipment and sale on the spot market. Because of the geographic concentration of metallurgical coal resources, most exports have been shipped by rail via either the Norfolk and Western (N & W) or the Chesapeake and Ohio (Chessie) railroad to the ports of Hampton Roads, Virginia, or Baltimore, Maryland. Nearly 95 percent of the overseas tons shipped in 1979 left the country this way (NCA estimate).

If energy forecasters are correct, and the U.S. steam coal exports expand to over 100 million tons per year (sales of $5 billion estimated in 1980 prices) coal would surpass grain as America's largest bulk export commodity. However, even at this level, coal exports would not exceed 15 percent of total industry sales (WOCOL, 1980). Thus, in terms relative to the domestic coal market, coal exports will remain of minor importance. Their real importance lies in the opportunity exports present for large coal firms (and through them their multinational owners) to encourage integrated reliance on fossil energy fuels which these companies will be in a position to supply.

The entry of large firms into the export sector will probably have a very slight effect upon the economic concentration and competition among firms in the U.S. industry. However, more interesting than narrowly defined economic or legal arguments over whether this newly emerging network will be an oligopoly or a prohibited restraint of trade is the practical question of what the effects of a market controlled by a few large externally owned firms might be. How are the emerging mechanisms, the network realignments, the strategic logics of action working to favor larger firms, and what difference will these changes make?

The U.S. coal export market has been the anomaly among coal market sectors. Its structure is the reverse of dominant industry trends. Overseas exports are predominantly handled by small, eastern firms on a spot sales basis, and the predominant product sold is bituminous metallurgical coal. Overseas exports have grown since 1970, although the reasons were tied to the world steel market rather than to the oil crisis of 1973 or to world electricity demand.

From 1980 to 1982 this anomaly was altered—not so much physically as perceptually. Huge steam coal firms which had previously ignored the export market began taking an active interest in increasing their involvement with coal export trade. They began acknowledging this sales sector and began shaping it to serve their ends.

## Large Versus Small Firms in the Export Market: Who Are They?

Even though fifty or even a hundred U.S. coal firms and cooperatives of small companies may eventually hold long-term steam coal contracts for foreign deliveries, during the time I observed the coal industry a handful of companies was beginning to effectively shape coal export policy and trade. Although other firms are also active, six to ten steam coal firms stood out as members of a core group influencing coal exports on many interorganizational levels. The case study which follows identifies the strategies and developing power of these firms.

The firms in the core group are all primarily steam coal companies (see Table 3.5). Together they produced about 25 percent of the total U.S. bituminous coal each year (roughly 200 to 830 million tons in 1980) (*Keystone Coal Industry Manual*, 1981). Each of the companies in the core group is capable of producing at least 20 million tons of coal per year, with the probable capacity, through reserve holdings, of meeting almost any level of export demand. The group includes the top five noncaptive steam coal producing firms in the nation. Additional firms are the fifteenth and twentieth largest U.S. producers, and two firms with heavy backing from large oil companies, which are expanding their production capacities for export trade.

The companies emerging as probable members of the core group are listed here in alphabetical order. *AMAX Coal* is the third

**TABLE 3.5. Industry Structure**
**Top Fifteen Producing Firms, 1980**

| Name | Tonnage (10⁶ short tons) |
|------|:---:|
| Peabody | 59.0 |
| Consolidation | 48.9 |
| AMAX | 40.5 |
| Texas Utilities | 27.6 |
| Island Creek | 20.1 |
| Pittston | 17.7 |
| NERCO | 16.9 |
| Arch Mineral | 15.8 |
| U.S. Steel | 14.2 |
| American Electric Power | 14.0 |
| Peter Kiewit | 13.4 |
| North American | 12.6 |
| Westmoreland | 12.6 |
| Bethlehem Steel | 11.7 |
| Exxon | 11.4 |
| Top 15 firms | 336.8 |

*Source: Keystone Coal Industry Manual, 1980.*

largest U.S. coal producer. It is a subsidiary of **AMAX** Corporation, an international metals and mining firm. AMAX Corporation is 20 percent owned by Standard Oil Company of California. *Atlantic Richfield* owns huge reserve lands in the west. Its coal producing subsidiary is Arco Coal. Atlantic Richfield has taken a strong interest in export trade and is expanding Arco's production capacity. *Consolidation Coal*, the second largest U.S. producer, is owned by the Conoco-Dupont conglomerate. Consol was a major steam and met coal producer and exporter prior to 1980. *Island Creek Coal* is a wholly owned subsidiary of the energetic and enterprising Occidental Petroleum Corp. Island Creek ranks fifth among U.S. coal firms. It has exported met and steam coal for many years. *Massey Coal Company* was a medium-sized producer of just 4–6 million tons until 1980. That year it received an infusion of capital and acquired new coal reserve holdings through a joint venture with Royal Dutch Shell Corporation (U.K.-Netherlands). As a result of the joint venture Massey's immediate capacity expanded to over 12 million tons. Massey, which had exported some coal prior to 1980, became more heavily concerned with export trade. *Peabody Coal Company* is the largest U.S. firm. Peabody is owned by a holding company which includes Newmont Mining, Ltd. (London), Williams Companies, Bechtel Corporation, and Fluor Corporation. These are multinational mining, engineering, and chemical firms. Peabody is probably the least likely of the six firms mentioned so far to enter the export market successfully, because of its midwestern and western locations and high proportion of high sulfur coal reserves. However, as the nation's largest firm, Peabody invested significant resources and prestige in entering the export market. These firms formed the most likely core group. There are several other possible entrants.

*Ashland Coal-Arch Minerals* are related firms which are owned by Ashland Oil and Hunt Petroleum Companies. Neither had experience in exports prior to 1980, but some of the activities indicated that they might become important core group members. Arch is eighth among U.S. coal firms—fifth among noncaptive steam coal producers.

In addition, if the export market continues to develop, the core group is likely to include one or more firms with primarily western production: such as Westmoreland, Peter Kiewit, North American, NERCO, Utah International, or Exxon Coal Group. These firms were all among the top twenty coal producers in 1980, which means that each produced at least 11 million tons of coal. By the end of 1982 it was too early to say which of the large western firms would become most dominant in export trade. Because of their connections to powerful outside owners, I believe that Utah International and Exxon are the most likely of the western firms to be important on the international scene. It is important to remember that among the firms mentioned in this core group, only Consolidation, Island Creek, and Massey had ever shipped even relatively small amounts of coal abroad prior to 1980.

## NOTES

1. Expected future entrants into world coal trade may include China, Colombia, U.S.S.R. (which currently exports about 25 million tons entirely within the Eastern bloc), India, and Sierra Leone.

2. This estimate is based on a speech by Ben Lusk of the Mining and Reclamation Council of America, (AAPA *Proceedings*, 2/17–19/81).

3. Long contracts, certainty of supplies, and the regularity of passed-through costs to consumers are probably why coal, unlike many minerals and extracted metals, is not traded on a commodities or futures market.

4. A recent exception and disruption in the regional isolation of steam coal markets was caused by demand for "compliance coal" (less than 1.2 lb. of sulfur per 1 million BTU) to meet the requirements of the Clean Air Act. This act has caused low sulfur western coal to enter markets in the east and midwest. Acid rain problems may bring similar results.

5. Exports to Canada are not considered overseas exports in this study, except when they are counted as part of total world coal trade. U.S. exports to Canada are about 80 percent steam coal. Volume has been about 10–20 million tons since 1918.

6. Consistent coal exporting firms have been Pittston, John K. Irish, John McCall, and Drummond Co. These are all metallurgical coal firms. Only Pittston is among the top fifty U.S. producers. Major steam coal companies which participated in export trade prior to 1980 were Consolidation, Island Creek, and A.T. Massey. Most other export sales were handled by brokers who arranged sales for small mining firms.

7. Due to South African exports filling in for production declines in West Germany and France world coal trade expanded slightly after 1973, although total coal use declined.

# 4 Historical Constraints and Opportunities 1980–82

## 1979: A TRANSITION YEAR FOR COAL

An eminent industry participant called 1979 coal's "watershed year" (Quenon, *World Coal*, 11/80), and this phrase seems apt. A new perspective about coal's future, as well as old attitudes and modes of operation, was evident. The year 1979 was also full of critical world events affecting energy. In the aftershock of each event additional focus in the international community shifted to the prospects and importance of coal as an energy source.

### World Events

Early in 1979 Iranian oil supplies were interrupted after the fall of the Shah of Iran. This second oil crisis brought about a price war which sent oil prices up precipitously. Oil prices doubled in less than twelve months (Kohl, 1982). The subsequent war between Iran and Iraq increased uncertainties about the availability of oil supplies. But more importantly, oil supplies were recognized as never before to be politically (as well as economically) vulnerable, and to be physically limited. Energy markets were shocked for the second time in six years, and western nations resolved to revise or hasten their oil displacement policies.

International organizations such as the International Energy Agency, the United Nations Economic Commission for Europe, the European Economic Community, and the World Coal Study renewed their discussions of the energy priorities of industrialized nations. Individual nations also began to revise and formally to adopt policies which would promote use of coal. Great Britain, France, Japan, Italy, and South Africa are some of the countries which announced that they would increase their reliance on domestic and imported coal. Japan, which had dealt with the 1973 oil crisis primarily by separating itself from western nations and developing closer ties with oil-producing nations (Sampson, 1975) was particularly adamant in its resolve to shift from oil to coal energy and to begin importing quantities of steam coal.

To pledge their mutual resolve and solidarity about avoiding economic ransom to uncertain energy supplies, western nations took cooperative policy action. The European nations and Japan, as members of the International Energy Agency, signed a set of general principles to expand coal demand, supply, and trade in May 1979. At the Tokyo Economic Summit in June 1979 they pledged not to interrupt coal supply contracts except in cases of national emergency. These decisions implied long-term repercussions for U.S. coal trade—the signatory nations were all potential buyers of American coal. Announcements of cooperative political intent had the effect of changing the relevant environment in which U.S. steam coal producers operated, making it more explicitly interconnected.

In June 1979, the International Energy Agency established an international advisory group on coal, the Coal Industry Advisory Board (CIAB). This group was drawn from top executives of coal producing companies and utilities in IEA countries. The CIAB was charged with the task of helping IEA nations plan for increased coal use.

## Industry Effects

The coal industry both in the United States and internationally did not dramatically change in 1979 from earlier years. Production and trade volumes around the world remained nearly level. Industries were being scaled back in Europe, while South African and Australian production grew slightly. In the United States *Business Week* called 1979 "bleak" (9/24/79) and "another bad year for U.S. coal" (10/29/79: 91). Although U.S. production recovered 100 million tons over 1978,[1] many observers felt that key markets were weakening because of continued uncertainty about the course of environmental regulations (Horwitch, 1979). In 1979, U.S. overseas exports achieved their "normal" level of roughly 40 million tons (double the previous year's total); but only 2.5 million tons of this was steam coal. By the end of the year there were predictions that in response to the oil crisis, U.S. steam coal exports might begin their awaited expansion, but this was not evident in trade volumes during 1979.

U.S. industry spokesmen were downright pessimistic about the future prospects for exporting steam coal. Donald C. Farnsworth, president of the Coal Exporters Association of the United States, and the CEO of Drummond Coal Co. (a met exporting firm), said it was unrealistic to expect American steam coal to play an important role in Europe or Japan. "We've priced ourselves out of the market," he told *Business Week* (8/20/79: 36). Stonewall Jackson Barker, Jr., president of Island Creek Coal, a major exporter of metallurgical and steam coal, was quoted in *Business Week* in October of 1979 saying "I see coal exports declining" (10/29/79: 91).

The U.S. coal industry had accommodated itself, by 1979, to new environmental requirements and was bracing itself for discussions of acid rain, revisions of the Clean Air Act, and reorganization of the Black Lung Trust Fund in the 1980 congressional session. These issues tended to concentrate the attention of industry executives on internal cost control. Recession was also beginning to hit the steam coal industry. Layoffs were announced almost weekly by the end of 1979. The soft market for steam coal meant that the industry had 100–200 million tons of overcapacity ready to be tapped at existing mines. This potential capacity was probably a major factor that sparked the initial interests of major steam coal firms in export trade.

## FURTHER CHANGES IN THE EXTERNAL SETTING BEGINNING IN 1980

### An Evident New Demand

In late 1979 a qualitative shift in overseas U.S. coal export demand became obvious. Foreign buyers, particularly Europeans, were set on purchasing American steam coal. Ships began to arrive at Hampton Roads, Virginia, for steam coal. A large steam coal shipment went to England's Electricity Supply Board in January 1980. It was the first delivery on a purchase commitment of 1 million tons. Delegations from France, Spain, Italy, Austria, West Germany, Belgium, Denmark, The Netherlands, and Japan arrived in the United States to scout for potential steam coal purchases. By the end of the year, overseas steam coal sales had grown to 16 million tons, almost six and one half times the 1979 total. At the end of 1981 steam coal exports skyrocketed again to 33 million tons. This level was sustained through 1982.

Coal had become an important strategic energy fuel after the 1979 oil-price escalation and disruption of supplies. Western nations resolved to buy more coal. They began actively to seek long-term contracts with U.S. producers.

U.S. coal export demand was also heightened in 1980 because of a coincidence of problems in competing coal supplying nations.

These events entered the U.S. industry's relevant environment and added to the sense of confusion and unpredictability in the U.S. coal export market. These historical events were selectively perceived and acted upon by organizational actors.

This chapter focuses on external events which began to impinge upon the U.S. coal industry in 1979 and 1980. Domestically oriented U.S. steam coal producers found that their area of relevant concern was greatly enlarged. Events and relationships which previously had little bearing on their operations and future growth now began to occupy their time and to exert crucial influence on their everyday activities. Steam coal producers became highly concerned about export trade.

Whereas previously the critical factors influencing U.S. coal exports were tied to metallurgical coal and to the world steel market, now they were tied to steam coal. The crucial factors were foreign electricity demand and siting of power plants, ocean transportation rates and availability of bulk carriers, inland fuel distribution systems, transloading technologies, foreign environmental quality standards, port operating procedures, the economics of substituting coal for other fuels, and the scientific and political progress of synfuels development. Such issues became important on a world scale. Although many of these factors were routinely considered by steam coal industry members in predicting their domestic sales, how they interrelated with world political conditions was only dimly grasped.

Accurate information on the new situation was also in short supply. In contrast to the voluminously detailed documentation of coal prices, transportation rates, fuel usage, and reports of public utility boards which were compiled weekly and used extensively in domestic coal sales, such comprehensive information was not routinely available for foreign transactions. Moreover, it was sometimes not clear to coal executives in 1980–82 what information they needed, or where to go to get it. Even after they began to identify their needs, they often found that the necessary information systems were not in place, data they needed were not systematically collected or compiled, and basic data had to be pieced together from many sources. On the other hand, long-range forecasts of expected trade looked highly optimistic.

## Trade Forecasts Created High Expectations

The forecasts of growing world coal trade which were being circulated in early 1980 unanimously predicted a huge increase in demand for U.S. steam coal abroad. These reports raised expectations and awareness about the need for domestic U.S. producers to look more carefully at export sales.

The consensus among world energy planners in 1980 was that the world market for metallurgical coal would remain stable or grow only slightly for the next twenty years. The volume of U.S. metallurgical coal shipped would rise from about 45 million tons in 1979 to only 60–70 million tons by 2000 (WOCOL, 1980, Vol. 2, Appendix 3). Therefore, metallurgical coal, the product which had been the backbone of U.S. coal trade for a century, was not expected to grow much over the next twenty years.

By contrast, even before considering the effects of the 1979 oil crisis, analysts estimated that steam coal trade would grow enormously by the end of the century. Planners from the International Energy Agency, World Coal Study, United Nations, U.S. Department of Energy, and other agencies and private consulting firms expected world coal consumption to double or triple by the end of the century. The reasons lay with stable or declining oil production and resources, limitations on feasible nuclear development, severely restricted natural gas resources, and as-yet undeveloped geothermal and solar energy systems. Coal was the most available fuel for world energy growth.

Because of limited domestic coal supplies in Europe and Japan, world steam coal *trade* would have to increase between three and ten times its 1979 level, from about 50–60 million tons to between 150 and 600 million tons, just to supply minimal world energy growth needs. These trade predictions stimulated the scramble to implement coal export sales among U.S. producers during 1980–82.

Much effort went into forecasting the probable market share of world trade that would be held by the United States. The World Coal Study concluded that U.S. steam coal exports could be anywhere from 65 to as much as 200 million tons per year by 2000. Even if the lowest prediction proved true, this was twenty-five times larger than U.S. steam coal overseas export sales in 1979. In January 1981, the Carter administration's Interagency Coal Export Task Force estimated that U.S. steam coal exports could reach 178 million tons and hold 38 percent of the worldwide steam coal market by 2000, if the U.S. industry acted quickly to secure customers, develop ports, and build adequate handling systems.

Pressure was building on U.S. coal companies to engage in export trade and infrastructure development. The consensus of experts was an important force propelling U.S. domestic producers into export sales. Findings agreed that steam coal trade would grow enormously, and that the only country with sufficient production capacity to support the massive exports the world would need was the United States.

## Significant Political Events: 1980

In 1980, several world political events coincided to make the surge in demand for steam coal at U.S. ports especially large. These events contributed to the atmosphere of unpredictability surrounding U.S. export trade. The surge occurred for several reasons, not all of which were immediately obvious or understood by U.S. coal producers. Much of the confusion in 1980–82 came from the unfamiliarity of U.S. producers with interpreting their foreign competitors and the unavailability of accurate information on world steam coal trade volumes.

In Poland, massive labor strikes and the formation of the Solidarity labor movement effectively shut down Polish coal mines for nearly four months in 1980. When mining resumed, it was on a much-reduced scale. The interruption of Polish coal supplies to Western Europe continued throughout most of 1981. Poland normally supplied about 30 percent of the steam coal imported into Western Europe (*ICE Report*, draft, Table 2-10). These exports were crucial to Poland and the Eastern bloc countries. They supplied much of their hard currency incomes. These exports were virtually cut off. Normally, Poland sent about 30 million tons of coal per year to Western Europe, 80 percent of it steam coal (NCA estimate published by The Energy Bureau, 12/6/81), but in 1980 and 1981 Polish exports dropped to less than 10 million tons (DOC telegram, 10/30/81; Markon, *World Coal*, 11/81). Western European nations looked to the United States to make up this shortfall in their coal supplies.

Australia experienced railroad and dock strikes in mid-1980 which disrupted export coal loadings at several of its ports. Australian exports were therefore several million tons lower than normal in 1980 and 1981. However, since most Australian coal is of metallurgical quality, the disruptions did not greatly affect steam coal movements. The effect was more psychological on buyers who perceived new investment and long-term commitments to Australian steam coal development as highly risky ventures. More significant than labor problems for the immediate market was a rise in fuel costs on Australian ships (a ripple effect from the 1979 oil crisis). Ocean freight rates on Australian ships rose about 20 percent, thus making Australian coal $4–$6 per ton more expensive than American coal in Europe. Europeans who normally bought coal from Australia turned to the United States.

The South African port of Richards Bay, although the model of a modern coal transporting center, was operating at capacity. Expansion plans would not be completed for several years. Long-term export growth from South Africa faced problems from both buyers and sellers. Antiapartheid policies in some European nations (notably The Netherlands, Ireland, Sweden, and Denmark) had marked South Africa as a nonpreferred trading partner. The South African government officially restricted export trade with quotas. While these policies did not noticeably limit South African exports during 1980–82, they threw doubts on South Africa's growth potential. Buying countries were encouraged to turn to the United States as a less problematic supplier of additional amounts of coal.

In addition to the conditions of trade in countries competing with the United States for coal sales, other world events also had consequences for U.S. coal exports in 1980–82. The Iran-Iraq war continued in the aftermath of the 1979 oil crisis. It had lingering effects on public opinion and government policy in Western Europe and Japan. These countries resolved in 1979 to move quickly and defensively to cover their energy vulnerability by diversifying sources of energy supplies. They explored ties to "stable" world coal producers and resolved to switch major portions of their energy feedstocks to coal. Policies that had been announced in 1979 were beginning to be felt in 1980.

Public pressure to rethink energy policies increased after the 1979 accident at a nuclear plant at Three Mile Island, Pennsylvania. Nuclear energy, which had seemed a way for resource-deficient nations, such as France, Italy, Denmark, and Belgium, to become independent of the political vagaries of world energy suppliers, was called severely into question in these countries. Thousands of marchers took to the streets in West Germany and the Benelux countries to protest the dangers of nuclear energy. Such public outcries and resistance to nuclear energy development enhanced the prospects for reliance on coal trade. France revised its all-nuclear energy plan to include more coal, especially in its cement industry and industrial heating markets. Italy began to consider steam coal imports.

The world environmental movement was somewhat deflected from the dangers of coal-burning by the nuclear disaster. Nevertheless, concerns about flue gas emissions, acid rain, and the "greenhouse effect" continued to be voiced. Most nations had legal restrictions against burning high sulfur coal. The prospect of burning more coal was considered a mixed blessing. In many ways, the technological treatments needed to relieve the pollution problems inherent in coal-burning looked preferable to the uncertainties accompanying reliance on other available fuels.

### Conclusions about the External Setting in 1980

The surge in demand for U.S. steam coal exports in 1980–82 occurred not just because of fuel shortages and price increases resulting from the oil disruption of 1979. Political decisions among western nations to alleviate their reliance on oil coincided with internal events that disrupted coal trade in several coal supplying countries, Thus, the increased demand for U.S. coal exports was caused by a combination of the political determination of coal buyers to buy more coal and the disruptions of normal supplies in coal industries competing with the United States.

These influences were not all immediately obvious or understood by U.S. coal producers. Many producers were, in fact, pessimistic about the long-term prospects of exporting steam coal. Nevertheless, a spate of impressive technical studies began to reinforce the notion that world coal trade and with it U.S. steam coal exports would grow enormously in coming years.

## Mood of Producers: Apprehensive Uncertainty

The new factors which entered the relevant environment of American steam coal producers in 1980 emanated from reversible strategic assessments and commitment decisions which could be traced to political and social values. They did not occur because of physical resource constraints or hard economic facts. In other words, it was not the physical lack of fuel elsewhere or a low price that brought buyers to the United States. Political actions and decisions (a war, strikes, public values shifts, a world council meeting) changed effective U.S. demand.

This reversibility made many U.S. producers nervous. They feared that the results of policy changes would be short-lived. Their unfamiliarity with international trade made many assume that social and political factors were intangibles that the industry might be better off without. The industry had few interorganizational strategies in place to buffer itself from the volatile political and social values which seemed to be influencing foreign trade priorities.

A cacophony of nations clamored at U.S. ports early in 1980 for delivery of steam coal. But how long would it last? How did the American companies interpret and respond to the confusing assortment of messages they were receiving? The newly presented situation was not objectively decipherable as a single, homogeneous environment. Instead, it was a situation capable of a variety of interpretations and therefore a variety of rational strategic responses, depending upon the goal or goals a particular firm or group of firms wished to achieve. During 1980–82 a core group of producers began to take proactive stances toward the tangible factors influencing their trade, and to shape these factors to their advantage. But the initial pressures on the industry came from foreign nations themselves.

*Foreign nations act: Limited goals became more long-term.* Early in 1980 many nations were hoping merely to cover the temporary shortfall in their coal receipts from Poland by buying coal from the United States. As that situation dragged on and as the imposition of martial law and virtual military occupation of Polish mines did not increase Poland's ability to predict exports accurately, these nations began to look at the United States as a more permanent source of supply. Both the U.S. State Department and private economic analysts began to predict that Poland could probably not regain its 1979 capacity for five years, and that future expansion of the industry was unlikely.

France and Japan had made the most ambitious political commitments to increase coal use. These two countries engaged actively in soliciting American partners for long-term mine expansion and reserves committed to exports. Spain aggressively sought steam coal for its cement industry. Finland, Denmark, and Belgium felt a sharp pinch from Polish shortfalls. Coal ships were already choking the two major U.S. coal harbors at Hampton Roads and Baltimore. By April 1980 existing portside loading facilities were strained to their limits.[2]

The two railroads which had formerly shipped primarily metallurgical coal for export were not equipped to deal with the handling problems of large amounts of steam coal. Steam coal needed space for large ground storage piles, rather than the complicated blending and railyard classification setups required for met coal. Railroad hopper cars were tied up for weeks in traffic jams, as shipments were inspected, licensed, and assembled for dumping into ship holds. Coal ships formed lines in ports where they accumulated waiting fees (demurrage) of $15,000 to $20,000 per day for two to six weeks. These charges would be added to the price of coal at its final destination.

In the long run these charges could price U.S. coal out of the world market and seriously jeopardize future trade. U.S. producers began to worry that the new export market that had been predicted and postponed since 1973 might evaporate before it began.

Steam coal producers were anxious to obtain overseas sales. However, they wanted to insure that the market was real by drawing importers into long-term sales agreements. Foreign buyers, on the other hand, would not commit themselves until they were able to assess the price competition and capacity of the U.S. coal industry and the seriousness of the U.S. government's commitment to support export trade. U.S. producers and railroads, meanwhile, had not invested in infrastructure in previous years, because they feared the coal industry's traditional boom and bust cycle. They would not invest now until they had long-term commitments in hand.

*Foreign pressure to expand and to revise industry procedures.* Foreign buyers did not want to become committed to excessively priced supplies and inadequate transportation facilities. They were more alert than the American producers to potential problems in U.S. infrastructure and handling systems, because they dealt regularly with more modernly-equipped coal exports throughout the world, particularly in South Africa and Australia. Foreign coal delegations were extremely vocal with their complaints. They actively pressured U.S. coal producers, ports, railroads, and government officials to improve coal handling methods. The involvement of potential buyers observing and commenting on U.S. export incapacities heightened the stakes of export trade for U.S. producers. They did not want to lose the respect as well as the valuable business of these potential customers.

Buyers (other than those on the spot market) were concerned about the long-term reliability of U.S. transportation infrastructure to support a huge increase in export sales. There were at least three foci of buyer concern. First, the U.S. had insufficient coal terminals to support present (much less the expected future) demand. Second, railroads were essentially dictators of U.S. coal prices. Inland freight rates regularly comprised half or more of domestic U.S. coal prices. Rates were inconsistent, were unrelated to distance, and were changed frequently. Potential foreign buyers felt that U.S. rail rates were often excessive. They wanted greater diversity and competition among transportation modes to get coal to export outlets. This meant that they wanted better service and more competition for the two dominant export railroads in the east; and in the west and midwest they wanted to encourage competition among rail lines, and between rail lines and other transportation modes, such as barges and slurry pipelines. The third focus of buyer concern was U.S. ports. Potential buyers complained about antiquated U.S. harbors and inadequate port depths. No U.S. port could accommodate the largest colliers in the world fleet. In fact, no U.S. port had greater than a 45 foot draft. This restricted full loadings to 70,000 dead weight ton (dwt) ships, whereas the world coal fleet was becoming dominated by 100,000 to 150,000 dwt vessels, which would have to sail partially loaded from U.S. ports. Several 250,000 dwt coal ships were already in use in Europe and Japan, and others were on order. To achieve the economies of scale which would come with large, full loads, thus offsetting higher U.S. rail rates and production costs, the United States would have to deepen its ship channels into coal harbors, foreign customers urged.

The problem of increasing loading capacity could be met by private industry.[3] Coal firms and trade groups began immediately to reassure potential customers, and to revise and expand current handling for the new needs. Railroads would have more flexibility under their partial deregulation by the Staggers Rail Act of 1980. But whether they would cooperate to offer foreign buyers stable, competitive freight rates remained to be seen. The port problem could not be tackled without major federal involvement. Active support from federal policy would be needed in one of the most entrenched and politicized pork barrels of the federal government: domestic waterway policy.[4] These issues posed challenging problems for U.S. producers.

The surge in world demand for U.S. steam coal in 1980 was a dramatic moment. It focused attention and heightened awareness along the coal chain on the need to revise essential handling systems for U.S. coal. The remainder of this study discusses the kinds of actions—strategies, goals, and tactics—that the industry pursued to meet this challenge and how its actions brought about changes in relative power arrangements among firms in the industry.

*Interpreting the strategies firms pursued.* The actions firms undertook and the strategies they pursued depended crucially upon how they interpreted the external environment. What kind of environmental uncertainty did they see themselves confronting? From the array of events and factors facing them, which did they focus on as problematic—as either looming threats or inviting opportunities—and how did they respond? Particular perceptions about what sort of uncertainty was confronting the industry lay behind the characteristic tactics and activities firms adopted. Firms had to disentangle the complex skein of "what environment was confronting them" and then to develop strategies to deal with that particular uncertainty. New patterns of interorganizational interaction emerged from these strategies.

Of course, the various perceptions firms held and the strategies they adopted were concurrent and overlapped in many situations. In fact, their multiplicity and variegated effects illustrate that it was not an objective, historical situation that was changing the industry. Realignments in the industry's interorganizational network originated with the perceptions and decisions of individuals—decisions which were changeable and open-ended. The fact that these realignments favored the largest U.S.

steam coal firms was a function of the power of their strategic decision-making abilities and the effectiveness with which they were pursuing their goals, rather than an indication of environmental necessity.

Important events were taking place in 1980 which were upsetting the normal world network or environment for U.S. coal exports. Those historical constraints and opportunities to which the U.S. steam coal industry usually responded were changing in significant ways. This complex situation provided a context for the five types of strategic and tactical realignments that firms pursued.

## NOTES

1. A long strike in 1978 disrupted production, and export levels were unusually low.

2. The question of how much physical port capacity for coal exports was available in the United States was a source of continuing investigation and confusion during 1980–82. I will discuss this issue in the chapter on sources of information.

3. WOCOL estimated that to achieve a moderate level of U.S. coal exports, private investment of $160–$495 million would be needed in new coal terminal capacity.

   Substantially upgrading railroad and inland waterway transportation systems would also be needed. This investment would also come mostly from private sources: roughly $740 million–$1.4 billion to upgrade these transportation systems. WOCOL concluded that these investments were within the resource capabilities of the industries involved.

4. Coal producers were aware that waterfront improvements would have to begin far ahead of actually delivering coal. New coal terminals would require at least from three to four years of licensing and construction time.

   Harbor improvements would be even more time consuming and difficult to obtain. The average lead time for improving a waterway in the United States under USCOE regulations is twenty to twenty-six years! If coal companies wanted to have deepened harbors in time to benefit from world steam coal trade expansion, substantial action would have to precede felt demand.

# 5　Entrepreneurial Activities

## Competition for Sales

Competition for overseas coal sales cut a double-edged swathe through the U.S. industry during 1980–82. This chapter explores the tension which emerged between prevailing standard operating procedures in the export coal market and new ways of doing business. Entrepreneurial activities to obtain new business realigned the industry's basic interorganizational patterns.

Increased export activity placed severe strains on the coal industry's standard operating procedures. Basic business assumptions were being challenged, breaking down, and changed. The boundaries of the old market were bursting, and energies were released in many directions at once. An atmosphere of opportunism prevailed. On the other hand, firms which were experienced in export coal handling (and the railroads that served them) had a stake in holding the market as close as possible to previous procedures (those with which they were familiar and within which they could operate profitably). Both of these styles of responding to export demand were strategies employed to increase the strength and competitive edge individual firms would have in the new market. Both styles indicated increased interfirm competitiveness and struggle for profitable survival in foreign coal sales. The prevailing perception by both groups was that the export steam coal market was virtually limitless, uncharted, and a grand opportunity. But whether they saw it as an invitation to new participants or as a potential threat to their dominance of sales depended on their particular perspectives.

*Simultaneous ebullience and caution: Perceptions of new business opportunities.* Through the mouths of their official spokesmen,

63

coal firms during 1980–82 looked forward to a robust and growing coal market abroad. Robert H. Quenon, CEO of Peabody Coal Company and a past chairman of NCA, announced to the world that "Coal's renaissance may be at hand" (*World Coal*, Nov. 1980). R.E. Samples, CEO of Consolidated Coal and 1981 chairman of NCA, wrote that the United States was "moving to realize a golden opportunity" to increase coal use (*World Coal*, Nov.-Dec. 1981).

Coal producers worked hard to outdo each other's deals. An unusual amount of creativity and hustle were evident in the actions of coal firms and their supporting industries.

At the same time, paradoxically, coal firms continued to be cautious about committing themselves wholeheartedly to foreign trade. They worried about the dangers of being overextended in a risky new area. Aggressive and innovative sales strategies were contrary to their normally conservative, production-oriented style of doing business. Although the export market looked like a long-overdue prospect for expanding their business, they retained a hefty portion of skepticism about its long-term permanence, and a certain fear about the spectre of overcompetition which might reduce profits on sales.

Hesitancy (born of the extremely large investments needed to increase production and improve transloading operations in the industry and a history of promises about increased coal use that had failed before) was a continuous drag on the rising kite of market expectations during 1980–82. The industry's deep-seated conservatism, however, heightens the importance of the shifts in patterns of interaction that did occur. In a generally skeptical and hidebound industry even small changes in basic patterns of delivery and sales are significant indicators of change.

Two quotations from well-known coal industry spokesmen illustrate the simultaneous optimism and circumspection that typified industry attitudes. Peter Vismans, a well-known trader for a Dutch brokering firm, summed up the ebullience of many about the coming of a more prosperous time for coal trade. "This is the start of it. There's no question about that" (*Forbes*, 8/18/80). But Vismans' bullishness was tempered by coal industry spokesmen who had insulated themselves from overoptimism through the years. Carl Bagge, president of NCA, expressed this well. "All of the warm rhetoric we've been basking in since 1973, all of the energy policies, all of the 'coal is the cornerstone' and all that jazz, hasn't amounted to diddly squat. . . . We see the projections. . . . We're the eternal optimists. It's got to happen sometime. We've been saying that since 1947. We've been saying something's going to happen" (Congressional Quarterly, 3/81: 68).

Yet, whether they believed it would be long-lasting or not, coal piers were becoming crowded by the evident demand for steam coal in 1980–82. Companies desiring to participate in this new and as yet unorganized situation plunged ahead, tossing around lots of ideas. They acted quickly, on the assumption that a new area of business was up for grabs.

In most cases, coal companies acted by trial and error without a single coherent plan, other than responding to the immediacy of unfolding events. The new market offered opportunity for expansion and for new ideas. The industry welcomed this invitation to unfettered capitalism. Questions remained: Who would participate successfully in this new market? How would relationships among coal firms be affected by new opportunities for export sales? The course of events revealed that large firms had the advantage in developing entrepreneurial activities.

*What are entrepreneurial activities?* For the purpose of this study, entrepreneurial activities simply mean those activities firms engaged in which focused directly on sales.[1] They were the autonomous, competitive strategies aimed at securing new business for a single firm or group of allied firms with foreign customers. Entrepreneurial activities were the responses coal firms made to the uncertainty of an increasingly competitive market situation. Entrepreneurial activities therefore embrace both the ebullient enthusiasm and innovative activities employed by firms trying to enter the market and the stand-patism of those who wanted to retain and extend as much of their current control of export trade as possible.

In network terms, entrepreneurial activities imply autonomous interactions in an almost perfectly competitive market situation. Survival and participation are based on price, supply, and other purely economic considerations.

## STRAINS ON STANDARD OPERATING PROCEDURES

The coal boom of 1980 continued long enough to make even skeptics at least want to hedge their bets that the market was real. However, even after demand continued at its unprecedented rate for a while, it was not in the interest of all industry participants to acknowledge that something new was happening. A conflict emerged between small eastern firms and railroads which wanted to maintain the status quo and the more expansionist large coal firms who were ready to change the marketing patterns of U.S. coal trade.

Small firms around Hampton Roads had fixed resources and were unable to expand. They had a stake in minimizing the new situation and emphasizing the adequacy of normal practices. The Norfolk & Western Railway became a major voice for these small mining companies and coal brokers who had handled up to two-thirds of U.S. coal export trade in the past.

Early in 1980 the growth in demand for overseas coal seemed a normal temporary surge. Major shipments were a flurry of spot sales originating from small mines in Virginia and West Virginia (CRS, 9/12/80). These mines regularly entered and withdrew from the export market, so the growth in demand did not appear extraordinary, However, when the boom continued through the spring and summer and then into 1981, as eastern ports became clogged, and as information circulated that the new demand was primarily for steam coal, major firms began to take a greater interest. As a result, usual procedures were called into question.

## Railroad Interests

The two eastern railroads (Chessie and Norfolk & Western) and the small eastern producers had a heavy stake in proving that they could handle whatever increase in coal demand came their way. They scrambled to accommodate all the extra business. However, their procedures (based on experience with metallurgical coal) were overly complex and inefficient for handling steam coal shipments.

For example, normal procedures required assembling all the railcars for a coal shipment with separate export licenses for each car. A ship was not loaded until its entire cargo was completely assembled in the railyard. A tardy shipment of two or three railcars from a small mine could delay assembling and dumping a 100-railcar load. This in turn meant delays in completing full shiploads of coal which might consist of several 100-car lots.

The lack of ground storage at eastern ports meant that coal had to be stored in hopper cars until it was actually loaded into ships. This tied up railroad rolling stock and further drove up the price of freight through per diem waiting fees which were levied on both railcars (paid by transshippers) and on ships (paid by the receiving broker in the destination port). By April 1980 the backlog of ships and railcars at Baltimore and Hampton Roads was becoming national news. By June 1980 over sixty ships were anchored in the Chesapeake Bay. This number rose to nearly two hundred ships before the mine workers' strike relieved congestion somewhat in March 1981. Four thousand railcars jammed up at Hampton Roads were waiting an average of four weeks (rather than the usual one) to load coal onto ships.

No one denied that there was a backlog at the eastern ports. The railroads contended, however, that it was being caused by a proliferation of new and inexperienced shippers who were unfamiliar with their procedures. Once the market "settled down," they argued, there would be adequate handling capacity at existing ports.

The two eastern railroads were the linchpins of coal export activity. Although forbidden by law to mine or broker coal, they owned all operating loading terminals and virtually all potential land for additional terminals on the east coast. Thus, they were situated favorably to control European coal trade. They determined the licensing, inspection, assembling of loads, and loading procedures at the two main coal ports (Baltimore and Hampton Roads). The critical activity of moving coal from its origin at a mine to its loading aboard a bulk-coal ship was almost entirely under the control of these two rail lines. To some extent they were happy to have customers lined up for coal. It was in their interest to try to keep the new business under their control.

Many of the normal procedures which were causing delays were due to inefficient railroad procedures. For example, ship queueing was handled according to railroad procedures. Ships were required to wait for berthing space in order of their arrival in port. However, if a ship arrived at port and found that its full load of coal was not available in the holding yard (even if it was expected in a few days) it had to get out of the queue until the rail cargo was complete. This caused exceedingly long lines of ships. Furthermore, there were no staging berths. Only one ship at a time could be accommodated at each pier, and there were only four piers operating on the whole east coast. (Two were owned and operated by Chessie, two by Norfolk & Western.) Valuable time was lost as ships moved into and out of loading positions. Cargo inspection was another bottleneck. The small mines served by these railroads could not afford laboratory facilities to certify the quality of their product. The railroads supervised these procedures at ports. But the number of cargoes and the centralization of laboratory facilities at ports caused confusion and excessive delays, especially if coal was not within specifications and had to be replaced from the original mines.

On a very prosaic level, normal railroad procedures at terminals were incompatible with continuously moving large lots of coal onto ships. Rail terminals worked eight-hour days and closed on weekends. This was frustrating to the bulk ocean-freighter crews who operated on continuous shifts, and often had to wait for rail service even after the ship finally got its berthing space.

Major coal firms became interested in these railroad practices by late spring. The Economics Committee of the National Coal Association (composed mostly of large firms) held a special meeting in May 1980, during which it surveyed industry sources for information about alternative coal export locations. NCA began a long series of conversations with the two railroads to get them to modify and streamline port handling procedures. Railroads and coal firms are not usually on amicable terms, but the export situation was further exacerbating their conflicting interests. Coal firms in the east were totally dependent on railroad cooperation and did not want to lose export sales due to their inflexibility or obtuseness.

*Chessie's export strategy.* The two railroads differed markedly in their openness to changing their operating procedures. The Chessie system was the first beneficiary of export sales. It provided the exclusive rail link for many eastern steam coal mines. Chessie also owned coal terminals at both Baltimore and Hampton Roads. It held contracts to ship coal for Island Creek, Consolidation Coal, and Massey, which were early participants in the boom. Chessie began to break all previous records for coal export loadings and to achieve a new record each month. From handling just 400,000 tons of export steam coal in 1979, Chessie jumped to 4.5 million tons in the first six months of 1980 (Senate, Energy Committee, 9/19/80). Chessie's export tonnage for steam coal reached 10 million tons out of its total 34.5 million export tons shipped in 1980.

Flush with its record success in the new export market Chessie recognized a need to modify current activities to handle all this business. John Collinson, president of Chessie, assessed the market by quoting the comic strip Pogo. "We have encountered insurmountable opportunities," he mused. And he added that if things were muffed now the boom could hurt eventual business more than if it hadn't occurred (*Coal Industry News*, 7/13/81: 16). Chessie responded flexibly with revisions of its ship scheduling policies to coordinate rail and ship arrivals and changes in transloading procedures to reduce waiting. It also increased dumping capacity by adding new work shifts at a current terminal, increasing it to full-time operation. Also, Chessie agreed to reopen an old pier at Hampton Roads at a cost of $3–$4 million, by August 1980. Collinson expressed the general view that the 1980 market was exaggerated by a convergence of events which were boosting short-term coal demand, but that the long-term market for U.S. steam coal was real. He also expressed confidence that Chessie could meet additional capacity demands by doubling or perhaps even tripling current loadings in the foreseeable future. Nevertheless, he did not expect significant growth in coal exports away from Hampton Roads and Baltimore.

Mark Gibson, director of coal exports for Chessie, expressed that railroad's view. "Though the export market looks tremendous, we are content to go with the terminals we have and improve them. . . . We feel confident with the producers taking a stake in export coal, not just coal. Then we can put money into our system knowing they have a stake and we can expect to see their business" (*Journal of Commerce*, 2/17/81: 18b).

Chessie had anticipated the market by conducting a study prior to the 1980 boom which marked out its current strategy. The report concluded that, although Chessie could feasibly expand its coal loading facilities at existing piers, the ground storage essential to large shipments of steam coal should be operated by coal companies. With the coal company rather than the common carrier railroad in charge of storage and loading, ship waiting times, car turnarounds, and licensing problems would be reduced, presumably because coal companies rather than railroads would be empowered to administer them more efficiently.

A concomitant of this change of ownership and control would be that the access of smaller firms to export sales would probably also be diminished. No longer would loadings be based on a time-priority or queueing sequence with large and small firms holding equal weight. Instead, a common stockpile of coal on land owned and administered by a large coal company would be drawn upon to move large volumes of coal quickly and efficiently through ports. Unit trains with favorable freight rates would take priority over individually assembled shipments from several mines. Large companies could inventory their overstocks of coal as cheaply in stockpiles at port as they could at mines, and hence they would have the advantage in quick turnaround "spot" shipments as well as continuous long-term loading. By providing their own freight cars, as large firms did for domestic sales, they could gain cost advantages too. All of these advantages would work against the small companies.

Chessie's proposal to modify its hold on export coal by selling off property and encouraging coal companies to develop terminals and handle ground storage seemed a way to reduce the railroad's risk. Incidentally, it would throw a great deal of export business toward the largest coal firms. The railroad, if aware of this potential shift in the shippers of steam coal, found it a blessing. In fact, Collinson saw it as a benefit to everyone. Space currently being taken up at the Chessie terminals by large firms would become available to smaller shippers, he said (Senate, Energy, Collinson testimony, 9/19/80). This would increase foreign sales opportunities.

*N & W's intransigence.* The attitude of the Norfolk & Western Railroad was quite different from Chessie's. Although not the nation's largest coal hauler (Chessie was), N & W was the largest railroad carrier of U.S. *export* coal. It handled mainly metallurgical coal exports from Southern Appalachian coal fields and, with the exception of a few poorly-maintained coal hauling roads, was the sole link with export markets for many small mines. N & W's operations were intimately tied to the port of Hampton Roads, where it had both of its export terminals. The steam coal boom was a mixed blessing for N & W. On the one hand it meant more interest in coal exports and more business. On the other hand N & W's facilities were adapted to shipping and blending of met coal, and it had little extra land in the congested port area it served. The bigger firms like Massey, Island Creek, Consol, and Pittston typically shipped on Chessie, leaving N & W as the main representative of the smaller mining firms. Any buyer frustration with outmoded and crowded facilities at Hampton Roads was bound to reflect poorly on N & W and perhaps reduce its dominance in the export market of the future.

John P. Fishwick, president of N & W, downplayed the 1980 market expansion and the need for basic changes. "We think the demand for metallurgical coal will recede over the next few years while the demand for steam coal will increase. The net will be, perhaps, an increase, but not a substantial one" (Senate, Energy, Fishwick testimony, 9/19/80). He portrayed congestion at Hampton Roads as a temporary problem, solvable with patience and standard operating procedures.

In the face of its potential loss of dominance of U.S. coal exports, N & W adopted an intransigent attitude about the coal market, refusing to guarantee fixed-fee unit train rates to large coal companies which were considering construction of new export terminals (Senate, Energy, Gore testimony, 9/19/80) and later moving to block development of land at Portsmouth, Virginia, to which it could assert a title. N & W took the position that a railroad was the proper operator of a coal export facility, because it had proven experience. Railroads, N & W argued, would serve both big and small producers equally and would thus maintain competitive prices in export sales. "Railroads have been in the coal export business for almost 100 years and know the problems associated with rails, terminals, and ships. We can do a better job of it." So said William Bales, Vice President of N & W's coal and ore division (*Journal of Commerce*, 2/17/81: 18b).

Fishwick dismissed the boom for "so-called 'steam coal'" (Senate, Energy, 9/18/80: 396) because he presumably judged that it could spell a loss of dominance by N & W in the coal export market. Instead, he emphasized the danger of overbuilding new facilities. New terminals could only take business away from the full utilization of the N & W piers at Hampton Roads. This is probably why he consistently overestimated N & W's capacity to serve the new market in spite of the evident backup of ships. He bragged that N & W could process four times as much coal as the present rate if it were not hampered by slow shipping procedures *(Coal Daily,* c. 6/5/80). His only concession to the new demand was to increase the fines placed on delayed coal cars in order to "motivate transshippers to more effectively control their own activities" (Senate, Energy, 9/18/80). Thus he hoped to cash in on the demurrage problem then holding up ships and railcars at Hampton Roads.

From the point of view of coal firms trying to enter the new market, Fishwick was most uncooperative. Former Senator Albert Gore, president of Island Creek Coal Sales, described Fishwick in his prepared statement to the Senate Energy Committee as an "immovable rock," blocking the development of new large-scale export facilities for Island Creek's expected foreign sales (Senate, Energy, 9/16/80: 233).

Fishwick, himself, said, "I am apprehensive about the demand, not the supply of U.S. coal for overseas sale" *(Coal Industry News,* 7/13/81). Fishwick wanted to rely on previous experience and standard operating procedures, as he waited to see if the long-term coal market was real. Hence, N & W emphasized the continuity of the current situation with the past, the need for short term solutions "to get the bugs out of the present system." Fishwick predicted that "When the current spot market for coal eases and more coal is shipped to the piers under longterm contracts, we expect these problems will subside . . . (Senate, Energy, 9/18/80: 413).

N & W admitted that it could not easily expand its facilities to meet the new market. It had no open land near its trackage and no unused facilities available for sale at Hampton Roads. Thus, it was unable to provide coal ground storage for steam coal. N & W's system of railcar storage and coal mixing were designed for metallurgical coal shipments which required preserving the identity of lots from many small mines. N & W's assessment of market opportunities and the strategies it used to cope with them were indelibly colored by its previous history as a dominant force in coal exports and its present desire to keep things that way. Fishwick's outlook on the new market reflected his resource position and the stakes he saw as problematic for his company.

Fishwick insisted that his unwillingness to modify basic procedures would protect the interests of the many smaller U.S. coal firms and of overall competitiveness in export sales.

> We have a viable spot market in this country because we have a lot of coal shippers, a lot of small coal shippers who produce coal when the market is good and don't produce it when the market is poor, and those are the coal shippers that have been kept in business and able to survive and thrive because the railroads operate a terminal facility as public facilities and give the same conditions and same charges to everyone. . . .
>
> What we have believed has been in the interest of this country and of the development of the coalfield and of the railroads is to encourage competition in the marketing price of coal by having a number of operators in the coalfield, and to some extent I think that advantage will be diminished by what is happening. (Senate, Energy, 9/19/80: 394)

He cast N & W in the role of protecting small coal firms.

> If we wanted to increase our tonnage without regard to being fair and equitable, we would give all our permits to the major shippers who have been in the business a long time and we could substantially increase the throughput, but this is not in the public interest. It is not in the public interest to close down the small mines in Kentucky, or Virginia, or West Virginia. (p. 415)

Translated, Fishwick's position was that competitiveness among the small firms (which he served) was preferable to a broadened competitive field which included various shipping procedures, large firms, and alternative delivery options. His strategy was to keep the market dominated by "old time shippers" as long as possible.

Thus, small firms and railroads that had established histories in coal exports (those who lacked the ability to expand) saw the new market as a potential usurpation of their dominant positions. This caused them to hold firmly to their known markets and procedures, to downplay new needs, or to modify existing policies as little as possible. Joel Price, one of the best known financial analysts of the coal industry shared this view. He scoffed at those who argued that new coal terminals were needed. "Where else," he said complacently, "could customers go?" (Senate, Water Resources, 6/12/81: 683).

## INNOVATIVE BUSINESS ACTIVITIES

The larger coal firms with capital to invest saw the new market as a grand opportunity—to expand into foreign sales, to break the hold of the two railroads on coal export handling, to provide an outlet for their production overcapacity. The main challenge of the new business was scrambling quickly enough to survive in the heavy competition for sales. Who could win stable long-term contracts?

The two eastern railroads and smaller companies were hemmed in by their fixed geographic locations and limited physical capacities. Although the east coast was the closest in distance to European markets, its mineral resource was expensive and becoming depleted; it was the most congested area of the nation for waterfront development. The railroads and smaller companies were trying hard to preserve the market in a way they could control. But companies that had not yet entered the export business or which were located away from the east coast tried to channel the new situation to their advantage.

Large coal companies began to embark on and announce a variety of entrepreneurial innovations to help them participate advantageously in export trade. Essentially they assessed their stakes as different from the go-slow attitude of Fishwick, the contentment of Chessie with existing solutions, and the self-assuredness of conservative analysts like Joel Price. They began developing new solutions to their problems.

Many companies were convinced that lack of coal export terminal space was costing them overseas sales volume. NCA vice-president, Constance D. Holmes articulated this dominant industry view in August 1980. Holmes said the United States had lost $400 million in foreign exchange and 10 million tons of overseas coal sales in 1980 because of inadequate transportation and port facilities (*Forbes*, 8/18/80). Large coal companies somewhat grudgingly revised their business practices to concentrate on sales and port handling as they never had before. Colonel James Baylor, a senior vice-president of Massey Coal, confided to his peers at an industry conference, "Like other producers of coal, we had no other choice. We had to get in the coal terminal business" (*Coal Outlook* Conference, proceedings, 11/10/80).

Large coal companies reoriented their delivery systems because of their perception that aggressive marketing activities were required to survive in the export market. Their attitude that their hands were being forced illustrates the strain being placed on old assumptions and the pressure building to alter old interorganizational relationships. Dan McQuade, another executive at Massey Coal, justified the decisions of coal companies to spend hundreds of millions of dollars on the new export facilities. "We're not going to be starved to death by inadequate export facilities," he told the *Wall Street Journal* (2/27/81).

*Assessing the market.* It is not that the large firms were correct in sensing the industry-transforming opportunities of a booming market and the railroads and smaller firms were wrong. Each attitude represented a strategy and view of its environment based on a specific assessment of a group's ability to capture new sales. In the early part of 1980 no one could know how prolonged or significant the demand for U.S. steam coal would be. Significant participants in the coal chain recognized immediately that basic assumptions about how the market would operate were not yet settled. The new market offered opportunities precisely because assumptions had not yet been mutually enacted. Market characteristics would be formed by the encounters of buyers with sellers at this early stage. The nature of interfirm competition for export sales—as well as the basic ways by which coal would be sold and shipped—were in many important ways being transformed.

## Export Terminals

The first place assumptions about coal export sales could be altered was in the control and capacity of coal export terminals. Almost weekly from May 1980 to May 1982 some major coal producer, engineering firm, railroad, or local governmental group announced its interest in building new coal export terminal facilities. By December 1981, *Fortune* magazine had counted forty-five new terminal projects at twenty-nine harbors on three coasts, Atlantic, Gulf and Pacific (12/14/91). These announcements were significant in two ways. First, they served as marketing tools and public relations strategies for announcing the availability of sales to foreign buyers. Second, for the structure of the domestic coal export business, they illustrated potential movement away from the concentration of export sales and Hampton Roads and Baltimore. They broke the traditional pattern of organizational and procedural dominance by railroads of export sales. These announcements for the first time raised the question of why just two railroads or even, for that matter, delivery by rail at all was essential to overseas steam coal trade. A decoupling of the enmeshed interests and organizational control of export coal sales by the two rail lines at Hampton Roads and Baltimore began to take place.

Planners set to work immediately figuring out how they could carry coal to export markets most inexpensively (House, Interstate and Foreign Commerce, 12/17/80). By late summer coal began to flow by barge to New Orleans to relieve congestion in the east and to test the Mississippi River as a major export trade route for coal (*Coal Industry News*, 8/11/80). Mobile, Alabama, which was an established met coal port, hoped to receive some overflow trade. Los Angeles experimented with test shipments to Japan. Virtually every port city on three coasts considered how it could get in on coal export business. Coal companies announced ambitious plans to build export capacity.

The initial leaders of this expanded competition were very large steam coal companies backed by oil and those which obtained financial backing from foreign buyers. One journalist cited the remark by the marketing manager of a coal equipment firm which explained the emphasis by oil backed firms on new coal terminals. "To them, [oil backed firms] terminals are a minor part of getting coal all the way to Japan" (*Journal of Commerce*, 2/17/81: 1).

*Traditional locations.* The first announcements were predominantly for terminals in the Baltimore-Hampton Roads area. The new terminals were planned with ground storage capacity that was unavailable previously in any east coast coal port.

Consolidation Coal (owned since 1966 by Continental Oil) announced a $30 million renovation project at Baltimore which would triple that port's coal export capacity from 10 to 30 million tons. Island Creek Coal (owned by Occidental Petroleum since 1968) said it would improve a 12–15 million ton former coal terminal in Baltimore for $20 million, and would put in 500,000 tons of storage space. A consortium of coal companies including Pittston, Old Ben, Utah International, Mapco of Tulsa, and others led by the New York engineering firm Soros Associates was considering building a 15 million ton facility on Marley Neck, a spit of land in Baltimore Harbor. Old Ben and Utah International were also multinationally-owned.

At Hampton Roads, Massey Coal Company (backed by a $680 million investment in its steam coal properties by Royal Dutch Shell) agreed to buy a shipping terminal at Newport News from Chessie plus sixty acres of land for ground storage. Total cost of this project was about $80 million. This would be the first ground storage at Hampton Roads. The Port of Virginia was studying a 40 million ton coal terminal with ground storage near Portsmouth in the Hampton Roads channel to be developed at a cost of $230 million. The port's ostensible concern was to protect small exporters from being muscled entirely out of the market by the aggressive large firms taking over control of delivery terminals. However, the port signed four major producers who agreed in principle to ship coal through the project (Massey, Pittston, Consol, and Cox Enterprises). This project was beset with problems and most backers pulled out of it by early 1982. The N & W later moved to recover the land for this terminal, thus temporarily blocking development of the only viable state-run coal terminal on the east coast which had a stake in helping small mining firms remain in the steam coal export market. These projects, in total, might increase capacity at Hampton Roads from about 50 million to over 100 million tons per year by 2000.

*New locations and new types of investors.* Hampton Roads and Baltimore were not the only locations from which steam coal could be conveniently exported. Soon announcements began to appear in the trade and national press for terminals outside the immediate Baltimore-Hampton Roads area. Wilmington and Morehead City, North Carolina; Charleston, South Carolina; Savannah, Georgia; Camden, New Jersey; Port Richard and Philadelphia, Pennsylvania; New York City and Albany, New York; and Boston, Massachusetts were sites being explored on the east coast. Mobile, Alabama; New Orleans and Baton Rouge, Louisiana; and Galveston and Corpus Christi, Texas, announced the interest of investors in expanding capacity in the Gulf area.

On the west coast, where there were no existing coal terminals and there had been no experience with coal shipping, at least fifteen ports indicated interest in coal. The range was enormous, from tiny Kalama, Washington (which shipped less that 1 million tons of all commodities in 1979) to the major shipping port of Los Angeles-Long Beach (which handled over 70 million tons yearly) (*U.S. Water-borne Exports and General Imports,* 1979). Eight west coast ports conducted feasibility studies of their harbors and surveyed potential sites for terminals to ship western coal overseas: Los Angeles-Long Beach and Sacramento, California; Kalama, Astoria, and Longview, Washington; Portland, Oregon; Vancouver, British Columbia; and Anchorage, Alaska.

None of these aspiring coal ports large or small had any coal export experience. However, they became potential actors in the coal exports network. The investors in announced projects included individual coal companies, consortia, states, local port authorities, engineering firms, and international companies. Some of the specific private interests which announced their intentions to get into coal export trade in new harbors were major coal producers (NERCO, Westmoreland Resources, Hunt Oil, Peabody Coal, and Consolidation-Canada), none of which had shipped steam coal abroad. Others were less directly related to coal production, such as mining equipment and construction firms (Wheelabrator-Frye, Williams Co., Harbart Construction), natural resource investors (Pott Industries, Houston Natural Gas), and international investment and shipping firms (Pacific Resources, Inc. [Honolulu], Sun El Shipping [Korea], Pan Ocean Bulk Carriers [Japan], Industrial Bank of Japan). The announcements showed a diversity of interests becoming involved for the first time in U.S. coal export trade. The U.S. coal industry's interorganizational network was coming to include a variety of large international firms.

Railroads, many of which had never hauled coal for export before (such as Seaboard Coastline, Southern, Union Pacific, Burlington Northern, Southern Pacific, Santa Fe, Illinois Central and Gulf, and others), agreed to upgrade their services and to provide dumping facilities and trackage at new sites. A few even considered taking equity shares in the new terminals. If carried out, these commitments represented hundreds of millions of dollars in capital improvements. The World Coal Study estimated that somewhere between $70–$175 million in railroad upgrading and $275–$785 million in new rolling stock would be needed to achieve a medium level of U.S. exports by 2000 [1980, Vol. 2: 472]). Railroads showed that they were ready to invest.

Several of the projects announced were mere puffery, such as Alla-Ohio Coal's project at Morehead City, North Carolina. The company declared bankruptcy by the end of the year. Some were made with little knowledge to support them and were withdrawn after preliminary investigations (Boston, Camden, Stockton [Calif], Sacramento, Savannah, Charleston [*Wall Street Journal*, 3/30/82]). But others, such as Mobile, New Orleans, New York, and Los Angeles-Long Beach, were undertaken with the commitment to follow through. Millions of dollars of planning, land acquisition, and engineering money was flowing toward establishment of new export terminals owned by coal companies or by international engineering and investment firms.[2]

Gene Samples, president of Consolidation Coal and 1980s chairman of NCA summed up the hit-all-targets strategy of major coal producers when he announced Consolidation's third major coal export project of 1981. The project involved participation in a consortium to purchase an export terminal at Vancouver, British Columbia. Samples said, "This is part of Consol's broad plan to assure greater participation in the growing world market for coal by providing adequate port facilities to handle our product" (*NCA Coal News*, 11/10/81). R.H. Quenon, Of Peabody Coal, noted what he saw as a significant change in the coal export market, but which probably revealed more about the attitude of major firms toward it. "Export coal has become a highly competitive business," Quenon said (*Journal of Commerce*, 11/5/80). Thus, he acknowledged that coal exports had become competitive for and a matter of interest to the country's largest firm.

Ports on three coasts were campaigning to enlist investments in coal export facilities. Major steam coal firms were becoming involved in export sales. This set the stage for geographically-based ad hoc groups and coalitions which would modify the export network. These coalitional realignments will be discussed later. Our current concern is with changes that took place simply because so many new entrants were vying for export sales. Large coal firms, ports, engineering companies, and foreign investors brought international perspectives, investment capital, and new ideas to export trade. They responded to the boom for steam coal sales overseas by trying to stake a claim in the new market. They shared the view that business could be attained by competitive pricing and service to foreign customers.

## Foreign Investments and Joint Ventures

Coal terminal development was not the only business tactic used to gain credibility for U.S. coal firms not accustomed to shipping steam coal abroad. Some firms adopted more long-term strategies of entrepreneurial innovation. They concentrated on making foreign contacts, arranging spot sales, providing new equipment and services to buyers, and the general strategy of inviting foreign joint venture arrangements.

Prior to 1979 foreign investment in American coal companies was insignificant. Just twenty-five of the three thousand firms in the industry were foreign owned. Only 25 million tons of the industry's 800 million tons of annual production was foreign controlled. Even more to the point, the foreign capital invested in coal firms was predominantly concentrated in small firms serving Canadian markets. A small amount of foreign influence may have occurred indirectly on two large coal companies through the foreign shareholders of their parent companies (CRS, A Congressional Handbook, 9/81: 223–24),[3] but this was a minimal level of foreign involvement for a major American industry. The overseas holdings of American coal companies were, by contrast, significant. Holdings, primarily in Australia and Canada, had a book value of $7.1 billion in 1979. But virtually no investments by foreign firms in U.S. companies involved production of steam coal for overseas markets in 1979.

Beginning in 1980, cash rich foreign firms (such as Royal Dutch Shell, British Petroleum, and Kawasaki Steel) began to try to secure U.S. coal assets. (Business Week, 9/21/81; Wall Street Journal, 2/27/81.) Pushed by the 1979 oil crisis, foreign firms and governments began to explore the U.S. for investment prospects. And different from the pre-1979 period, their primary interest seemed to be in large coal firms and major projects.

The investments by foreign governments and firms in U.S. coal companies were entrepreneurial activities in the sense that they increased the chances of these firms participating in foreign sales.

They encouraged coal development and brought about felicitous ongoing cooperation between U.S. coal firms and the foreign buyers and producers of steam coal.

The large size of these investments immediately made them the subject of possible government concern and regulation. Congress held hearings on possible amendments to the Mineral Lands Leasing Act of 1920 which would place a temporary waiting period on those foreign investments which might affect U.S. natural resource security (House, Government Operations, 8/80; House, Interior and Insular Affairs, 5/7/81; 7/16/81). Congress apparently wanted to protect the coal industry from unfriendly takeovers by foreign investors. The hearings were abandoned, however, when it was shown that coal companies were pleased with the interest of foreign capital in their industry.

Coal companies welcomed the infusion of cash and the possibility of new capital formation for expansion which these deals provided. Because mining and infrastructure development are time-consuming and heavily capital intensive; because labor costs in mining are high and relatively fixed; because public surveillance of coal prices and heavy competition keep profits low; the coal industry suffers chronic undercapitalization. Investments by foreign firms were seen as a way for the industry to overcome some of these problems.

U.S. coal companies saw foreign investment as beneficial to free enterprise. By this they meant it heightened their chances of successful competition among their U.S. peers.

Royal Dutch Shell (U.K.-Netherlands) was the first foreign firm to stake a definite claim in the U.S. export market. It had acquired three million-ton R. & F. Coal in the late 1970s. Shell then invested $680 million in steam coal properties and export improvements in a joint venture with A.T. Massey Coal Co. in 1980. It was the second largest foreign investment in the United States that year, and accounted for over 4 percent of total direct foreign investment (DOC, Foreign Investment, 1980, 1981). In this deal Royal Dutch Shell acquired half of total Massey assets. In 1981, Ashland Coal sold 25 percent of its production capacity (5.5 million tons of annual production) to Saarbergwerke, A.G., a West German utility which is entirely nationally and state owned. The deal reportedly cost the German government $102.5 million (*ICR*, 11/18/81). Carboex, the national utility fuel purchaser for Spain, acquired 10 percent of Ashland Coal in a $44 million deal. (*ICR*, 3/12/82).

Amax Coal and Occidental Petroleum (owner of Island Creek Coal) began to solicit joint venture arrangements to develop their export capacities. Amax announced in September 1981 a joint venture with Kawasaki Steel (Japan) to develop mines in Wyoming (*ICR*, 4/12/81). It was known that Amax was also seeking other joint ventures to "finance development of U.S. coalfields which could become major suppliers to Europe and Japan." (*ICR*, 9/25/81). One possible partner was Ruhrkohle of West Germany (*ICR*, 1/1/81). In July 1981, the Italian national power corporation (Ente Nazionale Idrocarburi, ENI) and Occidental Petroleum signed a preliminary joint venture agreement for $1.1 billion. Island Creek's annual steam coal production on the properties involved would increase from 7 to 10 million tons per year, with half of it going to ENI. Further expansion might be made to provide fuel for sixty Italian chemical plants (*NCS Coal News*, 3/16/81).

Another of the largest coal firms, Consolidation Coal, announced a joint venture and long-term sales agreement in June 1981 (*ICR*, 6/30/81) with Western Europe's biggest lignite producer, Rheinishe Braukohlenwerke, A.G., to develop five underground mines in southwestern Pennsylvania. Consol would develop the mines from which the West German producer was committed to take 24 percent of production and the Germans could also purchase an additional 24 percent each year if needed. This coal (up to 12.8 million tons for 28 years) would be shipped via the new Consol rail terminal at Baltimore. It was scheduled for the European industrial heat market.

Hence, five of the major steam coal firms I identified in Chapter 3 as key new actors in U.S. exports, became deeply committed to production for foreign markets through foreign investment deals that were unprecedented in the coal industry. The novelty of the arrangements being announced in the trade press added to the atmosphere of chaotic uncertainty about how and which firms would successfully negotiate for foreign sales. British Petroleum, for example, was known to be looking for deals, although none were announced in 1980–82. The criteria for how to sell coal abroad were unclear even after announcements were made. A general mood of disorganized scramble was the prevailing feeling in coal circles. Luck seemed as much a factor as anything else in obtaining foreign contracts. Connie Holmes, vice-president for economics of NCA and executive secretary of the Coal Exporters Association, called the export situation in 1981 "just insane" (conversation notes, 4/30/81).

Coal firms welcomed and to some extent prospected for these joint venture arrangements which they saw as a way to level the traditionally inconsistent coal export market. Foreign investment seemed a way to lock in future sales and guarantee participation in the future market. The cooperative joint ventures helped large coal companies share with buyers the risk of establishing new infrastructures and helped them guard against the uncertainty of variable market demand. Of course, these arrangements could also involve companies in cooperative relationships with new owners and buyers who might have little familiarity with and little appreciation of their critical concerns.

To some extent U.S. producers enjoyed the benefits of a seller's market. Foreign investors sought them out. Japan was notably active in looking for partners to develop railroad, port, and mining capacity near the West Coast. The Japan Coal Development Co., a consortium of ten Japanese utilities, sought partners for 10–20 million tons of annual export capacity in the west (*ICR*, 10/80). Another Japanese group considered developing the port of Los Angeles. The French government's coal development agency, CFP (Compagnie Francais de Petroles) circulated prospectuses on various projects, including building a coal terminal on the lower Mississippi River, a joint venture to operate coal properties of the Canadian-owned (and South African-controlled) Inspiration Coal Co. (*NCA Coal News*, 3/1/82), and acquiring mining interests and reserves in Kentucky. Reportedly, the French government would soon authorize an expenditure of up to $300 million for these coal supplies (*NCA Coal News*, 7/27/81). NERCO Coal and Taiwan Power entered a 60–40 joint venture to develop a steam coal project in British Columbia. The $46 million deal was to last 25 years (*ICR*, 10/81).

In these deals U.S. companies were not necessarily the initiators, but often willingly received proposals from foreign corporations. For example, Elf Aquitaine (France) proposed shipping Pennsylvania coal to New York harbor via Conrail and then loading it by offshore barge or slurry pipelines onto large ships (memorandum, 4/30/81). The significance of the plan was that none of the parties involved had any experience with shipping coal in this way. Costs, problems and advantages could be only roughly guessed at. The flood of new proposals challenged the industry's technical expertise to evaluate them reasonably. For example, rumor circulated that a Japanese shipping magnate was considering financing the channel dredging at Hampton Roads with his own funds (*ICR*, 5/12/82).

## Other New Sales Practices

U.S. firms were listening to any and all proposals, and trying to evaluate them. The transportation and marketing departments of large steam coal firms had often never dealt with problems of ocean shipping, tariffs, and port licensing. They had to become familiar with port practices. They began to be aware of the services and pricing options foreign buyers desired. Barge rates had to be compared with rail delivery to various ports. The prospects of mixing coals to lower sulfur contents for European markets where scrubbers are less utilized, were quickly investigated. Coal companies considered innovative delivery mechanisms such as slurry pipelines (one for as long as 1,500 miles), self-unloading ships, offshore terminals, ocean-going barges, wide-hulled carriers, and coal-burning ships as cost-saving incentives to encourage buyers. One equipment company offered to provide plexiglass covers for coal barges to prevent the moisture accumulation on the way to port which, some thought, caused spontaneous combustion of coal on long ocean trips.

Coal companies began to see the advantage that oil companies had retained for many years through their vertical integration into ocean transportation. By owning their own ships, oil companies controlled the cost of freight and avoided the volatile tanker market. Coal companies with oil affiliations found that they could promise guaranteed backhauls of coal on their parent company's oil-bulk-ore carriers (OBO's) which commonly carried imported oil to the United States. This service could give oil-owned coal companies a 10–20 percent price advantage over other American coal in foreign markets.

Foreign buyers also desired contracting procedures and secondary services which were unfamiliar to the American coal market. These expectations put American companies on notice that they would have to change their ways of doing business. Most basic was the questioning of the terms of traditional sales. Coal was typically shipped to port by sellers on a contract which severed the producer's responsibility once the product arrived at port. Thus, coal sales were made based on a "free on board" (FOB) price, which excluded ocean freight charges, demurrage, and port destination fees. Throughout the rest of the world, coal was shipped through to its destination port, hence the responsibility for efficient port handling, demurrage, transloading, and ocean freight was partially borne by the seller. This "cost, insurance, freight" (CIF) method of contracting for coal was much preferred by foreign buyers.

In some deals U.S. companies found that secondary services such as technical assistance in meeting environmental requirements, sophisticated equipment to upgrade domestic mining industries, and (in the more underdeveloped countries) even the provision of services like schools, roads, and rail or port infrastructure could increase the prospect of obtaining foreign sales. Some countries wanted to protect themselves against the outflow of dollars or perhaps could not obtain secure financing. They wanted to negotiate countertrade arrangements for coal. These unfamiliar ways of conducting coal sales presented challenges to firms trying to enter the new market. There was a great deal to understand. Companies had ample opportunities to show their flexibility and innovativeness in arranging such deals.

Entrepreneurial innovations reflected themselves in a few obviously changed attitudes and organizational structures *within* coal firms. At least two major companies, Consolidation Coal and Peabody, reorganized their internal sales divisions to make them more responsive to foreign business. Consol created an international sales division. Peabody (although hindered by its predominantly high-sulfur midwest production) decided to enter coal brokering and reorganized its marketing department to give overseas sales development greater prominence. More firms began to advertise their export capabilities in trade publications, and they became members of export trade associations.

## Large Firms Have the Advantage

Many of the business innovations noted here were highly dependent on large investments. They could not be implemented on short notice. Others, such as countertrade agreements, required a broad network of associations and contacts, and the ability to arrange complex deals in many related industries. Most innovations were possible only for very large firms who were willing and able to front significant capital investment in fixed improvements, or who could call on multinational support structures. The willingness of foreigners to commit resources to long-term improvements was encouraging to the still somewhat reluctant major coal companies. It was also shaping the profile of who would eventually participate in the export market.

Ben Lusk, president of the Mining and Reclamation Council of America, the major national association of small coal producers, articulated the emerging apprehensions of small coal firms. At a coal ports seminar in February 1981 he said, "The big question is whether the small or medium sized operator has a role in international coal exports." Although he concluded, "The big answer is YES!" he listed the enormous obstacles such as inadequate financing, lack of marketing capabilities, low credit, and poor transportation from mines that small firms would have to overcome (AAPA Proceedings, 2/17–19/81: 100–101). Lusk's conclusion was that the survival of small companies in this new market would be possible only with the formation of industry cooperatives and the direct intervention and support of small firms by government.

*The American Coal Exchange.* One innovation which might have aided small coal shippers was the proposal for an American Coal Exchange. Coal prices, tied down as they are by domestic regulation, long-term utility contracts, and heavy labor and transportation costs, had never posed an attractive prospect for commodity speculation on a futures market. The price and supply of coal simply did not vary enough. Coal futures were not traded on any U.S. exchange. Hence, the brokering of coal even in the volatile export market took place apart from the high-pressure atmosphere of international commodities trading. Furthermore, the brokering of coal for export was not officially organized or regulated. Unlike the grain exchanges at which individual farmers could market their crops through representatives bidding on specific sales contracts for that day's best price, coal was not bought and sold in any one place. Individual orders were prepared by a variety of independent brokers. Small firms were usually obliged to sell to larger producers who were themselves assembling orders. But in this situation the small producers were at the mercy of their individual brokers to obtain a good deal or to offer them a good price. Almost invariably they would not receive the full price of export coal. A trading exchange would increase the access of many buyers and sellers to possible outlets for their coal. It would also offer greater liquidity to cash-poor mining operations.

Shortly after the advent of the 1980 interest in steam coal a group of Virginia bankers and businessmen proposed the American Coal Exchange. The Exchange was to provide computerized brokering and trading services with particular attention to smaller firms for export coal sales. The organizers, primarily bankers rather than coal-men, were immediately subject to the ridicule of large coal firms and established coal traders for their inexperience with coal. They were suspected of trying to set up a futures market rather than a simple commodity exchange to facilitate trade.

Regardless of their motives, it does seem that a commodities exchange might have benefited smaller firms trying to ship steam coal. This view was stated by Ben Lusk at the AAPA Convention (2/18/81). To the extent that steam coal is a more substitutable product than met coal it might be possible to broker it though a central exchange mechanism. But this idea has confronted many obstacles. Large firms and traders essentially ignored the idea. They heaped scorn on the proposed organizers (*Wall Street Journal*, 7/18/80). In a situation where many standard procedures were being questioned some innovations were obviously unacceptable to powerful groups. In March 1981, less than nine months after its announced beginnings, based on the suspicion that the Exchange was illegally selling coal purchase (futures) contracts on an unlicensed exchange, the U.S. Commodity Futures Trading Commission (CFTC) temporarily halted sales and stepped in to investigate. The CFTC decided to sue in federal court, claiming that the Virginia bankers had defrauded investors of $1.5 million (*Washington Post*, 11/18/81). The future of the American Coal Exchange is at present uncertain. Its history so far does illustrate, however, the difficulty that new ideas favorable to small coal producers had in gaining a place in the coal export market. The flexibility and international connections of large coal firms give them inestimable advantages in entering and maintaining a strong presence in this new arena.

*Rampant inexperience.* In many new ventures U.S. firms were sought out even if they were not explicitly prospecting for deals. Their appeal to foreign customers was often their large size and secure reputation within the American domestic industry. Any lack of export experience was deemed irrelevant.

Unaccustomed activity led to some curious gaffes as large, supposedly sophisticated firms began operating in novel situations. For example, one large company obtained a contract for a trial shipment of steam coal from New Orleans to Taiwan. The ship contracted to carry the coal was impounded in port and the cargo temporarily seized for the ship's previous nonpayment of customs fees. This problem, which could easily have been avoided, was industrywide news. It is hard to know how widespread such mistakes were. But the admissions by many coal people in public meetings of their ignorance of foreign trade and its basic expectations testify to the fact that great confusion prevailed.

*Proactive global strategies.* Although the predominant tenor of entrepreneurial innovations from 1980–82 appeared haphazard, some very large firms were engaged in more aggressive policies of expansion and encouragement of foreign coal sales. These firms were typically involved in global strategies of development and diversification, usually as the instruments of their parent owners. These firms were not at all bound by consideration of the American steam coal market as such, and many preferred instead to place their developments offshore. For example, Exxon (a huge holder of reserve lands in the western U.S. and a producer of western and midwest coal) preferred to develop an offshore base in Colombia for its international coal exports. It had concluded a deal with the Colombian government in 1979 to develop coal resources, a port, and railroad infrastructure there. Long-term committed shipments were arranged to Denmark (27 million tons over 14 years to begin in 1986) (*ICR*, 10/23/81). Exxon was also building a massive synfuels plant in Rotterdam, which might eventually be able to process its high sulfur Illinois coal. Such strategies preceded the 1980 boom. They showed evidence of significant long-range planning and deliberate deployment of resources on the part of internationally-aware corporations.

Another example was Occidental Petroleum. With Armand Hammer's personal touch, Occidental negotiated an arrangement to provide housing, schools, railroads, port facilities, technical equipment, and expertise for a huge surface mining project in China.[4] It was the largest foreign joint venture in China's history, $230 million, and might yield 210 million tons of coal per year, some of which would be exported to Japan (*ICR*, 2/82). The deal hinged on Hammer's willingness to take coal as the primary form of debt repayment; coal which he would then sell on the international market. Within the U.S. steam coal industry this deal was considered both an amazing coup and a terrible risk. Island Creek Coal was not the most experienced U.S. firm in the techniques of surface mining. Hammer had perhaps oversold his company's expertise in the face of many American competitors. Second, other producers thought that holding coal instead of cash in an undeveloped world coal market could prove profitless. Nevertheless, the deal illustrates clearly the kinds of enterprising and flexible sales techniques that were beginning to shape a new international market for coal and which were favoring the largest firms. Hammer's deal would bring a whole new area of the world, both buyers and sellers, into viable competition for goods: The world market would expand. Hammer later obtained lenient offshore oil drilling rights for Occidental Petroleum after concluding this coal agreement. The coal deal may have been a part of a larger strategy focused primarily on oil.

There were other global strategies related to steam coal exports. Standard Oil of Ohio (Sohio), owner of Old Ben Coal, earmarked $2 billion for coal reserve development over the next ten years, with the prospect of increasing its investment even further if synfuel development took off (*ICR*, 2/12/82). British Petroleum, the controlling owner of both of these firms, previously had joined with Ruhrkole International of West Germany to explore coal reserves in Colombia (*Business Week*, 9/21/82). Atlantic Richfield, Utah International, and Consolidated Coal joined with an Italian firm to develop coal in Indonesia (*ICR*, 2/12/82). Arco Coal, which had entered two metallurgical coal joint ventures in Australia in the late 1970s, began to explore various port sites in the Canadian northwest (especially Canada's Rupert's Bay) and to experiment with oil-coal mixtures for pipeline deliverability (*Journal of Commerce*, 2/17/81).

Each of these internationally negotiated agreements to develop steam coal heightened the competition that U.S. firms would encounter in world sales. International deals greatly increased the scope of the U.S. coal firms' competitive network.

## Contracts Signed

But what finally was the bottom line? Did the frantic scurry for new business result in significant long-term sales? The long-term agreements desired by potential steam coal exporters, both to steady the market and to provide development funds to improve export capabilities, proved remarkably elusive. As I have mentioned, countries were reluctant to commit themselves immediately to long-term contracts in the United States until they could assess the market and the U.S. government's attitude to coal trade. The shippers they were dealing with were inexperienced in international trade and naturally, buyers did not wish to tie themselves down too soon.

By February 1981, according to William Mason, president of the Coal Exporters Association, not many long-term contracts had been signed, and those that were, were for relatively small amounts of coal (*Journal of Commerce*, 2/17/81). The spot market was apparently still the predominant conveyance of coal overseas (*Journal of Commerce*, Glasser, 2/17/81).

Yet coal was moving in new ways. N & W railroad announced January 30, 1981, that it had signed its first hauling contract for coal from a central Appalachian field to Hampton Roads for export (*ICR*, 1/30/81). The transshipper was ATIC (the French government's coal purchasing arm). Getty Oil claimed to be the first to send western steam coal (about 200,000 tons) to Japan in January 1981 (*World Coal*, Jan. 1981: 15). Getty said it could expand shipments to two million tons per year. The first shipment of Illinois steam coal went to Europe in June 1981: 125,000 tons from a Freeman United mine to a cement company in Spain. Delivery was through New Orleans by the Illinois Central and Gulf railroad (*Coal Industry News*, 6/19/81: 4). By February 1982, in perhaps the most remarkable event of all, U.S. Commerce Department data showed that New Orleans had surpassed Hampton Roads as the largest U.S. steam coal port (NCA, *International Coal Review*, 2/12/82).

However, few long-term arrangements had been worked out even by the middle of 1982. Most countries made clear that they wished to diversify their coal orders among the world's four or five major exporting countries. In this spirit they scouted the U.S. for the best available infrastructure and suppliers. The deals announced, although amounting to more contracted steam coal than had been sold abroad before the 1980 boom, were disappointingly small compared to expectations. Island Creek contracted to the Israeli Electricity Corp. for up to 400,000 tons between 1982 and 1984. Consol, Freeman United, and Exxon's International Colombian Resources would together send 9.9 million tons over six years to the Irish Electricity Board. Utah International also obtained a contract with Ireland for seven million tons over twenty years. Diamond Shamrock would provide ATIC (France) with 2.5 million tons over four years. In the only announced activity by smaller firms, a newly formed cooperative of eighteen small producers, the Big Sandy Coal Producers Association, aided by a guaranteed loan from the governor of Kentucky and the Appalachian Regional Commission, arranged a multi-year commitment with ENI (the Italian utility) (*Coal Industry News*, 9/25/81). Many discussions were underway: Consol with Reinishe Braunkohlewerke (West Germany); Ashland with Carboex (Spain); Diamond Shamrock and Peabody with ATIC (France). But actual sales were insignificant compared to industry hopes.

Foreign buyers made clear that they were also talking to potential U.S. competitors: Japan to Canada, China, Australia, and Colombia; France to South Africa; Denmark and Finland to Colombia; West Germany to Australia. It became evident to those American producers with the ability to reflect and with a stake in the outcome that pure grit and scramble would not be enough to secure and maintain a strong presence in international coal sales. Other strategies, based on more sophisticated assessments of the situation, would be needed.

## Summary: The Effects of Entrepreneurial Activities

Stresses placed on standard operating procedures for delivering export coal during 1980–82 widened the field of competition for sales among coal exporting firms. Entrepreneurial activities, focused on obtaining business from foreign customers, increased the number of viable market actors, changed assumptions about sales procedures, and fostered creativity in developing options for delivering coal overseas. New patterns of interaction became evident.

Activities such as new delivery modes, terminal building announcements, innovations in contracting and handling procedures, and foreign joint ventures realigned the industry's sales procedures. Public statements indicated that a group of major U.S. firms were becoming involved in exporting steam coal. Among these were many firms that had never exported coal before. The basic network, the daily associations taken for granted in U.S. coal trade, were being realigned.

Entrepreneurial activities were undertaken in the context that success in overseas steam coal sales was uncertain and more highly competitive than previously. Firms plunged into areas where they had little or no expertise, in efforts to satisfy potential customer expectations. They embarked on hit-or-miss plans to change delivery patterns and other basic assumptions about delivering coal abroad. They stumbled and created curious and embarrassing situations for themselves.

Only a relatively few firms achieved long-term contracts for steam coal delivery by the end of my observation in May 1982. However, major steam coal firms with global strategies for obtaining overseas business seemed to be gaining the advantage in initiating competitive entrepreneurial activities. This advantage is likely to continue.

The scramble for market participation realigned the steam coal industry's interorganizational network, by increasing the intensity of interaction among firms and expanding the number of firms competing for market shares. Random transactions, including luck, seemed to characterize the arrangement of power in the interorganizational network. A greater variety of American coal exporters were competing for business, but which firms would eventually control this business over the long-term was not at all clear. Becoming clearer was that major firms with great domestic market power and foreign resources had entered the network, and that they had many potential advantages over smaller firms in the competition for steam coal sales.

Entrepreneurial activities were but one layer of new network interactions taking place in 1980–82. They were based on the implied or explicit perception that the export market was a relatively simple market challenge. Hit or miss strategies to participate profitably in this increased competition were the goal.

In the following chapters I will discuss four additional types of interorganizational interactions which began to occur during 1980–82. All have already been glimpsed in embryo. Each pattern of network interaction was based, not on an objective difference in the environment, but on the kind of uncertainty to which organizational actors were implicitly trying to respond.

For example, as firms realized that they had serious foreign—not just domestic—competition for foreign sales, their need for reliable information about foreign markets, competitors, mining conditions, and production capacity increased. Few firms had monitored the conditions of foreign steam coal before. Here was a new·source of uncertainty they would have to take into account. The availability and accuracy of technical information became a new area of problematic concern. It resulted in strategies for organizing, deploying, assimilating, and disseminating information and expertise. The organizational realignments which resulted from this area of concern are discussed in the next chapter.

## NOTES

1. Hence, entrepreneurial activities (although often innovations) do not have the *necessary* connotation of innovativeness and risk that is often associated with entrepreneurship in other studies. Entrepreneurial business-oriented activity is used here to denote network activity in which the individual firm acts directly for its own profit; and individual firms are the primary unit of interorganizational interaction. The term is used in contrast to the other types of network relationships I will be discussing: informational, coalitional, supraorganizational and macroinstitutional; each of which focuses on different units of interaction and presents different rationales for interorganizational interaction.

2. An interesting financial wrinkle about the development of new coal terminals was that very little private capital would end up being spent on these projects. Coal terminals were eligible for tax-free industrial revenue bonds to finance companies' investment costs. Government and the U.S. bond-buyer would be partners with coal firms in the development of coal export facilities. The availability of this financing probably was influential in encouraging coal firms to make commitments to build new coal terminals.

3. One example of this is Old Ben Coal Company, a 10 million-ton per year firm, which is owned by Standard Oil of Ohio (Sohio). Sohio is in turn controlled by British Petroleum Company.
   The second major example is Colowyo Coal, an expanding western firm which is 50 percent owned by W.R. Grace (United States). W.R. Grace is in turn 31 percent owned by the Flick Group of West Germany. (CRS, *A Congressional Handbook*, 8/81: 223–24).

4. Hammer's negotiation with the Chinese even involved an extensive cultural tour of his personal art collection within the People's Republic.

# 6 New Sources of Information

Information became a newly-valued resource for coal firms during 1980–82. An enormous amount of information poured forth from general news media, trade journals, government reports, conferences, and congressional hearings. Much of this information issued from sources that had not previously been active in coal. New sources of information emerged specifically in response to a widely-shared perception that the environment for export trade was increasingly complex. Coal companies used new sources of information to develop their specialization and expertise. They committed their energy and resources to information-gathering and analysis as a strategy to increase their competitive edge, and many developed new relationships with information-providers. These strategic decisions had important ramifications for interorganizational relationships in the industry's network.

The goal of obtaining accurate information with which to evaluate the overseas market quickly taxed routine information-gathering capabilities; it exposed industry members to information systems they had not used before; and finally it brought industry members together among themselves and with supporting groups in new ways. New information vendors emerged as purveyors and disseminators of information for a fee (as with consultants and journals) or because these services furthered their own strategic goals (as with trade associations and government). By developing information themselves, some firms were able proactively to shape the expectations of the new market to their own ends, and thus they actually attained influence over the environment they were responding to.

A new layer of realignments emerged in the industry's interorganizational network as new sources of information became institutionally organized. New sources of information became attached to the coal industry as supportive services with which firms developed multiple crossties. Thus, the interorganizational network of the industry aggregated into new clusters as a result of the desire to obtain accurate technical knowledge. Network relationships clustered around services which provided coordination and support. Information sources increased the level of confidence and expertise among U.S. coal firms. Yet we will see in the final section of this chapter that expertise and confidence did not accrue equally to all firms.

## SOURCES OF CONFUSION: THE ENVIRONMENT AS TECHNICALLY COMPLEX

Actors in the coal export situation perceived the new environment as technically complex. There were many questions needing answers. Some were purely factual, like port depths, the location of shipping terminals, freight rates, inland transportation options, and ship sizes. Others were more evaluative, such as what was *causing* the U.S. coal boom; how much of a premium foreign customers would pay for secure U.S. supplies; how fast electricity demand and industrial expansion would grow in the Far East and Europe; and most important, whether the demand for American steam coal would last.

The lack of information (and the amount of misinformation) even on factual issues was obvious. Examples came out often in congressional testimony. For example, when Joel Price, a popular and well-known coal analyst, debunked the need for deepening American ports, no one on a Senate panel could dispute his contention that foreign receiving ports were not deep enough for large ships. Carl Bagge had to scramble during a lunchtime break to get figures to show that Price had his facts wrong (Senate, Environment & Public Works, Part 1, 4/21/81). In another example, E. Morgan Massey, speaking as chairman of NCA's Transportation Committee and as the CEO of A.T. Massey Coal, got his explanation of port operation so confused as he tried to explain NCA's position on port fees to a House committee that Congressman Robert Roe had to help him out (House, Public Works, 6/17/81). There were many examples of such misstatements.

Businesses are tempted to cover up their lack of information about technical issues. Many studies have shown that fear of negative repercussions in hierarchical settings and competitiveness among departments work to reduce candor and admissions of ignorance. So it is a mark of the extreme stress in the coal industry that evidence of uncertainty about technical prodecures showed through as much as it did. Coal spokesmen blamed their confusion on lack of foresight, inexperience, and the complexity of many intersecting issues. It was evident that they saw the exports market as a challenge to their knowledge and to their current capabilities.

William Boyle, a newly appointed coordinator of export trade for Consolidation Coal Company, summed up the feelings of many coal people at one of the first coal export hearings when he candidly remarked, "I am not totally familiar with all the export factors" (House, Interstate Commerce, 12/17/80: 43).

Admissions of surprise and some consternation about the new market pervaded the coal chain. According to Carl Weber, a vice-president of Chessie, ". . . if we go back to October 1979, sometime before that, I am sure that we didn't foresee this terrific upsurge in the demand for steam coal nor did any of the coal producers, nor the exporters. If we had I am sure that some one of us would have got moving a little faster than we did" (House, Interstate Commerce, 12/17/80: 81).

The factors causing the surge in U.S. steam coal demand were also matters of confusion and apprehension, as noted at the same hearing by Representative Clarence Brown of Ohio.

> One thing I think is remarkable and we haven't mentioned it, but all of this increase in both metallurgical and steam coal has occurred at a time when you have got a general economic slump going on all around the world.
> I am still unclear in my mind, whether that represents dramatic shifts to the U.S. market from an Australian market, screwed up by shipping costs, or whatever the factors are.
> That bothers me still, and I don't know. (House, Interstate Commerce, 12/17/80: 96)

Congressman Brown never isolated what was causing the boom. His suggestion of the anomalies present in 1980 was based on fear that the coal boom might be a temporary bubble. He did not even identify the disruption of Polish coal exports to Europe, which was a major factor in the expansion of U.S. coal exports from 1980 to 1982.

The industry needed help overcoming its ignorance on factual issues and sorting out the complex influences on causal questions. But it was not immediately clear in all instances to whom it should turn. About all that many consultants could offer their clients was reassurance that everyone was confused. Zachariah Allen, a respected coal analyst at the financial firm of F. R. Schwab Associates, noted the general lack of knowledge and experience at a coal industry seminar held shortly after the steam coal boom began.

> Finally, it is important to remember that this is a new business for everyone involved; for the buyers as well as the sellers. Many of the problems we have seen developing between European buyers and U.S. sellers have been due to lack of experience on both sides of the transaction. As time goes on we believe the experience will tend to rationalize this business. We believe it is one well worth pursuing but that the pursuit must be well thought out and carefully executed if it is to be a profitable business. (The Energy Bureau, conference proceedings, 12/6–7/80)

This admission of a gap in information and experience common to all members of the industry is noteworthy coming from one whose professional reputation rested on giving accurate advice.

Command over technical issues quickly became a premium that U.S. coal firms sought and for which they were willing to pay. The way to overcome confusion and uncertainty about the technical issues in the environment was to develop better information-sensing and evaluating capabilities. Zachariah Allen was one of a number of consultants to emphasize that command over technical issues was the most viable strategy U.S. coal firms could use to gain a competitive edge over the competition they would face from producers in other countries. "The coal marketer who can participate in and contribute to the technical and economic analyses that take place during the new plant planning process will be the successful marketer of steam coal in the 1980s" (*World Coal*, No. 4 April 1980: 44).

## INFORMATION-GATHERING AS A STRATEGY

Direct evidence expressed by firms of their desire for new information (as opposed to that expressed by consultants or Congressmen) is difficult to obtain. Privately, participants admitted their ignorance, but it was risky to announce it publicly while buyers were shopping around for potential trading partners. In my experience industry members were privately aware of their lack of knowledge and spent considerable time trying to fill themselves in. A transportation director told me, "Frankly the Europeans consider us a bunch of rank amateurs where coal trade is concerned" ( conversation notes, 2/17/81). He followed this with a list of coal export areas he did not yet understand, such as backhauls, transshipping arrangements, and foreign port fees; and that, he claimed, other firms were well versed on because of their oil-company connections.

It is also evident from a variety of unobtrusive measures that new information was desired and was being sought. For example, attendance at seminars and conferences, preparation and dissemination of technical reports, subscriptions to journals, interaction with other industries for information about handling of coal, and the obvious inaccuracies and later retractions of information given in speeches and congressional testimony attest to the fact that industry members were scrambling to fill in their knowledge about important factors in the chaotic situation. Consultants and consulting services became important sources of new information.

For what kinds of new information did coal companies feel a need? How did this information become organized into supporting services that would serve and extend the interorganizational network? Finally, how did new sources of information affect the power arrangements in the industry? In other words, which firms could make use of these new sources of information and why?

The emergence of new information sources is inferential evidence that they represented responses to needs and problems that the coal industry was trying to solve. At first glance this reasoning may seem to be an example of the causal fallacy *post hoc ergo propter hoc*. However, most of these new sources of information required companies to commit their time and resources to obtain the technical advice being purveyed. The survival of these information services depended on industry interest and monetary support. Therefore, industry attention to these services is a reliable indicator that they were becoming important parts of the industry's supporting network.

*What kinds of information did companies want*? To judge by the topics of industry seminars, articles in trade journals, and government reports, industry participants wanted information in several related categories. Generally speaking, none of this information had been important to steam coal producers prior to 1980. Topics that received most attention were:

- engineering estimates of the current capacities and handling systems at U.S. ports.
- information about port depths, dredging costs, and large-ship economies which would help control the cost of ocean freight.
- accurate data about the volume of current and expected U.S. (and world) coal trade.
- information about port depths, coal handling systems, and environmental regulations in foreign countries.

- country-by-country information about the preferences and factors affecting the buying patterns of potential U.S. trading partners and customers.
- general knowledge and intelligence about world competitors.
- forecasts of the expected sizes, destinations, and costs of the U.S. export sales from various ports.
- general political and social insights about how to sell coal in specific foreign countries.

The above categories go beyond the information individual firms often developed or sought about handling systems, special contractual services, or individual markets to implement their own marketing plans. Information-gathering of this limited sort was included in the entrepreneurial activities discussed in the previous chapter. This chapter concentrates on industry realignments which resulted from commonly identified gaps in substantive knowledge.

*How did the desire for new information become organized around new providers?* Coal companies looked first to their traditional support systems—engineering firms, financial and economic consultants, trade associations—to provide them with the kinds of information they desired. Government also took an active role in providing reports about this potentially huge area of foreign trade. Information provided in general media coverage and commentary was extensive, but whether industry people took this as authoritative or as merely a barometer of the outside world's awareness of the export situation is not certain. One Board of Directors postponed approving a new coal terminal project after *Fortune* magazine suggested that U.S. ports might become overbuilt. The article may have been invoked as a convenient excuse for more deep-seated reservations, but it indicates the influence of the general press on important investment decisions. In general, the information provided by the general press is not what I mean by new information sources. Although its sheer volume was impressive,[1] the general media did not become a significant factor in the technical system by which coal might be actually conveyed to foreign markets. The new sources of information important here took an active promotional interest in furthering the market for U.S. export coal.

*How did new sources of information affect industry relationships?*

1. *New supporting groups.* In general, potential and current exporters became more heavily reliant on the data-gathering, synthesizing, and coordinating capabilities of supporting service groups.

New journals and reorganized old ones, subscription consulting services, trade press reports, and stronger coordinating roles by NCA and the Coal Exporters Association became important sources of needed new information. The coal industry network was altered and extended to include roles for these new groups.

2. *Government-industry cooperation.* Government-commissioned reports and augmentation of trade information services solidified the partnership of coal firms with the federal government in promoting U.S. coal trade. These reports and services showed that government agencies and coal industry people were both working toward the goal of increasing export trade. This nurturant interest by the federal government in the development of the coal business was unique in the industry's history. The federal government was casting itself in a servicing role to the coal industry.

3. *Increased interpersonal interactions.* Conferences, seminars, and trade meetings brought new members of the export market together for face-to-face interactions. These meetings, which were usually sponsored either by outside groups or trade associations, became valuable forums for venting problems, exchanging ideas, and making new sales contracts. They encouraged a less parochial outlook on the part of coal companies, and reinforced instead their interdependence with ports, with rail and barge transportation, and with buyer concerns. Exporters came to rely on these interactive sessions for increasing their personal contacts and expertise. The groups which arranged these conferences enhanced their own importance as coordinative organizations within the inter-industry network and they attained a measure of leadership in the export market as auxiliary services coordinating coal trade.

4. *Proactive uses of information.* Very large coal firms (and a few other groups) saw an opportunity in the information gap to serve their strategic ends. They prepared detailed analyses and trade forecasts and presented them in a form that would promote their individual interests. Such forecasts amounted to public relations hypes designed to tout their own capacity and readiness to engage in the new market.[2] Such practices are common and accepted in many industries, although new to coal. In this way, large coal firms became the providers as well as the consumers of new information. Because they appeared knowledgeable, other network participants turned to them for expert technical data. Thus, the large firms developed a strategically preferred situation in which they were looked to for guidance, gained credibility with purchasers for their breadth of knowledge, and attained leadership in influencing the expectations and important policy considerations that would affect foreign trade.

The purpose of these forays into information preparation was not to provide objective research and unbiased market analysis but information which was forensically oriented to the support of their own interests and ends. The large firms had more resources to devote to planning and analysis than the small firms and, if they were new in the export market, they had strong incentive to tout their capabilities. On the other hand, many small firms who had established themselves in foreign met coal trade had only their geographic proximity to traditional ports and their record of past sales to prove their ability to compete.

In these four kinds of realignments the unifying feature was modification or displacement of older sources of information and the emergence of new sources on which the industry could rely. The industry's network grew more clustered with attachments to supporting groups. It was extended by contracts with other industries and with international buyers and sellers beyond its normal range of associations. Each of the four new sources of technical information is discussed more fully below.

## NEW SUPPORTING GROUPS

*NCA's role*. Accurate trade data to establish the volume of coal being shipped, where it was going, and how to handle it became the first source of concern for potential shippers. NCA and the Coal Exporters Association were the usual transmitters of official government trade statistics to the coal industry.

Since 1970, NCA had assembled coal trade statistics gathered by the U.S. Department of Commerce into a semi-yearly report called *International Coal Review*. This tabular report on coal export trade volumes and values, of course, mainly concerned metallurgical coal. In 1980, NCA began to issue *International Coal Review* monthly and to supplement it with additional reports. An issue appeared almost every two weeks. But the format of the Department of Commerce's data lagged behind the changes in coal trade taking place. Coal firms wanted to know how much steam coal and how much met coal was exiting from each major port. Not until 1978 had official statistics even distinguished between metallurgical and steam coal exports. It was the end of March, 1981, over a year after the steam coal boom began, before government statistics provided separate figures for met and steam coal exports from individual U.S. ports. NCA was sometimes called upon to make informal estimates of trade. This information lag as the port situation was changing led to wildly varying estimates of the amount of steam coal tonnage being carried through various ports. It increased confusion among fledgling steam coal handlers, but it also heightened NCA's importance as a repository of useful information.

The NCA Economics Committee (composed of two dozen industry corporate planning executives and two NCA staffers) tried to provide the industry with some guidance about shipping and port capacities. The committee met in May 1980 to pool its limited knowledge about the equipment at U.S. coal piers. A report was issued in June 1980 by the Coal Exporters Association. In the memo accompanying this report the NCA Economics Committee acknowledged their meagre knowledge about the basics of export trade. Little information was known and none had been confirmed about capacities of potential U.S. coal piers—even those on the east coast. (NCA memo, n.d. [5/80]; CEA Report on Coal Export Port Capacity, 6/80).

NCA and the Coal Exporters Association were doing their best to distribute what little information they had about the emerging boom, but the new demands were beyond their normal expertise.

Another indication of NCA's scramble to assess the export situation was shown by the Economics Committee's constant revisions of expected yearly export totals: upward three times in 1980 and four times in 1981.

NCA and the Coal Exporters Association put on special efforts to rise to the occasion. They began supplementing *International Coal Review* with issues on the foreign coal trade of competing countries. Often this information was culled from newly emerging world coal trade publications or was drawn from existing data which had become relevant to potential exporters for the first time, such as the coal trade data of the European Economic Community. NCA also took an active role in setting up seminars for its members on topics of current interest to U.S. foreign coal trade. Through these seminars—on ocean and rail transportation, on contracting, on foreign environmental regulation, etc.—similarly situated individuals within member-companies got together to discuss common problems and to upgrade their knowledge. The NCA annual conventions in 1980, 1981, and 1982 gave prominence to topics and invited speakers related to international steam coal trade. The NCA trade newsletter, *Coal News*, carried articles on the coal export situation in nearly all of its weekly issues throughout the 1980–82 period.

NCA served as the offical host for foreign coal buying delegations visiting the U.S. Carl Bagge, president of NCA, estimated that the association hosted at least fifteen delegations in 1980 and as many in 1981. NCA therefore was becoming an important conduit and repository of information on foreign coal trade. Its vice-president, Connie Holmes, the head staffer of CEA, was sometimes the catalyst for financial deals between NCA members and foreign buyers. Her economics staff (which was also the staff of the Coal Exporters Association) provided analysis and brought together legislative proposals on the port development bills which were being presented in Congress.

NCA's role in foreign trade gave it a higher than usual profile in the coal industry. NCA became the nearest U.S. equivalent to the Energy Planning Boards and official coal producing organizations typically found in most foreign countries. Foreign buyers looked first to NCA for information and occasionally for advice. Thus, NCA emerged in an important coordinative role. As NCA was called on more, its expertise grew, and by the end of 1981 it was reorganized with a separate department of international trade, headed by Connie Holmes. NCA's specific activities as a coordinator of U.S. coal trade and policy development will be taken up in the chapter on supraorganizations. Here I merely wish to point out that NCA was being looked to in new ways and for new kinds of information and leadership on foreign coal trade. These new demands enhanced NCA's visibility and expanded its coordinative and supportive roles. Even major members of the U.S. coal industry were more reliant on NCA and CEA services.

*Trade journals.* An enormous amount of the written material which crossed the desks of corporate planners in the major coal company where I worked consisted of specialized trade publications. These ranged from magazines, newspapers, and newsletters to statistical studies, technical reports, and the proceedings of conferences.

Trade journals are supported almost entirely by heavy subscription fees from the industries they serve, rather than by advertising. Therefore, they are tied more obviously to subscriber opinion than is the general press. They combine information needs and communication among industry participants with frankly promotional and public relations articles. Consequently, it is important when these journals are altered or new ones emerge. Such changes indicate that new kinds of concerns are requiring attention and that information needs are being displaced onto new sources. During the time I observed the coal industry a number of journals emerged with an emphasis on world coal trade and U.S. steam coal exports. More significantly, several of the more traditional journals altered their formats to acknowledge interest in steam coal export trade information.

The *Journal of Commerce*, a widely read business daily, followed the exports story with avidity. It ran lengthy multi-part features on coal export trade. *Coal Industry News,* a specialized biweekly with circulation of 11,500 also covered coal exports in depth especially the announcements of new coal terminals. Coverage of the story was so extensive it would be hard to imagine a business executive involved in coal, bulk trade or exporting in 1980–82 who had not at least heard of the emerging situation. This increase in available information was one major way the U.S. coal industry was becoming more internationally aware about its possible role in world trade.

*Coal Daily,* a newsletter published by a Washington-based business publishing service, had frequent articles on the export situation. It focused especially on the progress of port legislation before Congress. This kind of news heightened the industry's awareness of its dual stake in exports with the port industry, and enlightened industry members about the activities of important congressional committees and members of Congress involved in port and water policy.

NCA's weekly newsletter *NCA Coal News* devoted enormous space to coal export stories from 1980 to 1982. It was considered the biggest development of the two years, in spite of looming reauthorization of the Clean Air Act and revision of the Miners Pension Fund, which would have important economic repercussions on the industry (*NCA Coal News,* year-end summary 1/4/82). *Coal Now,* the MARC newsletter also covered developments related to exports for the smaller firms.

Pasha Publication's, *Coal Outlook,* a weekly newspaper, devoted much space to the exports story. It concentrated on trade statistics, features, and analytical articles, and perhaps most important, it sponsored industry seminars on topics related to export trade.

*Coal Age,* founded in 1911, is one of the oldest and most widely read periodicals in the industry, with a circulation of 21,000. In April, 1981, *Coal Age* added to its format a column called "Port Watch," which promised to summarize shipping conditions at all major U.S. ports. Ship brokers, railroads, and port authorities would be contacted for accurate information. Needless to say, port traffic had not been of great interest to *Coal Age* readers prior to 1980.

*New publications also emerged.* The *Financial Times* of London began publishing a coal newsletter in September 1980 which was specifically oriented toward international coal news. In cooperation with *Coal Outlook,* the *Financial Times* began compiling international information on coal trade, transporation, development projects, and coal sales agreements for *International Coal Report.*

This newsletter ran to about fifteen or twenty densely-packed pages every two weeks. The articles were the first exposure U.S. companies had on a regular basis to news about coal trade and coal industries abroad.

*World Coal* was a London-based magazine with a circulation of 10,000 which began publishing articles on the world coal industry for an American audience in 1976. It had such a long jump on the emergence of the American market that many well-known American companies did not subscribe. *World Coal*'s feature articles were usually based on firsthand observation of coal industries not well known to Americans: Soviet Union, Canada, Australia, the U.K., Germany, Venezuela, India, South Africa, and China. Although the emphasis was on mining technology rather than on coal trade, this coverage provided those U.S. producers who read it with insight into their competitors in other parts of the world.

*World Coal* was self-conscious about its pioneering role. In the editorial marking its first five years (March 1980) the editors announced that they had brought the world coal industry together by publishing articles on deliberately non-American topics. *World Coal* acknowledged that the pace of growth of world coal trade had not been as rapid as it had predicted in 1975, in the wake of the 1973 oil crisis. The editors hoped that "Now in the early 1980s we are perhaps back again where we stood in the spring of 1975" with an opportunity to expand and coordinate world coal trade. Although world coal trade was finally expanding, *World Coal* had not yet found the proper formula for its message. By March 1981, it had dropped from monthly to bi-monthly issues and by the next winter it was offering to give subscriptions free of charge to any American companies interested in foreign exports. The precariousness of the magazine does not necessarily mean that its emergence was unimportant. Two chairmen of NCA (the presidents of the largest and second largest U.S. coal companies) published optimistic articles in its pages in 1980 and 1981. World trade origin and destination figures were published here earlier and more thoroughly than anywhere else. It prepared an annual international directory of coal exporters, *The Annual Buyer's Guide*. The magazine seemed to have a sense of the whole world's coal trade, without the usual American or western biases which often omitted consideration of eastern bloc nations. Because it came about when it did and because it filled a gap that no other regular information source had identified at the time, *World Coal* is a good example of the kind of information source on which American coal exporters would increasingly rely if world trade continued.

It would be an overstatement to say that these new journals became powerful shapers of coal industry opinion and strategic action. Instead, their emergence reflected a demand for and reliance on new sources of information which would best be supplied by groups outside of, even if related to, traditional industry support groups. They were sustained as part of the industry's network by commitments of resources and time to their continuance by top managers who apparently were allocating their own time in order to give priority to these new information sources.

In the company I observed, coal executives at both middle and upper levels began to reach out for information to these new trade journals and to publications of other industries—such as railroad and waterway journals, shipping digests, engineering newsletters, port publications, and even grain industry export information. They also read government newsletters of executive agencies—to which they had not previously subscribed. These journals were carrying articles and information about export coal for the first time. This kind of cross fertilization (and a good deal of repetition of key factors) heightened the sense of multi-industry interconnectedness which was emerging.

*Consultants.* Financial and economic consulting services were a third group providing up-to-the-minute technical information and advice. Many of these consultants had been affiliated with the U.S. coal industry for years and were reorienting their services to include analysis of steam coal export trade. For example, a number of New York financial analysts (Dean Witter Reynolds, Kidder-Peabody, F.R. Schwab, Merrill Lynch, and Chase Manhattan Bank) offered subscription services to regularly published coal reports in which they evaluated investment and business conditions in the industry. Each firm added analysis of steam coal exports to its regular coal reports. For the leading coal analysts at these firms the steam coal export market meant simply extending their knowledge of metallurgical coal markets to include factors relevant to electricity-producing steam coal. However, this was easier for some to accomplish than for others. If the firm dealt typically with foreign investments and commodities trading, steam coal was just a new commodity to be learned. For analysts who had spent most of their lives concentrating on the domestic coal industry, such as Joel Price of Dean Witter Reynolds and later of Rotan-Mosle (Dallas), (who misstated the availability of deep water ports and of large ships to a Senate panel) the international steam coal market was more of an unknown.

Economic consultants with traditionally international and political outlooks such as Zinder-Neris (New York), and foreign-based brokerage houses saw an opportunity to offer subscription services about the international coal market which would not be tied solely to American sources. Zinder-Neris, Roskill Information Services (London), and Sheppards & Chase (London) were three firms that offered such services for the first time during 1980–82. (The Zinder-Neris newsletter folded after six months of publication.) Royal Dutch Shell proposed that an international coal information service be offered through the Coal Industry Advisory Board which would parallel international oil information systems of the major world oil companies.

These new participants in the coal industry were offering proposals which had to be evaluated in the light of a firm's goals, resource constraints, and expectations. Their stepping forward to offer themselves for membership in the coal industry's interorganizational network underlined the fact that in the international market coal firms would need many new kinds of intelligence, which they would probably not be able to get alone.

Accurate information on conditions within the United States (such as assessments of coal port capacities, dredging costs, ship economies, and transportation infrastructure) though presumably closer to the normal operations of the industry than international trade markets, was often beyond the expertise of the coal industry's usual engineering advisors. For example, the respected firm Data Resources, Inc., which provided a subscription coal service, embarrassed itself with a report in July 1980, which claimed that the United States had ample excess capacity at its coal ports to handle nearly 250 million tons of coal exports—triple the effective capacity. The trouble was that DRI had calculated theoretically, without observing the port situation, and without allowing enough time for equipment maintenance, moving ships into berths, and rail-ship coordination delays (Carey, DRI, 7/25/80). The report did nothing to explain why ports were backed up and why near chaos prevailed at Hampton Roads piers. Soros Associates, a well-known engineering firm, in a September 1980 report to the Department of Energy did only slightly better in describing the situation and remedies for it (U.S. Department of Energy, Overview of U.S. Coal Export Terminals, September 1980). No reports seemed to consider "effective" capacity (and therefore the constraints) caused by the port-inland rail links, lack of ground storage at eastern ports, and the long-term problems of railroad rate-making on regional coal supply and demand. The industry began seeking new consultants who could help it evaluate these issues.

Dredging costs and ship economies proved even more difficult to pin down. The engineering techniques being proposed were often untried and there were wide differences of opinion about their feasibility and economics. The economies of scale in large ships, for example, had to be extrapolated from the known costs of operating small freighters and might bear little relationship to the costs and even less to the prices charged for freight on proposed super-sized or coal-burning ships. International shipping firms, the IEA information service, and the U.S. Army Corps of Engineers were called on to help analyze these issues. Even trade data which were required by law proved difficult to obtain. The editors of *Coal Outlook* and a consultant from ICF, Inc. (another major consulting firm) expressed to me their difficulties getting accurate export data from the Gulf area because of the proliferation of small ports on the Mississippi River and the prevalence of midstream transferring of coal to ocean ships (conversations, 2/2/81). It later developed that steam coal exports from the Gulf Coast, were being incorrectly reported. Mobile's steam coal trade was added to New Orleans trade data with the collaboration of the Department of Commerce in order to protect the privacy of a single producer (conversation with coal industry planning executive, 1/21/83).[3] Such confusion was just one of many problems facing firms which were trying to make accurate market forecasts.

In these ways, technical information itself became a source of controversy and skepticism. Estimates could be easily used to favor one interest or another depending upon the assumptions on which forecasts were based. Many consulting firms being asked to develop objective analyses for private clients or government contracts were themselves partial owners of new terminal projects. For example, Soros Associates, A.D. Little, and Parsons-Brinkerhoff had all provided professional port capacity and feasibility studies while simultaneously being involved in planning new building projects. Hence, sources of objective technical information and interest in particular transactions could not be easily separated.

As industry members looked for guidance from outside experts who could reliably assess a complex situation they faced a dual recognition that: (1) special interests in particular ports or projects could color the information given by consultants; and (2) traditionally respected experts were inexperienced in collecting the information needed to assess this situation. Consequently the situation was open for a variety of new consultants and a deluge of conflicting advice. Port groups, terminal builders, government agencies, and coal companies began to enlist their own internal and external consultants who would give them tailor-made and usually positive recommendations to justify their strategic actions.

The consultants filled a new supportive role as sources of outside information on which coal industry actors now relied, but firms did not consider these additions to their interorganizational networks samples of greater dependency. Rather, they identified the information gap and generation of information to fill it as a proactive strategy they could make use of to shape technical information and business opportunities to fit their own ends. Consultants, of course, had a great stake in enlisting clients, and in touting the importance of accurate advice. Trade journals and the NCA were anxious to become more important support groups to the coal industry's foreign trade. New information services in support of export sales were modifying the coal industry's individually-competitive network. They added to it a set of alignments based on auxiliary affiliational relationships among firms and their specialized supportive services.

## GOVERNMENT-INDUSTRY COOPERATION

The industry's need for new information and government's willingness to supply it aligned the coal industry with several government agencies. In this respect government services and information became attached to the coal industry in ways similar to the alignments developing with consultants, NCA, and the trade journals. To the extent that government agencies supplied the coal industry with data and services to help it carry out its coal sales job, government was fulfilling the kind of auxiliary, supportive role which might be filled by a private group. However, government-industry cooperation also carries with it the implication of official endorsement and political support beyond simply the supply of information. This kind of realignment of business-government relationships, implying a joining of purposes by government and industry, is what I have called macrocooperation. These two aspects of government-industry interactions are impossible to separate practically. In the interest of space I will describe the more information-oriented aspects of supportive government activity in this chapter and discuss national and international policies of macrocooperation and their effect on the industry in Chapter 9. But the reader should realize that policy and services are interrelated. Even though I am arguing that conceptually they implied a different pattern of interorganizational relationships, many individual examples of government-industry cooperation would serve as easily in one category as another.

*Government reports and forecasts.* Commissioned government reports set the terms and expectations about foreign coal trade, and they provided important incentive for the industry. The energy and resources poured into documentation of market factors important to exporting coal showed the federal government's interest in fostering and promoting this new business.

Technical reports supportive of increased coal exports appeared throughout 1980–82. The U.S. Department of Energy commissioned several coal energy demand studies. DOE issued a Coal Exports Study in 1979 which stated official U.S. export policy at the time. This study endorsed previous OECD projections for increased steam coal trade and presented a wealth of technical information to the U.S. industry. It also identified the "appropriate government role."

> Since U.S. coal exports are generally considered competitive, the simplest and perhaps most productive U.S. Government role is to provide political support to expanded coal trade, reducing investor uncertainty and encouraging accelerating the private sector investment decisions necessary to expand coal exports. If basic political support proves inadequate, or if developments indicate that improved economics are necessary to expand coal trade at a desirable rate, the U.S. Government can consider more direct and extensive support. (DOE, Coal Exports Study, 1979: 27, reprinted in Senate, Energy Hearings, 9/16-18/80: 165)

*Moving U.S. Coal to Export Markets* (June 1980) and the more significant *President's Interagency Coal Export Task Force Report* (ICE), were attempts to follow up on the stated policy of information-gathering and interagency support of, without active intervention into, the industry. They were also impressive attempts to coordinate the policies of various cabinet departments.

*Moving U.S. Coal to Export Markets* was prepared by four cabinet departments with coal industry consultation. It was a first-cut at comprehensively laying out the domestic coal exports situation. Although quite unexceptional in its recommendations, the report indicated a high degree of executive agreement on this "private" trade issue. It implied that government agencies (Army Corps of Engineers, Commerce, Energy, and Transportation) would work together and would help coordinate the efforts of their various industry constituencies to promote coal export trade.

The more dramatic example was President Carter's designation in the spring of 1980 of a cabinet level Interagency Coal Exports

Task Force composed of fourteen government agencies and executive departments.[4] The ICE Task force operated under the direction of Deputy Secretary of Energy, John Sawhill. The lengthy report and twelve volumes of appendixes which issued from this effort in January 1981 showed extraordinary consensus about the coal export situation. The ICE Task Force gave coal exports a place of visibility within the U.S government that went symbolically beyond simply a supportive or service role. Yet, the main task actually pursued by government was still the provision of technical data and information.[5]

*Documents on port congestion.* The federal government prepared various documents which helped the coal industry understand port issues and evaluate port development policy. As port congestion increased during 1980 and 1981, both Congress and the executive branch needed better information about the capacity and operation of ports. This information, provided primarily for the purpose of federal policy-making, was also useful to coal exporters. Long-awaited reports under preparation by the U.S. Army Corps of Engineers on the dredging of various ports took on new significance to the coal industry.[6] The impact of port and inland waterway user fees had also been under study, and coal firms found the analyses in these reports helpful in assessing the impact of port fees on coal trade. The federal government thus provided an enormous amount of data both to assist the coal industry and for its own policy evaluation purposes.

*The World Coal Study (WOCOL).* Although not strictly an example of government-sponsored information, the World Coal Study was a semiofficial project too important to be overlooked. Backed by funds from the Department of Energy and private industry, WOCOL had already begun before the 1979 oil crisis. The World Coal Study was headed by Professor Carroll Wilson of MIT, a senior researcher and former chief administrator of the Atomic Energy Commission. It was formed in October 1978 to follow up on the previous work of the Workshop on Alternative Energy Strategies (WAES) which Wilson had also headed. The WAES had concluded in 1977 that world oil supplies would fail to meet increasing demand before 2000, and probably between 1985 and 1995. WOCOL was an ad hoc nongovernmental committee involving high-level individuals from sixteen countries representing government, industry, and research. The charge was to see what coal could do to replace oil in meeting the world's energy needs. Although Wilson insisted that the representatives were involved only as individuals and not in their official capacities, funding by the U.S. government and the exalted membership, which included former high government officials and industry representatives from coal, oil, engineering, and utilities of each of the member countries, implied some approval by the U.S. government. The U.S. group included coal industry-related officials from Atlantic Richfield, Bechtel Corp., AMAX Minerals, and Shell Coal International. WOCOL was fortunate in its timing. A "Final Report" was presented to Congress and the report was published in May 1980 just as the surge of steam coal exports was choking American ports.

The impact of the study was greatly heightened by the direct physical evidence of increasing demand for U.S. steam coal. WOCOL predicted that total U.S. export demand could possibly reach 350 mtce (including about 280 mtce of steam coal) by 2000 without endangering American domestic security or resource capacity. This was much higher than most American producers thought feasible at the time. Because of its large resource base and relatively developed infrastructure, the United States was the only country deemed able to exceed 200 mtce of total exports (130 mtce of steam coal).

The thoroughness and detail of the WOCOL study were impressive. American producers who had scoffed privately at WOCOL's preliminary estimates of steam coal trade (and even at DOE's which were much lower) revised their skepticism as they saw U.S. steam coal and total coal exports exceed WOCOL's High Case expectations for 1985 by the end of 1981. They began to speak more bullishly at conferences and congressional hearings about the prospect of expanded trade. WOCOL, along with other international reports, placed pressure on U.S. coal producers to seize a vast opportunity.

*Effects of government reports.* With minor differences about the levels of exports being predicted, the many reports issued on the export situation were quite consistent. They all predicted unprecedented export demand; they all called for government-industry cooperation; and they all encouraged joint planning and interindustry coordination to remove bottlenecks in the export transportation chain. They all also stopped short of recommending an active policy of intervention by the U.S. government. The federal government's role was to be that of partnership in promoting and supporting coal exports. The coal industry's interorganizational network became extended to agencies of the federal government with which it had little or no association in the past. The basis of this association was analogous to that of a consultant the industry might hire for technical advice. Reports provided technical grounding, a massing of data and forecasts, that in other circumstances the industry might have had to obtain privately. Government enlarged the expertise and technical competence of those firms able to expend the time and resources to make use of it.

*Government information services.* Ongoing, informational, supportive services to the coal industry—analogous to consulting services offered by the private sector—expanded beyond usual expectations. The State Department's commercial attachés began collecting information about foreign buyers and foreign coal markets from their posts abroad. Commerce and State Department officials briefed coal executives before they undertook sales trips. The Department of Commerce increased its analytic capacity by adding more refined numbers to its industrial classification code so that large steam coal users could be identified more easily. DOC also published a worldwide list of agents, distributors, importers, and potential end users of coal which was soon available to coal firms. Commerce Department officials also began collecting data about harbor dredging projects in other countries. The Maritime Administration promised to issue quarterly updates of coal terminal projects to keep the industry informed about the availability of handling facilities for shipping coal. National Security Council staff indicated their interest in helping to keep coal industry members informed about policy issues which might become involved in coal trade. Government effort focused on helping to expedite foreign sales. The emphasis was on giving the coal industry the freedom to expand into a new market: clearing the way for free enterprise to take effect through partnership with federal authority.

## Increased Interpersonal Interactions

Industry seminars and international conferences represented another kind of opportunity for network extension based on the need for information exchange. These meetings, where problems could be aired and contracts made among a variety of different industry members, proliferated during the years 1980–82.

*Industry seminars.* NCA performed a coordinating role by hosting informational seminars for members of the coal industry on specific topics related to coal exports. Such seminars included an international Transportation and Handling seminar in New Orleans (7/7–8/81), NCA's 2nd annual Handling and Storage Symposium in Chicago, (1981); the West Virginia/Appalachian Coal Export Conference (4/20/81), and a World Trade Luncheon sponsored jointly with the State of Virginia (5/21/80)(trade press announcements).

Holding industry seminars was not new for NCA, but heavy concentration in port cities, on export issues, and on speakers from export-related service industries was unusual. The American Association of Port Authorities also took an active role in encouraging buyer-seller-transporter interindustry meetings, such as the AAPA Coal Ports Seminar at Mobile, Alabama (2/17–19/81), and the Coal Ports West seminar at Sacramento, California (9/16–18/81 [proceedings, and brochure]). These are only a sampling of the seminars held.

Industry seminars usually drew from 200–500 participants and included 20–50 speakers and panelists. Attendees often included representatives from ports, barge and water interests, railroads, coal, banks, oil, engineering firms, utilities, consultants, government, and foreign buyers. Probably very little new information was obtained by well-informed participants at these sessions (although they sometimes drew impressively-qualified speakers). They served primarily as ways to introduce and disseminate basic knowledge to industry members, to raise awareness of interindustry issues, to reinforce optimism about the coming market, and to enhance the leadership and status of those who were invited to speak. In these ways industry seminars extended the interindustry network of associations and personal contracts that participants could rely on to conduct their new business. Contacts made at seminars might be unexpectedly called on later to build interindustry coalitions in order to achieve particular legislative or policy goals. They might also help identify authoritative sources who could provide specific technical advice. Attendees often returned to their companies with increased enthusiasm and enhanced knowledge about the new factors coming to affect their participation in coal trade.

Many seminars were sponsored by trade journals and other information vendors. *Coal Outlook* sponsored several export conferences (Mine to Market 11/16/80, "What's Ahead for Coal?" 2/12–13/81, and International Coal Trade 5/4–5/81). The *Journal of Commerce* jointly sponsored the Coal Trade Summit (6/10–11/81) held in New York. The Energy Bureau (12/6–7/80; and 9/80) and Lloyds of London Press (5/24–25/82) also sponsored these sessions (proceedings and trade press announcements).

Often these meetings might be no more than "talk fests" where the same participants met over and over to cover more or less the same ground. John A. Creedy, president of the Water Transport Association (a barge industry group) speaking at the Coal Trade Summit in New York (6/10–11/81) warned that talk might be diverting the industry from the goal it should be aiming for.

"If we had dispatched a boatload of coal for every talkfest on coal exports in the past two years, we would long since have buried our customers in the stuff" (*Coal Industry News*, 7/13/81: p 12).

The public relations role in conferences was particularly strong when the sponsorship was a port. The Virginia Ports Conference was among the first. It was held June 3, 1980, and attracted a bevy of international buyers and coal company representatives. The Japanese, Belgians, and French took the occasion to warn of high railroad rates and unacceptable port congestion. (*Richmond Times-Advocate*, 6/13/80 and *Coal Industry News*, 10/6/80). Portland, Oregon held a conference on Coal Exports to the Far East February 2, 1981, sponsored by the state (*Journal of Commerce*, 2/17/81). New York's Coal Trade Summit had broader sponsorship (including NCA, *Journal of Commerce*, and the Maritime Association of New York) but it was in part a frank bid to show off that port's potential as a coal port. Yet speakers in New York included Ulf Lantzke, the executive director of IEA, a representative of Spain's coal importing organization, technical papers on ship size and freight economies by the international ship brokering firm, Simpson, Spence and Young, chief executive officers from major coal producers and from the three major export coal hauling railroads, N&W, Chessie, and Conrail (Schneiderman, *World Coal*, Sept.-Oct. 1981: 68–69).

The AAPA's Coal Ports Symposium, jointly hosted by the Port of Mobile, did not include quite such an illustrious list of speakers, but it attracted over 400 participants in February 1981 and was slightly less of a public relations extravaganza for the port than some of the other port-sponsored seminars. The speakers included representatives of railroads, coal companies, foreign buyers, banks, and numerous ports. Carl Bagge, president of NCA, remarked in his featured luncheon speech on the rapid pace of change in the export network that the conference itself illustrated: "Who would have thought even two-and-a-half years ago that the port association would have attracted 500 people from around the world to a conference such as this" (AAPA Conference proceedings, 2/23/81: 23).

Participants in Mobile included about thirty who were obviously from foreign ports or represented foreign international coal industries or buyers. Twenty of the twenty-five participants from the U.S. coal industry represented large coal companies. At least twenty attendees were representatives of oil companies. The remainder were a gamut of port representatives, engineering firms, terminal owners, shipping firms, consultants, bankers, journalists and unidentified business people.

From the program it appears that this "seminar" was not primarily an informational meeting. The topics covered were elementary and familiar to all. It was instead more of an international public relations and sales conference of top executives and planners from many industries who had not been brought together before in this way.

*International conferences.* International conferences served to invite visibility, good public relations, and the chance to get to know coal exports people throughout the world. Many first-of-their-kind international conferences were held throughout the world during 1980–82. In 1980, NCA and the Coal Exporters Association hosted their first U.S.-Japan Coal Conference at Norfolk, Virginia. It was followed with a second conference in 1981 at Lake Tahoe, Nevada, presumably, to fulfill the Japanese desire to assess the feasibility of western coal exports. By 1982, the U.S.-Japan Coal Conference had become an annual event. Carl Bagge proposed to use its format for other NCA sponsored conferences for buyers from different parts of the world.

In January 1982, Carl Bagge and Sir Derek Ezra, chairman of Britain's National Coal Board, cochaired a World Coal Markets Conference in London designed to extend to Europeans the interactions which had started successfully with Japanese and other Far Eastern customers. At this international conference, which 200 people attended, Bagge proposed that an annual U.S.-European Coal Conference be convened to build a "solid foundation of partnership" between the United States and other coal consuming nations (*NCA Coal News*, 1/25/82).

Among the other international conferences announced in trade journals were New York's Coal Trade Summit in June 1981; the "first international" coal trade, transportation, and handling conference in London in August 1981 (*ICR*, 9/10/81) which drew 830 delegates; the "first international" Symposium on Coal, September 7–9, 1981 at Ixtapa, Mexico (*ICR*, 10/81); the first annual Pacific Rim Coal Trade Conference January 18–19, 1982, in Hawaii, sponsored by Pasha Publications, (*ICR*, 12/18/81); and the third annual Australian Coal Conference scheduled for April 19–22, 1982.

It is unlikely that important sales agreements came out of these conferences—at least none can be pinned down from published information. But clearly coal industry people were getting together more frequently with foreign buyers rubbing shoulders with investors and foreign government officials whom they had not previously known. They were considering business trips to far-flung parts of the world as part of their normal duties.

For example, in the firm where I worked, the middle-management transportation director began taking Japanese lessons. New coal brochures were prepared in five foreign languages (Spanish,

German, Italian, Japanese, and French). Top executives attended classes at Berlitz to prepare for trips to China and to France. The expertise of staff members who knew the languages, political systems, and customs of foreign countries took on new significance. Foreign trips were planned to Spain, France, Netherlands, Germany, Japan, China, Finland, Belgium, Greece; and delegations from foreign countries were given tours of the company's mines and were entertained socially.

Even if only superficially, coal producers were involved in a more interrelated world industry. A representative of Japan's Electric Power Development Corporation explicitly stated the need for wider cooperation at the Pacific Rim Coal Trade Conference: "Coal producers, consumers, trading companies, railroads, and ports must work together in a spirit of cooperation to insure the further growth and mutually beneficial relationships that the export market can afford to all parties" (*NCA Coal News*, 2/1/82). In answer to this challenge and in recognition of the value of the new international conferences and information exchanges taking place, C. R. Moore of Getty Oil Co. (a western coal producer) remarked at the same conference that developing a bond of friendship into a commercial business relationship between individual companies "will be the most significant factor in determining a long term market share for the western U.S." (*NCA Coal News*, 2/1/81).

Moore's remarks confirm that international conferences were valuable to the fledgling coal export business as places to exchange information—although not solely in the technical content of the presentations made there. His statement evokes our informal notion of the value of "social networking." This function of international conferences is highly important to understanding what was happening in the coal industry.

Industry seminars and international conferences which had not existed on these topics prior to 1980 were now becoming an expected, even an institutionalized part of U.S. export trade. People were coming together to meet and get to know each other. They were checking out relationships which might eventually last ten or twenty years, if a contract was signed. In this context the American coal industry leaders, especially those from major firms, felt confident they could make use of their past experience. They were accustomed to nurturing long-term relationships between buyers and sellers, and they knew how to build confidence and the aura of reliability.[7] Coal producers began to rely on the new contacts and exchanges of information which international conferences made possible.

The relevant network of associations for coal brokers, transportation managers, sales vice presidents, and even for the senior management officials of coal firms was rapidly becoming broader and more complicated. These officials were moving quickly to master (or at least become conversant with) the technical information demands of international coal trade.

## Proactive Uses of Information

A few major participants identified lack of information about the new market as an opportunity they could use to influence the expectations of the new market to their advantage. They commissioned reports or themselves became sources of information which favored their interests.

Ports were the first group to recognize that they could gain business by energetically promoting themselves as capable of exporting coal. In coordination with the entrepreneurial activities mentioned in Chapter 5 (such as issuing brochures, sponsoring conferences, and announcing their own terminal projects) several ports engaged consultants to study the regional economic benefits which would accrue from steam coal trade. For example, New York, Norfolk, Baltimore, New Orleans, Sacramento, and the Columbia River around Portland, Oregon, all commissioned studies (see attachments to congressional testimony, Senate, Energy, 9/16–19/80; Senate Foreign Relations, 4/28/81; and Bentz 7/81). These reports predictably showed that great benefits could be attained from construction and new business development. They also minimized any physical drawbacks of a particular port, and showed that coal trade would fit in compatibly with whatever other trade was currently being carried on.

As I have mentioned, the consultants engaged in these studies were not always totally objective with respect to the huge construction and engineering projects being proposed. Often they had financial interests in the projects being considered. Ports and their consultants formed mutual admiration societies in which both were cognizant that the right kind of information could have high material payoff for both parties. In these situations there was no such thing as an objective observer or a neutral situation. Consulting firms fed their clients and coal firms encouraged consultants to use the best possible assumptions favorable to their interests. There was no example I found, for instance, of a published feasibility study unfavorable to rapid investment and port development. This type of authoritative information and positive forecasting I have called hype.

Hype was often supported by sophisticated input-output studies and capacity and trade growth calculations, but it was at origin colored by an advocacy purpose: to shape critical expectations and thus the key factors in the environment influencing steam coal delivery and trade proactively to the benefit of particular interests.

Through hype and political clout New York, New Orleans, and Los Angeles-Long Beach had emerged by mid-1981 as the ports which most people agreed were the most viable for increased steam coal trade—along with the traditional coal shippers of Hampton Roads (Norfolk) and Baltimore. Small ports like Charleston, Savannah, Kalama (Washington), and Sacramento (averaging 5–20 million tons of commerce yearly) did not have the resources to push themselves forward as insistently, although they were as near or nearer to coal supplies. Philadelphia, Mobile, and Portland (Oregon) were somewhat more unexpectedly also losing out.[8] Of course, proactive strategies were not the only reason that the large ports became more visible. Their very size meant that they were politically stronger and were backed by more powerful congressional and state interests. Ports represent regional growth, jobs, tax revenues, and a host of other economic benefits to their local areas. Big ports were not about to let their less powerful sisters beat them out of a grand opportunity for new business if a little effort could secure this business for themselves.

Other groups created situtations that would shape the assumptions on which the new market would be conducted (even if only to turn the tables on what might have been a disadvantagious situation). For example, the marketing department of the Illinois Central and Gulf Railroad (ICG) distributed a lengthy "analysis" of its ability to deliver steam coal unit trains to New Orleans. ICG had never previously handled export coal, and was located in an area of high-sulfur coal reserves not considered most desirable by foreign customers. Furthermore its trackage closely followed the Mississippi River from central Illinois to New Orleans, on which barge rates for hauling coal were one-third the cost of rail freight. ICG was clearly fighting an uphill battle in trying to put itself forward as a coal export railroad. Yet the brochure, published in October, 1980, was widely read and cited even by official government sources, largely because it was one of the few reports available on inland transportation of export coal. This gave ICG a leg up at least in visibility on the coal exports issue.

Another example of hype was the way the Western Governors' Policy Office (WESTPO) used its prestige to promote coal exports. A WESTPO Task Force issued a lengthy report called "Western

U.S. Steam Coal Exports to the Pacific Basin" (excerpts reprinted in Senate, Energy, Vol. 2, 9/16/82). The report predicted great potential for coal exports from the western states. Again, the strategy was to get a jump on a potentially disadvantageous situation and attempt to turn it around. Western coal, though plentiful and cheap to mine, is far from ocean ports. To interest Asian customers in this resource, the Western Governors realized that they would have to take an active promotional role in providing information to analysts and to customers. They would need solid-looking information in order to establish their place and not be overlooked in the new coal export network.

The coal industry's usual proprietary research groups (Edison Electric Institute and the National Economic Research Associates) were unusually silent on coal export issues. Probably this is because their close ties to utilities and the many geographical differences of opinion among firms in the coal industry about how to implement export trade made exports a problematic issue. However, the silence of these more traditional industry research groups left room for even more hype and strategic initiatives by individual firms. For example, Consolidation Coal, Exxon and Peabody each issued their own authoritative estimates of coal use and trade.

Peabody's report was an interesting example of hype by an individual coal firm. The company prepared an analysis of the effect on steam coal exports of deepening the Mississippi River to 55 feet from the Gulf of Mexico to Baton Rouge (Peabody report, 2/28/81).

The report analyzed a project proposed by the Corps of Engineers which had been in the works for several years and had only recently been recognized by Peabody as relevant to steam coal exports. Peabody's analysis concluded that the project's yearly cost would be returned from eight to twelve times over cost each year from 1985 to 2000 if added steam coal exports were included in the cost-benefit ratio. The report said that twice as much steam coal would go out through the port of New Orleans by 2000 if the river was deepened to 55 feet. The report also made predictions about the distribution of overall U.S. steam coal trade by ports and the regional economic benefits which would accrue from steam coal exports through New Orleans.

More interesting than the findings of this study are the uses that were made of it. It was presented formally to the U.S. Army Corps of Engineers in a public hearing on the deep draft project. Then, it was made available through a press release to the media, and as a result was widely cited in the trade press. Peabody advertised its availability with full page notices placed in the *Journal of Commerce*, (6/15/81). Peabody reported that it circulated over 200 copies of the report in response to requests from all elements in the coal export chain. Particular interest seemed to be shown by investment and international shipping firms. Through this document Peabody (which had not yet shipped any coal overseas) reaped the benefit of being identified as an authoritative commentator on the export market. It also boosted its credibility as an exporter through New Orleans as an exit port.

The Peabody report was used to support the port development bill. It was sent to key congressional friends (later was reprinted in the *Congressional Record*) and to Louisiana local politicians. Key cabinet members received hand-delivered copies. The promotion of itself as a source of technical information helped Peabody to establish a position of leadership on export trade in spite of its inexperience in this area. The strategy paid off later when legislative and executive staff members asked the company for advice in analyzing proposals for port development bills. The company's vice-president for government affairs played a major role on NCA's Harbor Dredging Task Force which led the coal industry's coalition on port development issues. Hype from this company, which was foremost in the domestic steam coal industry, showed that it was staking out exports as an area of serious interest. Through its mastery of technical knowledge, Peabody showed that it wanted to be taken seriously in the development of coal export policy and trade. (Sources for this section are Peabody Coal Company's public relations department.)

## Large Firms Held the Advantage in Obtaining and Using New Information

In the examples I observed, marshalling and institutionalizing sources of information to support a U.S. coal export market generally favored the largest coal firms, and lessened the hold of small eastern producers and brokers. The expertise needed in information handling and interpretation, and the management sophistication needed for new and more complex international marketing, were more available in or obtainable by large firms. They had the resources to invest in sales forces, in scanning and monitoring of technical data, and in shaping policy through preparation of proactive analyses and reports. They contributed the most in dues to NCA and could therefore expect its consideration of their information needs and interests when seminars were planned, when legislation was analyzed, and when foreign visitors asked for advice.

The use of consultants, subscriptions to journals, information services, and invitations to speak at important inter-industry gatherings were also much more available to large firms. Large companies could more easily afford to attend and participate in national and international seminars and conferences where information was exchanged and contacts made for later sales, than could small firms. In the three cases where I saw lists of conference participants, all of the speakers (except those representing trade groups) and roughly 75 percent of attendees from the coal industry were from large firms (*Coal Outlook*, Mine to Market Conference, 11/80: Energy Bureau, 12/80; AAPA Conference, 2/81). Among the coal industry spokespeople before Congress, only one among fourteen companies represented was from a firm as small as 2 million tons.

Large coal firms may also have benefited from the attendance at these meetings of their oil or other large industrial owners. Over thirty representatives of big oil companies attended the AAPA convention in Mobile. These companies sent specialists in international economics, fuels research, transportation, and shipping. Although I do not know whether these people later contacted the staffs of their subsidiary coal producing companies, it does not seem improbable. These specialists were in some ways better able than coal executives to analyze the export situation. Almost all had more international experience that coal people. The heavy ownership of major coal companies by oil and engineering firms made them much more likely than small coal firms to receive expert advice from parent staff.

Creating documentation and promoting themselves as authoritative sources of information made large coal firms apt to be asked to contribute their knowledge to government panels and offical industry presentations on export issues. These official and semiofficial roles further increased their status and aura of technical competence and kept them abreast of inside news and policy concerns which enhanced their analytic capabilities further.

Peabody, Consolidation, Amax, Island Creek, Massey, and Atlantic Richfield representatives were invited to give their interpretations of coal market growth, sales, and the factors affecting steam coal trade in the conference proceeding I read. On the contrary, no small firms had speakers on these programs. Prepared speeches by large firms frequently consisted of insights gained from participation on *other* panels and study teams. So conferences became a circulating pot of information shared by status leaders with lesser members of the industry. Size and status within the domestic steam coal industry greatly increased the access to competence. The distribution of expertise about the new market was beginning to hover among the largest steam coal firms.

## SUMMARY: HOW NEW SOUCES OF INFORMATION REALIGNED THE COAL INDUSTRY'S NETWORK

Coal officials were faced with a highly confusing and rapidly changing export situation, one which involved unpredictable variables and complicated interconnections among political, economic, ecological, geophysical and mechanical factors. Those who wished to take an active role in the new market sought information by which they could make sense out of this new market, and which would help them achieve their strategic goals of long-term foreign sales. They looked to their trade associations (NCA and CEA), to the trade journals, and to consultants to provide syntheses of new technical information. They relied on the reports and services of supportive government agencies. They developed new contacts and expanded network relationships through meetings and foreign conferences. They even prepared their own data and analyses. The groups providing information formed symbiotic relationships with the coal industry participants to which they provided reassurance and coordination. Coal industry actors became organized more obviously in clusters around these information-handling groups. New sources of information became part of the coal industry's interorganizational network, and industry producers began to see the world through the interpretative analyses that these new groups provided.

New consulting services, journals, and new roles for the NCA began to appear. New government documents and services became available from executive departments. Conferences and inter-industry seminars brought members of the coal industry into contact with buyers and with members of other industries with whom they had had little or no contact in the past. Hype increased the status and leadership positions of certain key groups.

New relationships did not arise automatically because of the imperatives of determinative environmental pressures. In fact, the technically complex environment was in many ways a creation of what overlapping sources of information said about it and of the fact that for the first time new actors were turning their attention to this sector of trade. New interactions (extensions and elaborations of the industry's interorganizational network) came about because major industry actors were pursuing the strategy of participating actively and at a high level of competence in the export market. To the extent that individual firms adopted this goal, achieving it required them to become informed about technical issues. The problem they saw was the lack of technical information available to help them enhance their expertise. Each competing firm was trying to handle (or to manage) complex information more deftly than its competitors. This striving for competency can be compared to striving for specialization and for meritocratic recognition. Inherent in the pattern of interactions involving new sources of information was a struggle to become expert at providing services and technical support to knowledgeable and discriminating customers. It seems safe to infer that the resources being committed to support newly emerging sources of information would not have been committed had firms not hoped that they would obtain direct material advantages as a result.

The striving for meritocracy came about as interorganizational relationships clustered around those firms and those sources of information which showed that they could handle complicated data convincingly. Leadership in the network was moving toward firms that could turn new data deftly to their own ends.

Using information as a proactive strategy to change a firm's position and effectiveness became an important source of realignment in favor of large coal firms in the coal industry's interorganizational network. Proactive strategies added to the advantages available to large firms. They became active in soliciting new sources of technical expertise and they were more visible than small firms at interindustry conferences and associations.

## NOTES

1.  Major news features about coal exports appeared in *Business Week, Dunn's Business Month, Economist, Forbes, Fortune,* and the *National Journal.* Over 100 articles and editorials covered issues related to international coal trade and the world market in the *New York Times* and *Wall Street Journal* in 1980 and 1981, compared to eight in 1979.

2.  In the category I have called hype, I am not primarily talking about perpetration of deliberate misinformation. Although there was some evidence of this in the export situation and it caused considerable confusion, it was probably not widespread. (Note for example my mention later in this chapter of the Department of Commerce's deliberate falsification of trade volume statistics from New Orleans.) Instead, I am talking about the liberty taken by individual firms and other interests as they capitalized on the extreme fluidity and indeterminancy of the developing situation, by presenting information calculated on the best-possible assumption favorable to their interests.

    For example, a widely distributed brochure prepared by the Port of New Orleans, and ostensibly based on various economic analyses claimed that by 1990 the port could export 100 million tons of coal. (WOCOL had predicted only 120 mtce for the entire country in 1990!) The estimate was considered a wide overstatement and example of puffery even by coal exporters interested in the New Orleans area. Still, the *feasible* capacity was available at the port in land, access to coal reserves, rail and barge infrastructure, and port experience with large ships and overseas sales to make even this claim not totally dismissable. Grain exports had taken an almost equivalent leap in the previous ten years. (Sources: Port of New Orleans, brochure, 10/31/80, E.J. Bentz & Associates, 7/81).

3.    Deliberate misrepresentation of trade data was compounded by the inconsistency of information from one department of government to another. The Department of Commerce recorded export cargoes at their point of loading. The Army Corps of Engineers counted all shipments which traverse a port as exports whether they originate in a port or are through traffic. The two methods are incompatible.

4.    Participants in the ICE Task Force included the Departments of State, Interior, Commerce, Labor, Transportation, Energy; Assistant to the President for National Security Affairs; Department of Army (Corps of Engineers); Office of Management and Budget; Council of Economic Advisors; Council on Environmental Quality; Environmental Protection Agency; Export-Import Bank; and United States Trade Representative.

5.    The following passage from the executive summary to its final report makes the primacy of ICE's informational role quite clear.

> . . . [The Interagency Coal Export Task Force] assembled existing data, and developed significant new *information* regarding the international coal market. It undertook *analyses* of apparent problems underlying coal exports. It served as a *clearinghouse* for ideas and information among those who had interest in coal exports. In many cases, it helped to bring parties together for possible mutual and national benefit. It served as a point of contact for foreign representatives both to *obtain current information* on developments in the United States and to register concerns. Finally, the Task Force contributed to a *public awareness* of the fact that increased coal exports will serve both the domestic and international interest of the United States. . . . We do not see the Task Force as an invitation for recommendations which necessitate Federal intrusion into the free market, and, with a few significant exceptions, we view Federal action or new initiatives as generally inappropriate.
>
> The report, therefore, will set forth *information useful in understanding the process* by which United States steam coal exports can be increased, including current problems; ideas pursued, but for reason, rejected or deferred for others to consider; and *conclusions reached* by the Task Force on major situational factors—such as estimates of foreign demand for steam coal. (*ICE Report*, Draft for public comment, Executive summary, p. 2, reprinted in House Committee on Merchant Marine, Hearings: Port Development, Part 1, April-May, 1981, p. 532. Italics mine.)

6.    During 1980–81, the Army Corps of Engineers presented reports recommending dredging the harbors of Norfolk, Mobile, and New Orleans-Baton Rouge to 55 feet. Each of these reports had been in preparation for at least five years, and none considered the recent upsurge in steam coal export trade. (USCOA 7/80; 10/80; 12/80).

7.    In the course of a lunch discussion with coal executives representing three different firms, they compared themselves favorably to executives in the oil industry because of their more highly personalized and differentiated service to

their customers. Oil company executives were said to be impatient, because so much of their sales volume is based on the economics of strictly price-dominated markets. Coal, by contrast, was said to be a much more leisurely and patiently pursued business. Customers and sellers must get to know each other and match each other's needs (field notes, 5/22/81).

8.  This growing assumption about where new business was likely to develop was the more remarkable because New York, although a huge export port, was practically nonexistent as a bulk shipper (handling less than 15 million tons in 1978). Los Angeles-Long Beach, although experienced with exports, did relatively little bulk trade.

By contrast, ports like Mobile, Philadelphia, and Portland were all experienced bulk shippers,but dredging at these ports would be extremely expensive. By mid-1981 Mobile, Philadelphia, and Portland were being pushed aside by the hustle of port contenders who could control more of the economic and political variables. Hype, clout, and all-important political connections were arbitrating the distribution of steam coal export trade.

# 7    *Coalitional Activities*

## WHAT WAS COALITIONAL ACTIVITY?

In addition to increasingly competitive business interactions among coal firms and their efforts to outdo each other through mastery of technical information, combined strategies to secure political goals began to emerge during 1980–82. Coalitional activities focused the ideas and energies of individual firms on commonly desired strategic ends. Actors in the coal industry began to arrange themselves into groups and to seek alliances with other industries which shared their concerns about export trade. Coalitions betokened collaborative inter-firm relationships, although they did not make network interactions more predictable. Jockeying and bargaining for favorable treatment were the prevailing styles in these network interactions. Coalition membership was temporary. Groups broke up as soon as individual members felt they could get a better deal by bargaining alone or by moving to another coalition.

Although other coalitions also emerged, the main coalition I will use to illustrate these relationships was an ad hoc action group which arose in the coal industry to achieve political action on coal port legislation. Port development legislation is a fascinating and significant issue around which to orient. The coalitional activity surrounding it was extensive and for the most part public, and it absorbed a great deal of coal industry time and effort during 1980–82. It is the best illustration of how coalitional activity rearranged power in the coal industry.

The coal industry's Harbor Dredging Task Force did not represent a long-lasting interest with a fixed constituency and identifiable power base that would permanently restructure the U.S. coal industry. Instead, it was a fragile alliance maintained only while the immediate goals of allied firms remained concurrent. In fact, it was often difficult to keep even this temporary consensus operative. This coalition dissipated once the port development issue stalled and new issues distracted the participants to other lines of activity.

Despite the short life of any one coalition, however, the pattern of temporary collaborative interaction represented a realignment in the coal industry's network. This chapter will show how the coalitions that developed around coal port legislation brought about a new layer of interorganizational relationships.

## Perceptions of a Limited Market

*Why coalitions occurred.* Coalitions, like the realignments of interorganizational relationships previously discussed, emerged in response to a new challenge which industry members perceived. Many firms feared that industry sales might be artificially restricted and the U.S. share of exports limited below its potential if the federal government failed to support the physical changes needed to encourage foreign coal sales. Firms formed coalitions to try to influence factors which were beyond the industry's direct control. Industry members undertook coalitional strategies after apparently having determined that individually they had little influence on the policies they wanted changed. They then sought the additive power of combined action.

Coal firms feared that their ability to compete in foreign markets would be constrained by the shallow depths and inadequate harbor services in American ports. These restraints, they felt, would put a cap on their ability to supply U.S. export coal and would tend to confine whatever trade did occur to current coal ports. Coal people showed their apprehension in numerous pleas for coordinated public and private action.

For example, Robert Daignault, marketing manager of Youghiogheny & Ohio Coal, outlined the vulnerability of nontraditional coal exporters to factors beyond their control at an early informational hearing on the prospects for midwestern coal export trade.

> [A]s far as a Midwest producer or an Ohio producer is concerned, the only way that we can participate in this market is for it to be a long-term market, and for consumers overseas to look at it as a long-term market. The consumers overseas need some positive reinforcement from the U.S. Congress, from private enterprise in this country, that we are going to do something about the problem, and we are going to modernize our ports and upgrade our railroads and waterways so we can supply these countries with coal for 100 years to come. (House, Interstate and Foreign Commerce, 12/17/80: 36–37)

Coal people consistently spoke of their dependence on outside factors which might limit export sales. This mutual perception of looming constraints caused coal firms to cast their lots together. Coal industry interests petitioned the federal government asking for contract guarantees, harbor improvements, and reduced delays in the handling of licenses for onshore and harbor maintenance projects. They considered these government supports essential to achieving a favorable share of projected world export coal trade, and in making requests they acted together.

Senators and Congressmen from coal states were quick to publicize the industry's need for supportive federal action. Politicians could see many potential benefits for their home constituencies and for the nation from increased coal trade. They cooperated with the coal industry in presenting its case for government support. By late 1980, the factor receiving the most attention as critical to expanding U.S. coal exports was coal port development. The coalitional strategies that developed in the coal industry around this issue can be clearly observed in the public record.

James Beddington, assistant vice-president for Consolidation Coal Sales Co., was one of the many industry spokesmen who identified the need for federal action in this area and the dire consequences of failing to act.

> Port development is one of the most important keys to U.S. participation in the world steam coal market. The coordination of government regulatory requirements at all levels is urgently needed so that development of port capacity can proceed on a timely basis. . . .
>
> The competitiveness of the United States in the world coal trade will hinge upon our ability to move expanded volumes of coal through our ports. (Senate, Foreign Relations, 4/28/81: 157, 158)

William Mason, 1980 president of the Coal Exporters Association, called port and transportation facilities "the single most important constraint which could limit our participation in the growing coal market" (Senate, Energy, 9/18/80: 184).

Connie Holmes, speaking for the industry, told the House Committee on Merchant Marine which was considering a port development bill, "Without these actions [improvement in the coal export delivery system], we do believe that the United States is quite unlikely to take a major and full advantage of the opportunities that await us in terms of increasing our exports of coal and our exports of other commodities" (4/24/81: 122).

The coal industry was thus impelled into its coalitional actions in support of port legislation by a common perception that the industry needed outside help and had little time in which to accomplish complicated tasks. The generally held impression was, "That for these dredging actions to be of any use to America's coal export industry, the actions must be undertaken in the very near future and completed in 4 to 5 years" (Senator Warner, introducing port legislation, *Congressional Record*, 12/5/80). Such a challenge frightened and galvanized the industry.

Port deepening legislation became the carrier through which the coal industry attempted to achieve comprehensive changes in federal policy on terminal licensing and accelerated administrative and judicial review of port projects. Joint industry activities to obtain port legislation were motivated by the persistent perception—reinforced by many foreign buyers—that U.S. firms would lose business unless ports were deepened to at least 55 feet. Foreign purchasers took every opportunity to point out that U.S. ports were not up to modern world standards. None could handle fully loaded ships over 100,000 dead weight tons, although shipping firms estimated that these large ships would account for over 40 percent of world bulk trade by 1990. The directors of U.S. ports also spoke out on the need for federal investment in improvements. They quickly stepped in as allies of the U.S. coal producers. They provided testimony that U.S. ports were indeed outmoded compared to those in other parts of the world (Sedam testimony, Senate, Energy, 9/6/80).

U.S. coal companies, which had no direct control over the deepening of U.S. harbors, took united action out of their fear that port constraints would harm their growing business.

*Why coalitions for port improvement were necessary.* When compared with national policies of competing exporting countries, improving coal ports and guaranteeing against political reprisals on contracts were minimal industry requests. Other countries pursued aggressive export promotion policies. However, deepening U.S. coal ports represented a vast, potentially uncontrollable federal expense as well as a complex political issue. Many harbors were potentially appropriate for coal ports. How would the federal government decide which to improve? Traditionally, harbor improvement and maintenance expenses were entirely federally supported, justified by cost-benefit analyses conducted by the U.S. Army Corps of Engineers. But the Corps was frequently accused of inflating the potential benefits of improvements in order to obtain large engineering projects under its jurisdiction. Cost overruns had become the subject of bitter public inquiries. Project approvals and financing were also entrenched in an elaborate and highly politicized bureaucracy. The typical waterway project took twenty years to complete. Revising this system in any way would be controversial and would require concerted and effective effort.

Requests to dredge coal harbors were also coming at a time when the federal budget was groaning under elephantine deficits. The newly-elected Reagan administration wanted government services (like ports and waterways) to start paying for themselves on a more businesslike basis. The coal industry would have to present a case for dredging specific coal ports in this light. Yet, if the administration failed to expand ports for international coal trade it would be reneging on announced U.S. policy, and it would perhaps forego enormous balance of payments benefits.[1]

Through coalitional activity the U.S. coal industry hoped to garner its influence, to overcome traditionalism in water policy, and to impress on government officials the need to act quickly and decisively to deepen U.S. harbors. A coal coalition might be able to unite support behind proposals by which a new policy of harbor financing could be implemented. Acting alone coal firms would not have gained much credibility on these issues. But by combining their energies into coalitional strategies coal firms were able to present a powerful case, one which nearly achieved their goal.

*Commitment to joint strategic action.* Urged on by their similar shared perceptions of a common problem, coal firms began to work together to achieve their ends through political means. By early 1981, Carl Bagge was exhorting industry members to adopt a strategy of industry and interindustry cooperation on port issues. Bagge said 1980 had been the year of entrepreneurship; 1981 would be the year for coalitions.

> I suggest that now is the time for us to recognize and take full account of our commonality of interests and to forge a coalition to promote rapid development and expansion of our ports and greater use of coal. Let us bring together many and diverse groups—labor, commerce, industry, our public officials—to push for what has to be done.
>
> In Washington, they say it is time for "a new beginning." We cannot wait. We cannot wait. The nation cannot wait. I think we owe it to ourselves, and to the nation to get moving on it. . .to capitalize on our new opportunities. . .to meet our challenges successfully.
>
> Together, we can do it. (AAPA proceedings, 2/17/81: 28)

Bagge described coalitional activity as different from and more difficult than entrepreneurial competition, but equally critical to securing foreign business. He predicted that the coal industry would need to remain united if port development legislation were to make headway in Congress (Bagge speech, AAPA convention proceedings: 22–27).

Similarly, Ben Lusk of MARC, speaking on behalf of small coal producers, warned of the danger of infighting when joint action might result in positive gains for the whole industry.

> What are we doing? Talking alot [sic] and fighting over which ports to deepen. . . .
> We simply do not have time for this. We will be out of the coal export market if fast track status is not applied to dredging and maintenance dredging soon. If we do not act quickly to dredge, a golden opportunity for coal will disappear. . . . We can not allow the U.S. to lose these markets because our harbors are too shallow. (AAPA proceedings, 2/18/81: 103)

In spite of its challenge to Reagan administration promises to cut federal public works expenditures, port development legislation seemed to have a good chance of passage when first proposed. Broad interindustry concern about port congestion aided by the general public's desire for swift recovery from the 1980 recession favored it. A coal industry coalition seemed almost redundant except to head off opposition from environmental groups. However, as the implications of specific proposals became more clear, generalized support dissipated, and debate centered on the specifics of individual bills. Noncoal commodities, powerful federal agencies, inland waterway interests, and specific ports withheld their approval. The coal industry became the only major group that remained relatively united behind legislation. Although the falloff in support eventually damaged the port bill, the coal coalition was able to maintain a unity that was impressive and allowed it to orchestrate compromises being put forth.

## HOW COALITIONS DIFFER FROM OTHER INDUSTRY REALIGNMENTS

Chapter 5 presented the effects on the interorganizational network of competitive entrepreneurial activities. The steam coal market was viewed as a virtually limitless, magnificent growth opportunity. Competition and entrepreneurial activities extended and broadened the interorganizational network, and standard operating procedures were revised as many actors looked for new business. New domestic and foreign investor-producer-buyers were introduced to coal exports. Chapter 6 discussed the realignments which occurred as a result of viewing the market as a complex technical challenge. New vendors of information in government, the media, consulting firms, and trade organizations became attached to the coal industry as supporting groups. The new groups complicated the interorganizational network and created new network roles and interaction settings.

The changes in the interorganizational network previously discussed resulted from additions of newly relevant members to the network, or from the undertaking of new roles by older members. In both cases the structural arrangement of the network remained basically a pluralistic mob of participants elbowing each other for business with a minimum of vertical or horizontal coordination among the interacting units. Roland Warren (1967) called this style of network interaction "social choice." Through entrepreneurial activities autonomous interests competed for attention and market control. With informational realignments, individual units clustered around the technical advisors they needed to compete at a higher level of acquired expertise.

This chapter focuses on coalitions, which are temporary collaborative interorganizational structures. This makes them fundamentally different from the competitive forms of industry realignments I have discussed. Coalitions, although constantly shifting and transitory, create blocks of power and may exercise influence beyond the additive power of their individual participants. Although members of these coalitions retained individualistic reasons for joining together and ceded little power to the group as a whole, their collaboration nevertheless changed the texture of the pluralistic network by inserting into it a layer of articulated interests which were larger than those of any individual member. By agreeing to act together, firms changed their relationships to one another, becoming more collaborative and intricately linked in the area of export issues.

The final outcome of port development legislation is still undetermined. However finally resolved, issues articulated and the strategies represented by coal industry coalitional activities will remain whether or not this legislation proceeds further through the legislative process.

## THE PORT DEVELOPMENT BILL

### Issues and Proposals

So far I have referred to port development legislation as though it were a single, well-coordinated proposal. In fact, there were numerous coal port development bills with different sponsors and different specific terms. Congress very actively considered this issue during 1980–82. Eleven different congressional committees held hearings.[2] Six separate committees considered port development legislation. The government affairs representative of the company where I worked observed that port legislation received more attention than any other coal issue in the 1981 Congress. "Coal port development is very sexy in Congress," he reported to his department head (legislative meeting notes, 12/10/81).

*Senate activity.* Senator John Warner (R, Va.) was the first politician who scheduled hearings to consider what should be done about coal export congestion and the government's role in supporting coal trade. Warner began holding a series of informational hearings of the Energy and Natural Resources Committee in September 1980. Warner had promised representatives of the port and coal industries during the summer that he would introduce legislation to relieve congestion at Hampton Roads (*NCA Coal News*, 11/3/80). His hearings were intended to focus attention on that issue. Warner did introduce a bill shortly after the 1980 election. It called for dredging in selected harbors, streamlining the process of issuing permits for coal terminals, and accelerating the approval of port improvement projects (*Coal Now*, 11/4/80). Little was done with this bill, which died at the end of the lame duck Congressional session that preceded the new Reagan administration. Warner's bill was nongeneric. It named three specific ports for deepening. Quickly port leaders huddled and decided that they preferred legislation which did not name specific ports, thus inviting less opposition from their unnamed peers.[3] Warner's staff began to reconsider his proposal for the new legislative session. Coal and port leaders expected that Warner would introduce a revised version of his bill in early 1981; in fact he did not introduce a new version until late fall, by which time he had lost effective leadership of the issue.

Warner's approach had problems other than naming of specific ports. The purpose of Warner's bill had been to hasten the normal process by which designated port projects would obtain federal funds. It would not have altered the funding formulas by which ports were financed, although it sought to alter Corps of Engineers' procedures. Under its existing procedures the Corps of Engineers had conducted studies of Hampton Roads, Mobile, and New Orleans to determine the feasibility and benefits of deepening them to 55 feet. Baltimore had been approved for deepening since 1970, but because of environmental challenges had been unable to get congressional appropriations. Warner's bill named the three coal ports currently considered good risks by the Corps as special cases to receive accelerated funding. Warner wanted to promote his own state's port and its interest in coal exports. However, he had not correctly judged the political context of his bill.

First, the Senate Energy and Natural Resources Committee was not the normal assignment for a waterways bill. Water interests had powerful legislative friends who served primarily on the House and Senate Public Works Committees and on the Water Appropriations Subcommittees in both bodies of Congress. These friends would work hard to retain control of any bill affecting water interests. Warner was a new member of the Senate Energy Committee and consequently had little clout there. In the new session of Congress the Senate's Environment and Public Works Committee, particularly the Subcommittee on Water Resources, asserted its jurisdiction over port development issues.

On the other hand, the 1980 election had changed membership in the Senate from a Democratic to a Republican majority. This change favored Warner, who was a close personal friend of Ronald Reagan. Warner's interests would have some sway with the president. Still, the Warner bill was not one the new administration wanted to embrace. The Reagan administration's announced policy was to require user fees for full cost recovery of public works projects. Coal port development looked like too big an exception too early in the game to the president's budget advisors. A rumor circulated that Senator Warner personally asked the president to make an exception of coal ports because their potential contribution to economic recovery placed them in the national interest, and the president had replied "No way" (conversation notes, Senator Warner staffer).

Although realizing that his current thinking would probably not receive administration approval, Warner cosponsored with Senator Bennett Johnston (D, La.) and Representative Lindy Boggs (D, La.) Senate and House companion bills in the new legislative session which provided generic fast track consideration for coal ports. They eventually included a minimal cost recovery formula. Meanwhile, other proposals were also being prepared.

In March 1981, the administration submitted bills to the Public Works Committees of the Senate and House which would revolutionize the method of financing port and inland waterway projects. These bills required full cost recovery of existing inland and port operations as well as of any new dredging expenses. The administration's proposals were more concerned with revising federal waterway financing than with coal port development per se. David Stockman, director of the Office of Management and Budget (OMB) and the administration's spokesman, wanted to capitalize on sentiment supporting coal exports and would support port deepening only if it was accompanied by restructuring the financing of all port operations. The administration's bills did not include accelerated project approvals and streamlined licensing, the fast track provisions that the coal industry considered essential.

Senate Public Works Committee members were also beginning to take an interest in drafting port development legislation, although, ironically, the leadership of Public Works was now less favorable to coal industry issues than it had been under the Democrats. Jennings Randolph (D, W.Va.) and Daniel Patrick Moynihan (D, N.Y.), who had strong interests in coal, foreign trade, and ports, were replaced in key roles by Robert Stafford (R, Vt.) and James Abdor (R, S.D.) neither of whom had reason to support either coal or coastal ports. More significantly, the Republican staff counsel, Hal Brayman, had spent years trying to get an integrated federal water reform policy through Congress (see Reid, 1980). He felt strongly that water resource issues should be dealt with as a package, with inland and ocean port legislation together. Brayman considered the coal ports bill special interest legislation (reports of third party conversations with Brayman, 1/16/81; 4/23/81). Brayman's response to coal port improvement was that it should be part of comprehensive waterway financing reform. "We have been looking at this for a great deal of time. It is a problem of water policy far broader than deepening of one or two ports" (Brayman quoted by Madison, *National Journal*, 2/7/81).

Nevertheless, the Senate and House hoppers filled with bills naming favorite ports for accelerated dredging. By June 1981 at least thirteen bills had been introduced in the Senate and seven in the House. The ports favored included Baltimore, Charleston, Philadelphia, Savannah, New York, and the Texas and Gulf ports. The Public Works Committee eventually drafted a committee bill in the summer of 1981, which called for moderate cost-sharing, but the administration continued to insist on 100 percent nonfederal financing of ports. Committee hearings on coal export issues were held throughout 1981 where senators had a chance to examine factors important to the coal and port industries and to U.S. foreign policy.

*House activity.* Jurisdiction over port development issues also became an issue in the House, although it was resolved somewhat more amicably than in the Senate. Two committees asserted their authority: Merchant Marine and Fisheries, headed by Congressman Mario Biaggi of New York, and Public Works and Transportation's Subcommittee on Water Resources, headed by Congressman Robert Roe of New Jersey.

Biaggi acted first. He held a series of field hearings from April through June 1981 in preparation for drafting a committee bill to support coal port development. There were already several coal port bills in the House hopper—companion bills to the Senate's versions favoring specific ports and the administration's full cost recovery proposal. Biaggi saw an opportunity to draft legislation that would revise the administration's full cost recovery plan, obtain accelerated project approval for a few dredging projects, and include the port of New York as a viable competitor for U.S. coal exports. Although New York had no experience with coal trade, interest in it by shippers, land developers, and Conrail was strong.

Biaggi conducted hearings that revealed his desire to find a fair-minded compromise that would resolve the dilemma between the administration's insistence on full cost recovery and the need to act swiftly to reassure customers of American commitment to export growth. However, as the hearings began in the spring, groups began to form which would make compromise difficult. While the administration continued to insist on cost recovery, small ports and inland waterway interests were vehement in their opposition to any kind of local financing contribution. Biaggi tried to steer a course between these two groups. He also kept in mind his desire to help New York.

The House Public Works Committee was normally charged with drafting legislation affecting waterway projects. Congressman Roe held several joint meetings with Biaggi's staff. They determined that their outlooks were sufficiently compatible that they would work together to prepare a bill. The House Rules Committee granted joint oversight. Biaggi drafted a proposal for fast tracking projects and a fee formula. Roe's subcommittee later held hearings on general port development which incorporated consideration of coal port development issues. The two committees eventually issued a joint report to the House.

*Critical concerns.* Critical concerns in both Senate and House consideration of port legislation turned on financing. Fast tracking of proposals through an accelerated administrative and judicial review process turned out to be less controversial than port fees. Environmental groups were surprisingly mild in their cautionary warnings about coal port development. In public hearings they worried about the disposition of dredge soil, about noise, and about potential disruption of wildlife. However, coal port development seemed a lesser and more remote evil than many other problems associated with energy development. Environmental issues were blunted also because the location of coal port projects was not being specified. The largest and most obvious project—dredging the lower

Mississippi river from the Gulf to Baton Rouge—turned out to have beneficial effects. Dredging would enlarge coastal habitats for fish, wildlife and fowl by building up jetties along the river's edge (USCOE Report, New Orleans District, 12/80).

How to pay for coal port projects became the critical abiding issue. Port dredging was expected to be very expensive. Even if undertaken at only four major ports (Hampton Roads, Baltimore, New Orleans, and Mobile) the cost would be $1.5 billion. Annual maintenance on the improved harbors would amount to over $100 million annually. Just as important to nontraditional coal ports, existing approval methods provided no procedural way to decide among several ports which ones to fund.

## Interindustry Positions

*The coal industry coalition.* As early as the fall of 1980 a coal coalition began forming to obtain coal port legislation. The American Mining Congress (AMC) and NCA decided to work together on this issue. The coal industry's trade associations anticipated that legislative initiatives might occur as a result of congestion in coal harbors. Also, they anticipated that the recommendations of the Carter administration's Interagency Coal Exports Task Force Report (ICE) would include port deepening legislation. These trade associations polled their members asking to what extent they should become involved in these issues. After polling its Coal Policy Council, the AMC decided, "We should join in a coordinated effort with the National Coal Association as the lead trade association. This is an expanded assignment for AMC . . . " (AMC memo, 12/22/80).

The professional staff at NCA, particularly Carl Bagge and Connie Holmes, were to take the lead in representing the coal industry's interest in port development. AMC would perform backup analysis and information dissemination to its membership. Bagge and Holmes became actively involved in legislative hearings, coal export panels, and the analysis of various bills. They both tried to increase interindustry support.

NCA established a special task force of industry participants to push for port dredging legislation. Chaired by Ashland Coal Co., this six-member Task Force on Harbor Dredging interacted with congressional staffs, with ports, and with other trade associations. The members of the Task Force were Ashland Coal Co., ARCO, Consolidation, Massey, Peabody, and Utah International. They were aided by Connie Holmes' staff at NCA. The Task Force developed proposals and analyses and drafted specific legislative language for congressional staffs who were preparing port bills during 1981–82.

The members of NCA's Task Force on Harbor Dredging were six very large coal firms, four of which had not previously participated in export trade. Through NCA these large companies could pool their energies and expertise in order to press for government support for port dredging legislation. The NCA Harbor Dredging Task Force became the coal industry's voice on port development in Congress. Members identified themselves in congressional testimony as speaking for NCA, CEA, or the American Mining Congress. By implication their views stood for those of the coal industry. As this coal coalition gained expertise and confidence, it solicited support from coalitions in other industries with whom it could combine forces to help put its message across.

*Water interests.* The coal industry's Harbor Dredging Task Force met with water industry associations to try to develop joint approaches to port legislation. Water interests were generally in favor of port development, but the inland group vehemently opposed any kind of user fees. Ports, represented by the American Association of Port Authorities (AAPA), were less adamant. This group became active in working with coal interests to achieve a port development bill. None of the water organizations had the budget of NCA, but they did have powerful congressional supporters who could help with port legislation.

Water interests were seriously split over user fees. The administration's waterway cost recovery proposals linked inland waterways and ports. Shallow water interests felt they had been tricked by the passage of a small fuel tax in 1979, and they refused to accede to a user tax of any kind.

Inland water interests maintained their trenchant opposition to user fees. This kept the water industry from having a united position on port development legislation. The National Waterways Alliance, an interindustry organization, cautioned its members that Congress was serious about user fees, and that the waterway industry "must come to grips with the cost-recovery issue" (National Waterways Alliance memo, 4/14/81). However, the only action taken by inland interests was to call for further studies of the impact of inland and port fees on various ports and on total export demand. The refusal of barge companies to consider port fees even caused some tension between them and their parent firms, which in some cases were coal companies.

On the contrary, port directors were aware, through their international contacts and trade associations, that user fees were levied in many ports of the world to raise revenue and to regulate traffic. Port directors, however, had a different problem. Ports were notoriously jealous of one another. Each port's situation was unique.

No port wanted to sit idly by and see its revenues taxed to pay for the deepening of another port. So, devising a fee formula that all U.S. ports would back proved to be a major challenge. Small and large, eastern and western, Great Lakes and ocean ports did not have the same concerns.

The AAPA working with Senator Warner floated a first suggestion on cost sharing in the early spring of 1981 (company memo, 3/20/81). Cost recovery could be handled through a tax on the value of ocean-going (import and export) cargo at all ports. The money would be placed in a trust fund and then drawn out according to a priority system established by the Corps of Engineers for deepening projects that the Corps deemed eligible. The trust fund would theoretically protect ports which had low current tonnages of coal or other commodities, but which showed the potential to become viable deepwater export harbors. The use of an ad valorem tax had another advantage. It could be kept very low, adding only about $ .10 per ton to even the most expensive cargoes. It would be minimally disruptive of existing trade/port patterns (CRS report, 6/26/81).

The main problem with an ad valorem tax was that highly valued cargoes (such as furniture, liquor, automobiles, and other merchandise) did not need deeper harbors. Large bulk cargoes were typically low value (such as gravel, bauxite, crude oil, chemicals, grain, lumber, and coal). In fact, coal had the lowest value to ton ratio of any deep draft commodity. Yet an ad valorem tax would mean that the higher-cost cargoes would pay for coal's immediate benefit. Though not disruptive of current trade, an ad valorem tax was soon found to be politically nonviable. Warner's staff, which had shown the most interest in it, soon dropped it from consideration. But port directors and policy makers had at least made a start toward thinking about various options for cost recovery.

As time went on ports became significantly split over cost recovery proposals. New York wanted a completely local financing system. Baltimore, which had an approved port deepening plan, wanted to accelerate scheduling, but to keep full federal funding for dredging. Los Angeles had naturally deep water and could therefore stay out of the deepening fight, except that it opposed all uniform national fees whether ad valorem or of another type. Hampton Roads and New Orleans wanted federal funding, but were willing to accept some local share. Small ports, such as those on the Great Lakes, ports in the south, and at the mouth of the Columbia River, felt their needs were being shunted aside in the rush to consider formulas which would favor large loading centers. Carl Bagge offended Great Lakes ports by admitting that they were "off our radar scopes" for coal export trade (*Coal Industry News*, 7/13/81:11).

The source of tensions among ports was that cost recovery-formulas would have quite different effects on them. National uniform fees would be kept low, but ports with low or no maintenance would be paying for the improvement of their competitors. On the other hand, locally calculated fees would favor the ports that already controlled most commerce. Large trade volumes would provide a larger pool of fees from which to repay expenses, thus keeping per ton costs at large-volume ports low. Over time, more trade would be drawn to those ports where fees for commerce were lowest, thus exaggerating the advantages that larger ports already held. Western and southern ports knew that they would suffer from locally financed schemes.

In contrast to the deep splits among water interests, NCA and the Harbor Dredging Task Force showed a coherent and united coalition working together.

## Coal Coalition Activities

*Coal's acceptance of port fees.* Carl Bagge, president of NCA, indicated the direction he thought the coal industry and its allies should pursue. He foresaw the greatest threat to coal exports as failure to achieve port deepening fast enough to meet growing export demand. At the AAPA convention in February 1981 he therefore called for "reasoned balance" among objectives and the need to avoid "rigid absolutist approaches" to port financing. User fees, he said, were not an unthinkable option if they would help achieve prompt federal action on dredging. Bagge, a longtime Washington insider, judged that cost sharing would be the price of obtaining coal port legislation.

> [W]hen you take into account the present reality of the country's fiscal health and the Reagan Administration's well-publicized intent to cut federal expenditures and strike a balance in national accounts, there seems to be a clear message for us. It is that no time should be lost in considering what financing alternatives exist—and which of them may be most desirable—for reducing the demand on the federal treasury, and thereby reduce the potential for delay in attempting the [sic] make a political decision on where to dredge first. (AAPA proceedings, 2/17/81: 26)

Bagge's announcement shocked many coal producers. His position was not confirmed by the NCA board until several weeks after he announced it. In the meantime, he tried to forestall division in the industry by circulating copies of his AAPA speech to all NCA members. In this way he apprised them of the need for united industry leadership to achieve port legislation and of its bottom line (NCA memo, 2/25/81). Bagge's announcement also frightened subsidiaries to the coal chain, particularly inland water interests. He was suggesting that the coal industry accept the notion of sharing the cost of deep draft projects without even putting up a fight.

Bagge's position placed the coal industry between the hardline fiscal reformers at OMB and those water interests who wanted no nonfederal fee contributions. These were the two "absolutist approaches" that he feared threatened the coal industry with a stalemate on port development.

At the NCA board meeting in early March that followed Bagge's AAPA announcement, his position on shared financing of ports was formally confirmed, but not before skeptical questioning by coal producers (Massey testimony, House Public Works, 6/16/81: 68). NCA's board agreed in principle that some cost sharing to support ports was necessary, as long as it was applied equitably to all commodities and was tied to an effective method of accelerating authorization of port improvement projects. NCA's thirty-member Transportation Committee was given the job of fleshing out this position. In April the Transportation Committee reported to NCA members that the industry should accept cost sharing of 25–50 percent of construction cost for deepening coal ports (NCA memo, 4/27/81). Maintenance should remain a federal expense.

In retrospect, it is surprising how quickly the coal industry accepted the necessity of port fees. In the past it had bitterly opposed severance taxes, mine safety fund charges, and land reclamation costs. The ease with which the coal industry accepted the notion of contributing monetarily to port development illustrates, I think, the seriousness of its fears about losing foreign business. It also shows that the industry was trying to overcome its vulnerability to inadequate ports by building as much public support for improving them as possible. The industry accepted the political reality that to gain important future benefits it would need to compromise now. Accepting a modest port fee would demonstrate the industry's good faith and would allow it to influence other geographic and economic considerations as port projects matured. The coal industry, which had received few examples of government support in the past, calculated that its future sales were worth the price of some initial cost now. Since most producers expected that they would be able to pass on port charges to foreign customers as they now passed on demurrage fees, they felt that they had little to lose by accepting the principle of cost sharing.

Within NCA the acceptance of local cost sharing was supported by large coal companies. Both the NCA board and Transportation

Committee were dominated by large firms. Like Carl Bagge, the government relations representatives of large coal firms were savvy observers of the Washington scene. They had come to the conclusion that port legislation would require some form of user fee even before Bagge made his AAPA speech. These lobbyists were privately urging their CEO's to accept cost sharing (coal firm memo, 2/25/81). Port fees for dredging, if applied to all cargo would add only a few cents per ton to coal (which would probably be passed on to foreign buyers anyway). This seemed a small price to assure the huge volumes and long-term commitments that technical reports and foreign coal customers forecast. Large companies also needed to justify to their stockholders and parent firms the resources they were committing to huge coal terminals—terminals which would be most cost efficient when handling large orders in ships that needed deeper channels. For these reasons large firms accepted the political necessity of port fees to obtain dredging. Industry representatives thought that the various pressures on the United States to expand export coal trade would induce OMB's Stockman to settle for less than 100 percent cost recovery, if he was able to claim a partial victory for waterway financing reform.

Companies that had had contact with foreign buyers were aware that American conduct on port development was being closely watched. Foreign buyers were waiting for signs of U.S. commitment. A legislative impasse within the coal industry over fees might thwart enthusiasm for American coal and emphasize that U.S. ports and coal producers were more concerned about petty differences among themselves than about the long term volume of sales. Coalitional strategies were in part meant to impress upon foreign buyers that the coal industry would do its part—that it was indeed serious about overcoming obstacles to foreign trade.

By April 1981, even Hal Brayman, the longtime advocate of a unified approach to waterway reform, head staffer of the Senate's Environment and Public Works Committee, acknowledged that a rationale was building for a ports-only financing bill. Perhaps the best way to achieve waterway financing reform, he admitted, would be by splitting off ocean port development from inland projects (third party conversation, 4/23/81). The principal issues were how much ports should have to pay and how fees would be assessed. Would fees be determined on a national basis or through port-specific local formulas?

Unlike ports, the coal industry was not deeply divided over these issues. Individual firms calculated that they might gain a few cents' advantage per ton by shipping through Hampton Roads, Los Angeles, New Orleans, or New York depending upon how port fees were determined. Yet, with the predicted expansion of exports into the future, most large companies thought there would be several possible ports from which they would ship coal. The large producers represented in the NCA Harbor Dredging Task Force wanted to stick together to protect their fledgling market and to get a coal ports bill.

Ashland, Consolidation, Massey, and Peabody, members of the NCA Harbor Dredging Task Force, testified before several congressional committees where they reinforced the industry's willingness to participate in "equitable" user fees (letter from Task Force to Hal Brayman, 4/10/81). Representatives of these companies also worked almost daily with the Senate Energy, Senate Public Works, and House Merchant Marine Committees behind the scenes to draft proposals, consider funding formulas, and develop compromises with other interest groups.

The NCA Harbor Dredging Task Force favored generic port funding based on tonnage rather than ad valorem fees. Coal would bear the largest burden from this kind of formula because of its low per ton value. However, the Task Force thought that a tonnage fee was more politically palatable and would provide bargaining leverage with other commodities from whom they anticipated resistance to user fees, through their evident willingness to sacrifice to obtain fair legislation. The Task Force used this position in negotiating with petroleum, grain, and various port interests. The Task Force also favored differentiated fees at various ports. Port-based fees would provide the semblance of a market test to determine which ports would be deepened. Each port would have to convince bond buyers and/or state and local taxing authorities that its prospects for deep draft trade were a good risk. Only those able to pay back federal dollars would have them advanced for dredging projects. Thus, the Harbor Dredging Task Force adopted a position which would minimize delays caused by many ports competing for federal funds.

Still unresolved in the Task Force's thinking was the further issue of long-term harbor maintenance costs. The administration had proposed that maintenance as well as improvement costs be paid for out of local funds. The maintenance and Coast Guard operating services that harbors routinely received to keep their channels clear and safe would become local expenses. Obviously this change could have important political and economic implications. Yet neither the administration nor industry leaders had a clear idea of how much of such expenses coal (or any other commodity) could bear without crippling foreign demand. Coal companies had no history of steam coal exports to fall back on. Companies and policymakers were operating blind.

*Cabinet-level negotiations.* By May 1981, the administration's proposals for port financing had been reviewed and constituencies both inside the federal government and in various industries were aligning. Top coal industry CEO's decided to seek a meeting with cabinet officials to reinforce the seriousness of their concerns about export coal trade and the immediate need for port legislation. Four coal industry leaders met on May 15, 1981, with four cabinet officials. Representing the coal industry were Peabody's R. H. Quenon, Consolidation's R. E. Samples, Pittston's Nicholas Camicia, and Thomas Holmes, a board member of the holding company that owned Peabody Coal. The Reagan administration officials were U.S. Trade Representative William Brock, Secretary of Energy James Edwards, Secretary of Interior James Watt, and Undersecretary of Commerce for International Trade Lionel Olmer. The coal leaders emphasized two points: first, the need for renewing presidential assurances to foreign buyers about the sanctity of U.S. coal contracts; second, the need for administration policy including legislation in support of port development. The coal leaders emphasized that port deepening was "critical to the development of a stable coal export market" (issues memo, 5/12/81).

In return for legislation to accelerate approval and development of deep draft navigation projects, the coal leaders promised that the coal industry would support a cost-sharing mechanism of up to 25 percent of construction costs to be obtained through fees on all commodities shipped through the deepened ports. No mention was made of maintenance expenses. The coal leaders emphasized the role that coal could play in reducing U.S. energy trade deficits and in relieving allied nations of their dependence on foreign oil.

At the conclusion of this meeting the coal leaders were pleased. They considered government officials responsive to and supportive of their requests. They came away convinced that administration officials intended to act quickly to support U.S. coal export trade, including dredging legislation (summary memo, 5/15/81). The meeting led them to conclude that a compromise on port financing could be worked out.

This meeting brought about consolidation of the coal coalition in support of port legislation. Coal exports and port development held demonstrably great importance to key steam coal industry leaders. They had used precious political capital to obtain a meeting to discuss the issue with high government officials. At this meeting the positions they presented were not simply their own but were backed by the official endorsement of the industry.

Top administration leaders seemed to accept the coal leaders' proposed cost-sharing formula. They did not object to the level of local cost-sharing that coal leaders had proposed. This argued that the administration was amenable to a compromise. The leaders came away expecting to receive support on port legislation and anticipating imminent announcement of a new official U.S. policy promoting coal trade, either at the upcoming Ottawa Economic Summit (July 1981) or at the IEA Ministers meeting in Paris.

This meeting between coal industry leaders and cabinet heads invigorated the NCA Harbor Dredging Task Force. They interpreted it as a green light to press more actively for port legislation. The Task Force immediately began to contact other government officials at the Department of Energy, Department of Commerce, OMB, and on Capitol Hill, to explain their position and to circulate proposals for possible financing of port projects. The Task Force also actively solicited cross-industry coalitions to broaden support. NCA's Task Force began to concentrate on modifying OMB's hard line on 100 percent local funding of dredging and maintenance. They also concentrated on getting fast track funding and licensing clauses inserted into proposed bills.

But just as coal's coalition seemed to gain momentum, other interests both inside and outside the federal government began to express their doubts about the imposition of fees. Two incidents showed that broad support for dredging—once port fees were added in—was extremely fragile.

*Two tests of coal coalition unity.* Just two weeks after the principals-only meeting with cabinet officials, the Harbor Dredging Task Force thought that they detected a trial balloon by administration officials to test the coal coalition and the industry's willingness to support port fees. The *Washington Post* (5/29/81) ran a small article that cited a remark by Secretary of Commerce Malcolm Baldridge which sent the Task Force into a tailspin. Baldridge had apparently told a public gathering that federal funds were not needed for port improvement. The article said: " 'The business is there; the financing is there,' he said, 'I guarantee it.' Instead of drawing on federal funds, port authorities could increase users' fees on coal shippers to pay for development, he said." On seeing this article, Task Force members inferred that Baldridge was about to saddle the coal industry with the responsibility for paying the whole cost of dredging ports.

The NCA Harbor Dredging Task Force quickly tried to contact Baldridge and Undersecretary of Commerce Lionel Olmer who had been at the principals-only meeting to register their horror and chagrin and to point out that export coal trade would be killed by such heavy fees. They pointed out that dredging in four major ports was amply justified by studies completed by the Corps of Engineers even before recent evidence of coal export growth. Therefore, they argued, coal should not have to bear an inequitable portion of the expense of deepening ports simply because coal demand was coming into prominence before that for other commodities. Task Force members were left with the uncomfortable feeling that the administration might leave them holding the bag.

Once the Task Force reached Baldridge, however, a different story emerged. Instead of being presented with a plot to fob off the costs of deep draft on their industry, the members of the Harbor Dredging Task Force found themselves asked to help the government develop a reasonable fee structure. Commerce Department officials reassured the Task Force that the Department stood behind "equitable" financing reform, though the DOC admitted that it had little notion of how to accomplish this. The NCA Task Force realized that DOC had done little or no analysis of this issue. Considering how much effort had already gone into drafting legislation and into hearings on Capitol Hill, this admission was amazing.[4] It showed that if the Task Force could present its case, it might take command.

As soon as tonnage fees began to be discussed by congressional staffs and endorsed by the NCA Task Force, various commodities began to marshall arguments for why they should be exempt from a tax. Grain and oil as well as other bulk commodities would gain economies of scale in ocean shipping if harbors were deepened. Publicly, these commodities adopted a strategy of silence about port legislation, thus letting it appear that port deepening was primarily a coal issue.[5] However, they indicated through their friends that they did not look kindly on the voluntary acceptance of port fees. The Agriculture Department spoke for grain interests at Congressman Roe's Public Works hearings. Agriculture spokesmen claimed that grain, although a user of large ships which often sailed partially loaded, did not need deep draft (House, Public Works, 7/15/81: 1000). David Stockman was skeptical (Stockman testimony, Senate, Environment and Public Works, 7/16/81: 469–514).

A second test of the coal coalition's strength was prompted by its intertwining with oil interests. Petroleum interests were even more close-mouthed in public about user fees than grain. In the relative privacy of the June 1981, NCA board meeting oil companies did reveal their position. ARCO Coal, a member of the Harbor Dredging Task Force, joined several other oil-owned firms in objecting to NCA's insistence on all-commodity tonnage fees. ARCO proposed that only those ships loaded to a depth in excess of current harbor capacity be charged deep draft user fees. Other coal firms interpreted this move by ARCO as preliminary to a general and more threatening request by oil-owned firms that all petroleum tankers (which are lightered off shore and therefore do not use their full draft capacity in harbors) be exempt from user fees. ARCO seemed to be representing its parent firm's interests in making this proposal. Oil companies were perhaps also testing through their coal subsidiaries whether coal would be willing to pay the full price of deep draft.

NCA's top brass had gotten prior wind of this insurrection and was prepared. NCA chairman, R. E. Samples of Consolidation and R. H. Quenon of Peabody were able to push ARCO and the other oil-owned firms back into line and maintain the coal coalition by citing an analysis showing that coal-only fees would have devastating effects on coal prices and coal trade. Port fees as much as $3–$10 per ton would occur if coal were forced to bear the whole cost of deep draft (company memo, 6/5/81). Everyone knew that such huge fees would ruin export business. The course of the NCA board's discussion revealed another reason coal companies might want to break ranks. Port fees placed only on coal would favor exports from Hampton Roads, where fees would be $1 or less. Since Hampton Roads was already obtaining most of its tonnage from coal, coal-only fees would be lowest at this port. The eastern firms were interested in this.

In spite of the advantages to eastern companies including itself, Consolidation Coal convinced independent and nonoil owned firms that the potential advantage they would gain from a lower port fee was not worth splitting the industry and potentially losing out on effective port development legislation. The NCA board voted decisively to reject ARCO's reconsideration of NCA policy. The coal coalition remained for the time being intact.

The effect of these two incidents on the NCA Harbor Dredging Task Force was encouraging. Rather than finding that the administration had developed its position and fee formula for local port financing, the Harbor Dredging Task Force found that it could probably shape the thinking of government officials. In the second incident the Task Force gained confidence that the coal coalition was resilient even in the face of questions from oil-owned firms.

The Harbor Dredging Task Force began to work with William Morris, the Undersecretary of Commerce for International Trade, to whom they were referred by Baldridge and Olmer. Morris was coordinating work on the port development bill for the administration. The Task Force shared with Morris their analyses of port fees and the calculations used at the NCA board meeting which showed that huge fees would result if coal alone had to pay for deep draft. Confronted with these numbers, according to one Task Force member,

Morris "sucked air" (third party conversation, 6/6/81). He then volunteered that although the administration wanted to recoup most of the cost of dredging projects, the government felt that a fee of over fifty cents per ton would render coal noncompetitive.

This remark was a revelation to the NCA Task Force. Until this meeting with Morris the industry did not know the general magnitude of fees that government was considering. Their worst-case calculations had been running well in excess of fifty cents per ton. A Task Force member told me after the meeting that when Morris said fifty cents was the limit, "I was not about to disabuse him" (conversation notes, 6/6/81). The real point was that unlike grain and oil exporters who had some history to fall back on, neither the coal industry nor government officials had any real fix on how much fee coal could afford to bear. Compared to the current demurrage charges at Hampton Roads, which were adding $6–$10 per ton to coal a fee of fifty cents per ton seemed well within their means. After this meeting with Morris, fifty cents per ton became the benchmark that the Harbor Dredging Task Force publicly set as an acceptable fee limit, although privately they thought that they could afford to bear somewhat more. The Task Force continued to meet and work with Morris. It had established itself as a well-informed and realistic voice for bringing about port development legislation.

NCA's Task Force members were jubilant over the meeting with Morris. Two potential threats to the coal coalition had actually confirmed their leadership and expertise on the dredging issue, and they were in close touch as advisors to the main person in the executive branch who was charged with developing the administration's position. Task Force members felt that their top leaders' meeting in May was paying off.

Meeting with Morris also encouraged the members of the Task Force to present their ideas directly to OMB. Task Force members began to explore their contacts there. Glen Schlady, who had previously worked at NCA, Frederick Khedouri, head of the natural resources and economics section, and Stockman, who was taking a personal interest in waterway reform, received calls or visits from Task Force members. Although they obtained no promises, Stockman's testimony before the Senate Public Works Committee in July, especially his responses to questions from Senator Warner, seemed to indicate that he might compromise below 100 percent local port financing (7/16/81: 494–95). Stockman seemed to recognize that fees had to be kept reasonably low to protect foreign trade.

*Seeking interindustry alliances.* The general magnitude of a user fee did not settle how it would be assessed—whether as a national uniform charge or based on the costs and local cost recovery options at each port. Both methods were problematic from the coal industry's point of view, because both had implications for how fast action on port dredging could be completed. The Harbor Dredging Task Force now set out to look for allies who would help it to work out one formula or another.

The Harbor Dredging Task Force approached Ronald Brinson, the key staff person at AAPA. Brinson was a featured speaker at the NCA National Convention in June, and this provided a good opportunity to approach him about how the Task Force and port directors could work together. During a chance encounter on the plane flight back to Washington, Brinson and key Task Force member Christopher Farrand, the government affairs vice-president of Peabody Coal, discussed a possible way to finance port improvements. Farrand explained a proposal that the Task Force was working on. It separated new construction expenses from maintenance and ongoing operations costs and funded each differently. The formula offered benefits to both large and small ports. It called for setting aside a national maintenance fund of twenty-five cents per ton on all commerce through all ports. This fund would amply cover existing operations and maintenance in harbors and would also fund the maintenance on improvements for the four deepening projects most often discussed. The relatively low fee would not be burdensome to any port and would spread the cost of maintenance throughout the port system. New construction expenses for harbors desiring deep draft capacity, according to this proposal, would be paid on a port-by-port basis, through whatever financing mechanism an individual port might choose. Some options might be industrial revenue bonds, port fees, cargo tonnage charges, or commodity-specific taxes (AMC memo, 9/14/81).

Brinson saw the proposal as potentially saleable to ports. It offered small ports with high maintenance costs a fair way to avoid exorbitant charges for existing operations. They could also stay in the running for deepening if they could convince local financing agencies of their viability for local support. Brinson agreed to present the proposal to the AAPA Board of Directors as his own.

The same proposal was presented by members of the Harbor Dredging Task Force to Undersecretary Morris and to officials at OMB. It was taken to Hal Brayman at the Senate Public Works staff, and to the Biaggi Subcommittee, which was drafting the House of Representatives' Port Development bill. The Harbor Dredging Task Force felt it had found a workable formula that could unite ports behind a port development bill.

For several weeks it appeared that the coal coalition might have

hit on a solution to the funding dilemma that was holding up progress on port legislation. Biaggi and Brayman as well as Brinson approved of the plan. Once it was explained to them, most groups
could see merit in separating normal maintenance expenses from
deep draft construction funding.

Other events also worked in favor of this compromise.
Undersecretary Morris was formally named head of a newly created
Coal Interagency Working Group which was charged with coordinating coal export policy initiatives for the executive branch (*Inside DOE*, 7/24/81). The Reagan administration issued an official
coal export policy statement through Commerce Secretary
Baldridge. It promised to support port deepening legislation
(USDOC New Release, 7/17/81). Leadership of coal export policy was
transferred from the Department of Energy to the Department of
Commerce and was placed under Morris. OMB's role was not mentioned. Morris, being already aware of the coal coalition's positions
and proposals, was now favorably placed to bring them forward.
The coal coalition's efforts seemed to be gaining strength. In July
1981, it looked like the coal coalition might soon get a port deepening bill through Congress.

## Alliances Collapse

Although coal was able to keep its own coalition united and
focused on the goal of achieving immediate port development
legislation, it was not able to build a long-lived consensus for support with other groups. Bifurcated fee charges were not acceptable
to the AAPA. Brinson was unable to get the AAPA board to approve
the coal industry's compromise plan, or any other. Ports such as
New York and Los Angeles, which had very low current
maintenance and high tonnage, were unwilling to accept any sort of
national uniform fee to ease the burden of maintenance costs at
other ports. Speeding the process of deepening harbors was of less
concern than jockeying for competitive advantage among ports. An
indication of their lack of cooperation was that at Congressman
Robert Roe's hearings on general resources issues in July 1981,
twenty-two port witnesses requested time to present separate views
on port deepening!

By August 1981, ports had split into opposing camps. Big ports
formed their own coalition, the National Coalition for Port Progress,
which opposed any nationally imposed fee. Eventually this group
proposed its own legislation (NCA/GRC memo, 5/11/82). Small ports,
particularly those in the west and south, saw all local financing of
ports as threats to their areas. The Oregon Senators (Mark Hatfield

and Robert Packwood) joined by Senator Strom Thurmond (R, S.C.) and Senator Mack Mattingly (R, Ga.) and three Congressmen met with the president's counselor Edwin Meese to express their objection to port-by-port financing (AAPA memo, 8/3/81). Hatfield and Packwood vowed to block any port legislation that seemed unfair to their area. Since Packwood chaired the Senate Port Caucus and Hatfield served on the powerful Senate Finance Committee which theoretically had the power to gain jurisdiction over port fees as a tax, neither senator could be ignored.[6] In fact, the Oregonians' concerns ultimately caused the Public Works Committee's approved Senate bill to be set aside for the 1982 session. Senator Stafford, in deference to the objections from Hatfield and Packwood, did not call the bill to the floor, although it received a favorable report from his committee. The issue has hovered in indefinite limbo since March 1982.

No large, dominant, interindustry coalition continued to build for port development legislation. A critical moment had passed. Congressional committees continued to hold hearings, and both Houses eventually reported bills favorably for floor action, but the momentum to institute such a major change in the financing of major public works projects was not there.

Nevertheless, the coal coalition had succeeded in establishing itself as an important and knowledgeable force in port development policy-making. This role placed it in new associations with ports and with the federal bureaucracy. The coal coalition continued to meet with port groups and to propose compromises to individual port directors. In one instance a member of the Harbor Dredging Task Force reviewed and suggested revisions in a major port's position statement sent to the Biaggi Committee *after* it had been approved by the port director (conversation notes, 10/5/81). The Harbor Dredging Task Force met constantly with House and Senate committee staffs as they prepared to mark up legislation. They worked with members of the House and Senate Coal and Port Caucuses. They strengthened contacts with analysts at OMB, and fed data and proposed bargains to the Coal Interagency Working Group. Having lost its bid to orchestrate a broad interindustry consensus, it became a gadfly for change. Still pursued by the fear of losing future business, its desire to attain legislation at almost any cost remained strong.

*Final Efforts.* In a final effort at compromise, the Harbor Dredging Task Force proposed to senior officials preparing the administration's budget requests in October 1981 that the coal industry would accept 100 percent local funding of construction expenses in return for a federal port maintenance fund. This was a desperation move to get accelerated deepening of ports. The NCA board accepted this proposal in March 1982. Their hope was that this action would jolt OMB and the ports association into realizing that *some* kind of port legislation would be better than none.

This funding solution would help the big ports and would aid most major coal producers. Delays in waiting for federal authorization and funding of ports would be eliminated. It would also be good for OMB, which would save $1.5 billion and achieve a precedent for revising port financing. New York, Hampton Roads, New Orleans, and Los Angeles were the ports that could afford such a proposal. But the position was by now unacceptable to major political interests in broad geographic areas of the country. The coal industry's fear of losing future sales, which had prompted it to make such an expensive and drastic suggestion, was not shared widely enough by the allies it would need to pass legislation.

Senator Bennett Johnston of Louisiana, an ardent supporter and cosponsor of port legislation, noted the dissipation of support.

> No port wants another one to get deeper draft than it's got. Questions are raised by the railroads. Questions are raised by Stockman's shop about whether or not the traditional role of the Corps or if the budget can stand any money. And there is a lack of support from this administration. I must say I'm not too encouraged. (Senate, Energy hearings, 12/3/81: 55)

Organizationally, however, the coal coalition was remarkably successful at shaping debate on coal port development, even with its minimal expertise and experience in this area. Many proposals, including some specific language that it drafted, were incorporated into committee-approved bills.[7] Simply getting bills through hearings, mark up, and to an approved status with the major provisions important to the coal industry intact was a major achievement, given the original hostility of the Senate Public Works staff and the unfamiliarity of Biaggi with coal issues. Near the end of 1981 even OMB became more conciliatory.

When OMB offered a last ditch analysis of port development fees sub rosa to the Senate Public Works Committee, this analysis reflected the influence of the Harbor Dredging Task Force in framing the port fee issue. OMB proposed local financing of new construction combined with a twenty-three cents cap on maintenance expenses. The proposal avoided both excessive local fees and a national uniform tax. It also bore a remarkable resemblance to the bifurcated funding proposal devised by NCA's Farrand and AAPA's Brinson which the Harbor Dredging Task Force had presented to

OMB. OMB's proposal also adopted the same general magnitude of fees that the coal industry had indicated it would accept.

The Public Works committee amended its bill to accept a modified version of this OMB formula. David Stockman announced publicly that 'the twenty-three cents cap "satisfied the administration's requirements for local financing" (*Journal of Commerce,* 12/3/81). A new compromise was possibly in the works. The Harbor Dredging Task Force's efforts to bring about workable legislation and their contacts with administration leaders may have goaded OMB into a concession after all.

OMB's last ditch proposal was a Pyrrhic victory for the Harbor Dredging Task Force. The Task Force had pressed a consistent case for immediate action to hasten port improvements. It had also provided a template formula which clarified the issues and which helped ports and OMB zero in on their differences so that legislative proposals could proceed. If port development legislation is passed in the future, there are still many issues to be worked out. The vigilance of NCA's Harbor Dredging Task Force had made it an important force for change. It had held the coal industry together and had focused others on the need to consider serious solutions.

## Phasing Out the Coal Coalition

The status of Senate and House versions of the port development bill remained unclear in the 1982 session. Connie Holmes reported to the NCA Government Relations Committee (1/20/82), "According to committee staff, the senators are receiving no 'push' from affected industries to move the bill, so this is needed before we can expect floor action." Hatfield and the National Coalition for Port Progress continued to work for fee formulas that favored small or large ports respectively (NCA memo, 5/11/82). In the House, after a year of frantic activity, the Public Works Committee had not yet accepted Biaggi's bill. Special interest attachments threatened to bog it down. A seaman's union amendment requiring that U.S. ships and labor be used to export American coal would, if passed, render U.S coal exports so costly that the savings from deepening ports would be more than cancelled out.

By spring 1982 quick action on any bill looked unlikely, and the debates and issues were becoming routinized. The coal industry's Harbor Dredging Task Force was ready to take a lower profile. They wanted to take a less active role in articulating proposals and coordinating various interests, and let NCA monitor the situation.

The Harbor Dredging Task Force offered as much impetus to legislative action as was possible in 1981. It successfully articulated key elements of a bill acceptable to the industry and kept the industry united behind its proposals. When the momentum for approval slowed, the Task Force members tried last ditch efforts. When the issue bogged down again, they went on to other things. The loose, temporary coalition dispersed. Yet, the Harbor Dredging Task Force created a precedent for coal industry cooperation and influence over water policy and export issues. The coalition was an example of temporary coal industry cooperation and joint activity, especially among large firms, on export issues which had not occurred before.

## Large Versus Small Coal Firms in Coalitions

Members of the coal industry's Harbor Dredging Task Force were all major steam coal producers. They each aspired to attain a large portion of steam coal export trade. Consolidation Coal and Massey had previous export experience, but the other members of the task force (ARCO, Ashland, Peabody, and Utah International) were new to export trade. Peabody, Consolidation and Utah International were among the twenty largest firms in the coal industry in 1980. ARCO, Ashland, and Massey, though not as large, each had annual production capacities of about ten million tons. Both ARCO and Massey were among the top twenty firms by 1982. All six firms are owned by huge multinational companies. Four are subsidiaries of oil.

The Harbor Dredging Task Force did not include any small firms, nor was it particularly representative of shipments from the main export center at Hampton Roads. Consol and Massey would probably continue to use eastern ports, but the other four firms were primarily interested in Gulf and western ports; and Consol had many western properties.

The official positions taken by the NCA board followed the lead and advice of a task force of large firms with little combined export experience and with interests in developing coal export trade away from its traditional center. A few large firms directed the coal industry's position on user fees, the deepening of harbors, and the intricacies of fast track legislation, all of which would have important financial ramifications for every exporter. The Task Force, as we have seen, was also helping to shape the government's position on these issues as well.

The predominance of large firms would not have been remarkable except that prior to 1980 export issues had been handled by the Coal Exporters Association (CEA), an NCA affiliate organization composed primarily of export traders who often represented very small mining firms. The voices of NCA and CEA on export policy and port development began to reflect the opinions of large steam coal companies, particularly those on the Harbor Dredging Task Force. NCA's Transportation Committee also took a role in solidifying industry support behind port dredging and fast track approval of infrastructure. The thirty-member Transportation Committee, headed by E. Morgan Massey, was generally representative of NCA's overall bias toward the interests of big producers.

Large producers had the leadership status to influence the entire industry on port legislation. Large firms also had the resources to devote staff energy to finding out about port issues. Some had Washington representatives who could expand their list of contacts on congressional committees and in the departments of Energy, Interior, Transportation, and OMB, to include people related to ports, water, and export trade.

The power of large firms over export issues seemed both natural and inevitable to coal industry members. Still, it was a new and unprecedented development. To what extent this dominance of coalitional activity by large firms would ultimately harm small coal companies is hard to say.

Even those few public spokesmen who noted the special problems of small coal exporters were in favor of deepening ports. For example, Peter Vismans of SSM Coal, a trader who had dealt with small firms for thirty years, predicted transportation-cost problems for small producers (Senate, Energy, 9/16/80: 238). He urged the United States to act as quickly as possible to improve its ports so that it could remain competitive with other countries.[8] Ben Lusk of MARC made the same point at the AAPA Convention (2/18/81).

However, it is possible that once cost-repayment formulas became the key elements in coal port legislation, spokesmen for the small firms needed to reanalyze whether deepened ports would bring benefits to small firms. For example, the very large long-term shipments which dredging would make possible might be difficult for small firms to fill. In most cases, they could not offer dedicated reserves or specially negotiated prices. The development of coal ports competitive with Hampton Roads would diversify exports away from the area where most small mining companies were located. Finally, large firms desired fast track licensing to speed their building of coal terminals. Owning their own terminals would allow them to set their own rules of assembling and loading coal shipments. But, by implication, these efficiencies for large firms would widen the gap in performance efficiency and handling costs between large and small firms, and could possibly cost them sales.

There is no evidence that the small firms were aware of these

possible drawbacks from port deepening policy. I am suggesting only that with the shaping of issues and articulation of coal port policy
resting in the hands of huge steam coal firms, small firms risked
becoming tied to paying for a port deepening solution from which
they would receive little direct benefit and perhaps some harm.
Whether these considerations would have outweighed the expected
growth in sales for all firms because of the enormous increase in
sales volume is still a moot point.

I do not think that large coal companies had sinister motives in
orchestrating coalitional activities of the coal industry on export
matters. They simply moved in because they saw a job that they
thought must be done. Large firms argued that the benefits of port
deepening would accrue to the whole U.S. industry. This does not
mean, however, that individual firms did not hope to gain more
from export development policy than their smaller or more experienced peers. Members of the NCA Task Force extended their
scope of expertise, effective leadership, and political power into the
area of export trade. Large steam coal companies increased their
power over export traders and over smaller members of the coal industry who had been exporting coal for a long time. The large companies created a new political power center. Future efforts at
legislative compromise would have to acknowledge the issues they
had raised and them as political forces to be reckoned with.

## SUMMARY OF THE EFFECTS OF COALITIONAL ACTIVITY

The Harbor Dredging Task Force brought together a small
phalanx of influential steam coal producers. They developed a joint,
programmatic position on port development which served their interests. They became empowered to speak for the coal industry and
to commit it to political stands. The Harbor Dredging Task Force
became the dominant coalition in the coal industry on port legislation. The unity that the coal coalition was able to maintain within its
own industry became a source of political strength which made the
coalition persuasive in presenting its position to other groups. This
strength made them effective bargainers. Interactions with groups
outside the coal industry increased both the coalition's reputation
for expertise and the industry's leadership position.

The coal coalition's initiatives broadened the industry's network of interactions beyond its normal set of associations. Coal's
potential waterway allies (and potential opponents) became part of
its interorganizational network. Yet these groups interacted not so
much with individual firms as with the temporary consensus position

that the Harbor Dredging Task Force represented. In its negotiations with other groups the Task Force was always seeking the best
deal it could obtain for its members. The primary interest of the
coalition was in getting the best terms from federal legislation as its
members defined those terms. A good example of how these terms
might not necessarily fit the priorities of all industry members was
the Task Force's decision to accede to totally local construction funding in return for a federal maintenance fund. The concession
reflected the dominance of midwestern coal producers on the Harbor Dredging Task Force and their desire to protect export trade
from New Orleans, where maintenance expenses were extremely
high.

The implied environmental view, that market share would be
restricted without positive government action to deepen ports, led
to the use of temporary collaborative activities and zero-sum
negotiations with other industries, with government agencies, and
within the coal industry itself. The implied structural goal toward
which network relations of this type are working is an oligopoly
controlled by a small group of powerful firms. If resources are insufficient to go around, those firms astute enough to set the operational terms of the dominant coalition will gain control. True to the
oligopolistic tendencies in this layer of new interrelationships, large
coal firms were predominant actors in shaping the coal industry's
(and the country's) port policy.

*Theoretical observations.* Coalitions are collaborative bargaining units with limited mandates for joint action and with specifically defined, programmatic goals. Coalitions, therefore, represent
more complex intergroup network interactions than either entrepreneurial activities or information-based clusters of network
realignments. Coalitional activity is an intermediary between a random (competitive or clustered) network pattern and the more formally arranged, federative network interactions characterized by
permanent supraorganizations. Coalitions usually occur in
response to a perceived uncertainty or external threat which individual network members feel they need to control. By joint action
they hope to reduce this source of uncertainty and to bargain for a
desired outcome.

By comparison with network patterns in the following
chapters, coalitions do not transcend the decision-making authority
of their members. Coalitions merely agree temporarily to coact in
order to achieve the best possible approximation of an end that each
member desires. Although coalitions can act on behalf of larger
groups (as did the NCA Harbor Dredging Task Force), there is little or
no acknowledgment of ideals beyond the immediate gains members

hope to achieve. If new proposals and compromises were made by members of the coal industry's coalition, it was because each member was conforming to a political reality which advised it that each individually would be better off with *some* control over the deepening of harbors, rather than none at all.

Norms of agreement and consensus are very fragile in coalitions. This was illustrated when the coal coalition encountered a threat of dissolution from ARCO Coal at the June 1981, NCA board meeting, and when the coalition faded after significant further progress on port legislation appeared unlikely in March 1982.

Membership in the industry coalitions I observed from 1980 to 1982 was also quite flexible. Individual firms were constantly joining and withdrawing from specific coaction groups. For example, after its defeat at the NCA board meeting ARCO Coal withdrew from active involvement in the Harbor Dredging Task Force. Collaborative activity continued or dissipated depending upon the probability that a firm attached to reaching its ends through coalitional or other strategies. Coalitional network arrangements could therefore be considered analogous to interlaced webs which appear and disappear according to the adjudged probability of success in various available coaction opportunities.

The coalition in support of port legislation remained viable only so long as the time and effort expended on joint activity did not conflict with entrepreneurial tasks or with more pressing coalitional activities on other issues. This brings up another feature of coalitions. They are oriented toward immediate and decisive action. They tend to be more aggressive and innovative than supraorganizations which must base their stands on predetermined decision-making rules. Members of a coalition may present themselves as autonomous actors or as collaborative partners, depending upon which strategy is most opportune at the moment. This is also why once an issue becomes routinized, a coalition will likely dissipate or will reconstitute itself into a more permanent interorganizational structure. Coalitions are therefore ad hoc, flexible, and essentially disposable interorganizational structures. They survive only for an immediate purpose and if that purpose is achieved, or stymied, or if internal consensus breaks down, they dispel.

Finally, and in contrast to many previous explanations which have located the cause of coalitional activities in a hostile environment, coalitions do not arise from sheer environmental pressure. Like other realignments, coalitions require an intermediate step, identification of a particular environmental problem by organizational actors from an array of possible factors and selection of a strategy to address it. Coalitions are an important layer of interorganizational activity.

They arise when groups of firms identify restrictions of resources or growth as a common environmental problem and when they decide to address this problem through strategies which require them to act together in order to bargain with others. The common environmental problem leads them to adopt temporary coaction strategies. But their purposes never entirely meld. In coalitions, individual members continue to attempt to obtain benefits helpful to their own power positions in view of what they see as a restricted situation. Coalition formation remains, however, one of many strategic choices a firm could pursue. Coalitions are not brought on by unavoidable external pressures, but indicate instead the freedom organizational actors have to select the interorganizational relationships in which they will engage and the environmental issues to which they will respond.

## NOTES

1.  Failure to expand ports might eventually limit the ability of U.S. commodities to compete in international trade of all types. In the long run, inadequate harbors would raise the prices of both imported and exported goods and would brand the United States as an antiquated trading nation. If steam coal exports expanded as forecast, they would handsomely repay the extensive investments made in them by returning benefits of $5–$10 billion per year in expanded foreign trade. This would be a significant dent in the U.S. balance of payments deficits; estimated at $60 billion in 1983 (*Harvard Business Review*, 7/83).
2.  Informational hearings that touched on coal exports were held by the House Committees on Banking, Finance, and Urban Affairs; Energy and Commerce; Government Operations; Interstate and Foreign Commerce; Interior and Insular Affairs. Legislation was jointly drafted by Merchant Marine and Fisheries cooperating with Public Works and Transportation. Senate informational and legislative hearings were held by Committees on Energy and Natural Resources; Environment and Public Works; Foreign Relations; Finance; and Government Operations.
3.  Warner named Norfolk, New Orleans, and Mobile in his original port deepening bill. These ports decided that they preferred generic legislation because it would keep the fight for annual appropriations for dredging within the U.S. Army Corps of Engineers rather than have it fought out on the floors of Congress. These ports felt they had a greater chance of managing Corps politics than yearly congressional action.

    Also, generic legislation would create less interport enmity. It left open the possibility that unnamed ports could receive funds, and thus it encouraged ports to work together to obtain deepening legislation.

    Finally, generic legislation would diffuse environmental opposition to port deepening. Environmentalists would not know which harbor project to attack (internal memo, 1/6/81).
4.  One member of the Harbor Dredging Task Force privately noted the awesomeness of this situation. "What's staggering is that it seems nobody in

government has thought about this half as much or as carefully as we have done. It's staggering considering the billions of dollars at stake. (Pause.) It may also mean that we can slip something by them" (conversation notes, 6/6/81).

5.  Grain and oil companies admitted privately, and expert reports confirmed, that they would gain economies of scale in ocean shipping if harbors were deepened (conversations with grain and oil and reports Binkley & Shabman, 1980; Schenker & Brockel, 1974). The size of shipments in these industries was expected to grow, and already many ships loaded in American harbors were sailing partially loaded because of insufficient drafts.

6.  Packwood opposed any user fee saying, "There will be no port user fee enacted by this Congress—period" (*NCA Coal News,* 6/21/82). He circulated a petition on which he obtained over forty signatures seeking referral of user fee legislation to Hatfield's Finance Committee as a tax measure, where it was sure to be killed.

7.  The Task Force drafted the fast track provisions of the revised fall 1981 Warner bill and of Biaggi's committee-sponsored legislation. These were eventually copied into committee-approved Senate and House bills.

8.  Vismans argued strongly to Congress that small firms had much to gain from export trade expansion, but his very vehemence makes one wonder whether he saw more problems than he would admit.

> Many statements have been made that the new and large market for steam coal will mean that the exporter-trader and the small coal producer will be squeezed out of the market. This is an absolutely false statement. . . . We will offer a source of supply to small as well as larger customers, and through our domestic contacts can act as a ready supplemental source of supply to meet customers' unexpected needs. (Senate, Energy, 9/16/80: 237–38).

# 8    *Supraorganizations*

During 1980–82, two quite different events illustrated realignments in the coal industry's supraorganizations as a result of developing export trade. The Coal Exporters Association engaged in a lengthy protest of proposed railroad rate deregulation. This extended activity brought into focus the increasing overlap between two industry associations: NCA and the NCA-housed Coal Exporters Association (CEA). The course of CEA's protest and its eventual outcome showed that these two supraorganizations were being forced to reconcile their divergent positions because of widened interest in export issues. Both supraorganizations were realigned to reflect the interests of dominant industry members. Power was taken away from the Coal Exporters Association and was placed more directly in the hands of large steam coal firms. In the second example, members of the coal industry encouraged NCA to represent them in international negotiations about a serious safety hazard that potentially threatened coal export trade. Through NCA, the coal industry heightened its international prominence and reputation for integrity, as it sought to protect itself from regulatory intervention.

Different from the previous chapter in which I chose a particularly dramatic example of a coalition to illustrate coalitional strategies, these two examples of supraorganizational realignments are the primary ones that occurred during 1980–82. They were important because they involved the industry's export-oriented associations.

In both examples, supraorganizations were like shields that protected individual companies from involving themselves publicly with controversial issues. Supraorganizations inserted a layer of formal, official representative action between individual firms and what was perceived as an adversarial environment. Supraorganizational activities were strategies based on the perception that external intervention in the coal export market was a serious threat to be overcome. Supraorganizational activities sought legitimation for industry concerns and protection of individual members. They also lent a cloak of anonymity to individual strategic actions that continued to take place behind the scenes.

## WHAT ARE SUPRAORGANIZATIONS?

Supraorganizations are federations; they are constitutionally empowered, interorganizational bodies with stated membership requirements and rules for internal decision making. They are typically more long-lasting and more broadly focused than temporary, ad hoc coalitions. They may be leagues, councils, or trade associations. Usually they comprise similar organizations who agree to work together, more or less permanently, over a broad range of issues of common concern. Members agree to form a self-perpetuating institutional structure. Often the responsibility for implementing policy is delegated to a professional staff.

The members of a supraorganization are usually considered formally equal. Dues are a frequent criterion of membership. However, participation in an association's leadership and/or policy councils may be reserved for a select status group. Leadership is often established by longevity in the association, or by elections, but these often amount to pro forma confirmations of previous succession decisions.

In one recent study of this type of interorganizational relationship, Robert Stern (1980) identified the two roles of supraorganizations as regulation and coordination. He leaves out other roles such as dissemination of information, officially deputized representation, and advocacy of group needs. Although the members of a supraorganization agree to act as a unit on a range of continuing issues, their size normally prohibits them from reaching decisions unanimously. The usual decision rule is a majority vote of members or of a governing or executive board. This rule allows significant controversy to remain inside the association. Controversies over ongoing issues coexist with a high degree of agreement about the principles basic to the organization's founding. This cohesiveness normally preserves the association in spite of internal dissension. Still, internal controversy places supraorganizations in constant jeopardy of disintegrating, and this may explain why most supraorganizations avoid bold initiatives and precedent-shattering stands. In most cases, supraorganizations favor positions which are acceptable to as many members as possible. They often sacrifice consistency to preserve the possibility of continued joint action. This tendency to preserve themselves separates supraorganizations from most issue-based coalitions, although at times they may overlap. Consciousness of their own historical precedents frequently makes these organizations slow to change and conservative in taking action. Thus, any obvious alteration in the structure of a well-established supraorganization is an important indicator of stress.

Supraorganizations are subject to the same kinds of internal organizational behavior as other organizations and may have coalitions, interest groups, and power centers within them. Members of a supraorganization maintain their autonomy on all issues not covered by the federation, but officially they cede some of their decision-making autonomy to the group as a concomitant of agreeing to be represented by it. This does not hinder individual members from trying to influence decisions within the association's domain. But in an important way, the purpose of a supraorganization is to transcend the status and power accorded to the aggregate decisions of its members. Supraorganizations seek to legitimate their group's views and protect the group from outsiders.

The actions of supraorganizations can provide insights into power relationships in the industry or group that the supraorganization represents. This chapter discusses how two coal industry supraorganizations, although more conservative in their actions than ad hoc coalitions and thus more resistant to change, were nevertheless altered by the addition of new actions, new concerns, and new power struggles within them which came about as a result of coal export trade.

## Two Coal Associations

The coal industry has two related supraorganizations which had overlapping and sometimes conflicting interests in coal export issues: the National Coal Association and the Coal Exporters Association of the United States.[1]

*NCA.* The National Coal Association (NCA) is the main trade organization of the coal industry. It speaks for the industry in all matters except labor negotiotions.[2] NCA is the oldest and most powerful industry association. Founded in 1917, it has over 200 members and an annual operating budget of over $5 million (*National Trade and Professional Associations of the U.S.*, 1983). NCA includes about seventy-five coal producers, most of which are large companies. It also has roughly 125 affiliate members from industries such as coal brokering, equipment supply, transportation, resource development, finance, and consulting (NCA membership lists, 1982). NCA has its own building in Washington, D.C., and employs a staff of seventy people.

NCA is supported by dues which are assessed according to each member's size. The largest coal companies provide the most support and have the most say in the association. The NCA Board of Directors is composed of large firms, and its executive committees set policy. The 1980 board included representatives from fifty mining firms, but only about fifteen of these are really powerful within the association. For example, I was advised that NCA staff would appreciate informal interaction with me on technical issues because it would give them a chance to get "backdoor" comments and to judge whether or not they were pleasing their bosses in the large firms (conversation, 6/4/81). I found NCA staff to be extremely deferential given my own newness to the industry. The association's president is Carl Bagge, a lawyer and former member of the Federal Trade Commission. His job is to represent and promote the interest of the industry at conferences, speeches, before Congress, and in the departments of the executive branch.

Not all large coal firms belong to NCA, but the politically active companies tend to be members. Coal firms frequently coordinate their lobbying efforts through NCA, which provides them with contacts and background information. Fourteen of the industry's twenty largest coal producers are NCA members. Twelve of these are noncaptive firms, meaning that they sell coal on the open market; two are captive firms owned by steel. Of the six top-twenty firms that are *not* NCA members, five are captive companies. Captive firms probably calculate that they do not stand to gain as much from national protection and good public relations as do noncaptive firms through NCA.

*CEA.* American coal exporters have had an affiliate organization within NCA since 1947. Changes in the coal export situation put strain on the hitherto informal relationships between these interrelated organizations during 1980–82. The Coal Exporters Association of the United States (CEA) was originally founded to coordinate post-World War II shipments of coal to Europe under the Marshall Plan.

Only a few members of NCA are CEA participants. Until 1980 , CEA had only thirteen regular members. Just three of these (Consolidation, Island Creek, and Massey) produced steam coal. Most CEA members were international coal brokering firms or were relatively small producers of metallurgical coal. Counting Pittston, an exclusively metallurgical company, only four or five CEA members were major coal producers in 1979.

CEA activities are subsidized (70 percent) out of NCA's regular budget, and it uses NCA staff for its projects. Its annual expenditures, mostly on export-related conferences, averaged just $70,000 annually, not including the value of donated NCA staff time through 1980 (NCA memo, 1/16/82).

Since coal exports before 1980 were a very small part of total U.S. production, the services provided CEA were a rather unimportant part of NCA's total staff support. Many large companies otherwise active in NCA took little or no interest in CEA affairs, since they involved a very unpredictable market, mostly of metallurgical coal sales. CEA traditionally went its own way without direct supervision, approval, or oversight by the NCA Board of Directors.

Major coal companies considered CEA's interests narrow and cliquish. It was commonly accused of being an "Eastern producers' club" by other coal industry members (legislative meeting notes, 12/10/81). Although CEA claimed to represent between eighty and ninety percent of the firms exporting U.S. coal, much of this representation was through brokers who were CEA members and who arranged coal sales for small firms.

## Perception of an Adversarial Environment

The coal industry, usually through the representatives of its two export-related trade organizations, made many pleas during 1980–82 that government not interfere in the regulation of coal export trade. The industry wanted to keep exports a private-sector responsibility as much as possible, and thus avoid trade quotas, traffic controls, cargo inspection systems, and/or overregulation of transportation rates. Industry members felt that one of their attractions to foreign custromers was the relative lack of involvement by the U.S. government in exporting coal. The industry wanted to maintain this advantage, and it turned to its representative supraorganizations for strategies to head off the problem of potential government meddling in what it considered its business. This stance was a familiar position for coal associations. They were used to fighting off federal regulations on behalf of domestic business interests.

Coal producers who saw themselves as potential actors in an expanded export market turned to supraorganizations to protect themselves and the coal market in various ways from interference. In adopting supraorganizational strategies as part of their response to exports they exhibited their view of the environment as adversarial. Supraorganizational strategies offered the protection of joint action and formal anonymity on controversial issues. Firms used supraorganizational strategies to overcome their vulnerability to government regulation and to achieve comfort, strength, and relative safety in numbers as we will see below.

Statements and actions of industry associations as well as indirect indicators show that protection of the industry was an active concern. Indirect indicators, such as the membership in supraorganizations and the increased reliance on them for leadership and expertise, showed that industry members were relying on this form of collaborative, representational action to head off government interference.

Undoubtedly protection was not the only reason firms acted through supraorganizations. They gained information, and contacts, and some stature through their associations with trade groups (as the chapter on sources of information made clear). They could avoid duplicative lobbying expenses. Yet, for the biggest firms—many of which were quite active in supraorganizations during 1980–82—these reasons were probably not primary concerns. Big firms could accomplish most of their sales goals, foreign contacts, and information-gathering on their own. In fact, big firms sometimes felt that their participation in industry collaborative groups was a waste of time and effort (reported view of a senior vice-president). Yet, big firms were moving to join and to strengthen industry associations during 1980–82. Inexperience with export trade and apprehensiveness about the possibility of negative government intervention seem good reasons why. Also, the ability of supraorganizational activity to shield individual firms from direct identification with controversial issues (as in the "hot coal" issue described later) provided another rationale for supporting supraorganizational activities.

General articles and speeches consistently stressed the coal industry's desire to minimize federal involvement in export trade (*National Journal*, 5/24/80; 2/7/81; AAPA proceedings, 2/25/81; Senate, Energy testimony). Industry spokesmen stressed the need for relief from "burdensome regulation" and for freedom to show that American business could do its job. William Mason, 1980 president of the Coal Exporters Association, was one who gave voice to some of the industry's underlying fears at Senator Warner's first Energy Committee hearing. "I would like to emphasize that most of the actions which must be taken to expand our export market are in the hands of the private industry, the potential customers, and the coal suppliers. . . . This must be done within the confines of private industry and not through a proposed allocation system" (Senate, Energy hearing, 9/16/80: 184–85). Carl Bagge continuously stressed the need for very limited federal involvement in exports before the

Senate Foreign Relations Committee. (4/28/81: 142–43), as well as elsewhere. In the Clean Air Act, surface mining land regulations, and many health and safety standards for miners, the coal industry had significant experience with government control. The industry wanted to head off any movement toward this kind of role in the area of coal export trade before it began.

## CHANGES IN SUPRAORGANIZATIONS

*NCA Leadership.* The National Coal Association's role as protector of the coal industry took on some different aspects as a result of involvement in export trade. Many of NCA's activities have already been mentioned. NCA staff gathered information on coal terminal capacity early in 1980 through the Economics Committee. Staff tried to keep NCA members informed of the quickly-developing export situation. The Economics Committee revised and re-revised export forecasts.

NCA sponsored seminars for industry members on topics related to export trade. In this way it stood ready to help industry members meet the unfamiliarity of the current crisis. NCA gave testimony at numerous congressional hearings, spoke at conventions, and provided expert advice on panels. Often its information was hastily patched together, but gradually NCA was gathering a repository of information and was developing new sets of contacts to inform itself and to advise the industry on export trade. NCA staff often wrote speeches or provided information to industry leaders who were going to speak on export matters. In general, the industry leaned on its association to provide direction and analysis of the novel situation.

Connie Holmes, vice-president of NCA, held a pivotal role that demonstrates the overlap between NCA and the Coal Exporters Association. Holmes headed NCA's Economics Division. She was also the chief staff person for CEA. The leadership she provided in the analysis of legislative proposals and in working with the NCA Harbor Dredging Task Force gave NCA a higher profile than before on export issues. She consciously revised her own presentation of coal export issues from the views of eastern producers who dominated the Coal Exporters Association to a much broader national perspective more oriented toward steam coal. She often had to resolve disputes over policy between old-line CEA colleagues and the members of NCA who were just getting interested in exporting.

In mid 1981, the growing involvement of NCA in foreign trade was acknowledged organizationally. A separate division of

Economics and International Trade was formed with Connie Holmes as its head. Six months later an International Trade group was formed (*NCA Coal News*, 4/19/82). This built into NCA structure a permanent place for export issues.

Among other things, NCA began to portray coal producers as patriotically striving to help the national interest through coal exports. NCA had enjoyed few chances to take such high ground in the past. Coal exports offered the coal industry and its primary supraorganization the opportunity to improve their public images by linking coal to vital issues of national security and public welfare. In fact, many of these issues were being announced by experts and government officials even before NCA began reinforcing them. These issues made coal more cohesive as an industry and more willing to collaborate to achieve better export trade potential. NCA, the industry's major trade association, emerged stronger and more thoroughly unified as a result.

*CEA Membership.* One major change which occurred in coal industry structure as a result of 1980 export demand was the addition of new members to the Coal Exporters Association. Membership mushroomed from fifteen to twenty-seven members from 1980 to 1981 (*Keystone Coal Industry Manual*, 1980; 1981). Even more significantly, five of the new members were large steam coal firms: Ashland, Mapco, Peabody, Westmoreland, and Youghiogheny & Ohio (see Table 8.1).

CEA was obliged to suspend its rules to accommodate these prestigious new members. In the past CEA had required that new members export coal for at least one year prior to joining the association. The new steam coal members had not yet participated in foreign sales, but they wished to indicate (partly through their membership in CEA) their interest in foreign sales opportunities. CEA could serve as an important touchstone for contacts between foreign buyers and sales delegations. Now that major steam coal firms were becoming interested in export sales, their membership in CEA could not be delayed.

This influx of new members into CEA and the industry's generally heightened interest in export issues could be expected to change the importance of CEA as a semiautonomous part of NCA. Indeed, there was some evidence in 1980–82 that CEA was being gradually taken over and reoriented by interests dominant in the rest of the coal industry. CEA would no longer be an isolated group with interests only in metallurgical and in eastern coal. Cooptation by larger members of the coal industry brought CEA into a more formalized relationship with the NCA Board of Directors and with industry-wide NCA policy. This supraorganizational realignment in

**TABLE 8.1.**
**Members of the Coal Exporters Association**
**of the United States, Inc., 1979,1981**

| *1979 Members* | *Members Added, 1980–81* |
| --- | --- |
| Castner, Curran & Bullitt, Inc. | Anker Trading S.A., Inc. |
| Consolidation Coal Co. | Ashland Coal International |
| Cory Mann George Corp. | Calvert Coal, Inc. |
| The Drummond Co. | Coal Trading Corp. |
| Foreston Coal International | G & W Carbomin Coal Co. |
| John K. Irish & Co., Inc. | Mapco, Inc. |
| Island Creek Coal Sales | Peabody Coal Co. |
| Jno. McCall Coal Co., Inc. | Primary Coal, Inc. |
| Pittston Coal Export Corp. | Ruhkohle Trading Corp. |
| Sprague Coal International | Scallop Coal Co. |
| Stinnes Coal Co. | SSM Coal Co., Inc. |
| United Eastern Coal Sales Corp. | Virginia Iron Coal & Coke Co. |
| A.L. Watson & Co., Inc. | Westmoreland Coal Co. |
| | Youghiogheny & Ohio Coal Co. |

*Source: Keystone Coal Industry Manual, 1979;1981.*

the coal industry's network is discussed below. It was precipitated by CEA's decision to protest export rail freight rates on behalf of the whole industry.

*CEA's role expands.* Although prior to 1980 export issues were generally handed to the Coal Exporters Association by NCA as a matter of course, the relationship between the two groups had never been clearly specified. The addition of new members in 1980 and 1981 gave the CEA new coloration. Yet, in his statement in April 1981 before the Senate Foreign Relations Committee, Carl Bagge let it appear that CEA and NCA were cooperating autonomous organizations. Asked by the committee to address what role NCA would play in export trade Bagge's prepared statement reads as follows: "The final question you have asked me to address is the role of the association [NCA] in responding to increased demand for export coal. The Coal Exporters Association has taken the lead in these activities and the National Coal Association has assisted in any way possible" (Senate, Foreign Relations, 4/28/81: 147). Apparently, to Bagge as well as to the outside world NCA and CEA, though formally separate, were not likely to be in conflict. With the expansion of U.S. coal export trade, CEA expanded its scope of duties. Most were noncontroversial formalities, such as meeting with foreign trade groups, promoting U.S. coal overseas, disseminating information, and presenting the coal industry's viewpoint about export opportunities to federal and state governments. CEA also took the lead in negotiating with railroads over port congestion and in determining coal capacity at various ports. Connie Holmes was, of course, a key person in carrying out these roles.

Since the geographic concentration of the coal export market in the United States was potentially changing, even officially formal duties could take on political significance. As new members joined CEA it became more of a focal point for buyers who were looking for steam coal. The capabilities of American exporters could no longer be portrayed as hovering solely around Hampton Roads. Carl Bagge and Connie Holmes consciously tried to include in their representations of U.S. exporters indications of a broader, less eastern-dominated CEA. For example, note Bagge's testimony at the hearing cited above. "Finally, the major and most necessary role of the U.S. Federal government is the facilitation of port and harbor improvements on the east, the gulf and west coast. And I want to underscore at this hearing in Baltimore that our concern extends to the east, to the gulf and the west coast as well" (Senate, Foreign Relations, 4/28/81: 143).

Connie Holmes tried hard by her own account to inform herself about the possibilities of exporting coal from various ports by visiting them and by representing potential new and old coal exporters evenhandedly (conversation, 5/21/81).

## PROTESTING RAIL RATES

Transition of the CEA from an association representative primarily of export interests in the east to one that would represent all areas of the country contained many potential conflicts of interest. Protestation of railroad rate deregulation became an issue in which the traditional eastern interests in CEA vied for control of the association with newer export interests from the midwest and west. The struggle revealed how the industry and its supraorganizations were becoming realigned.

*Export coal: captive to rail.* Railroads and the coal industry have a close and often uneasy relationship. About 20 percent of total railroad business in the United States each year consists of coal hauls. Coal is often tied to rail as its only outlet to markets.

NCA conducted a study in 1977 of coal export rail rates which found that over 98 percent of export shipments at that time were carried by the Norfolk & Western or the Chessie system. Ninety-three percent of export shipments were captive to a single railroad or had no competitive means of transportation (*NCA Coal News*, 4/6/81).

Deregulation of railroad tariffs to provide greater competitiveness in rail rates was not particularly favored by the coal industry. In debate over the Staggers Rail Act of 1980, NCA had protested that railroads had monopoly control over coal producers in many areas and that these producers needed some protection from excessive rail rates. Congress maintained some protection under the Interstate Commerce Commission (ICC) for captive coal producers and devised a formula to determine acceptable costs-to-profits ratios in areas where alternate modes of transportation were scarce.

When the coal boom of 1980 hit ports, the effects of partial deregulation under the Staggers Rail Act were just beginning to appear. Railroad lines (particularly the Norfolk & Western and Chessie) were surprised by an immediate call for export deliveries. They wanted to cash in on the new business by increasing rail rates to Hampton Roads and Baltimore. They also wanted to channel overflow export business to their other service areas by lowering their normal rates for export coal to underutilized piers. Since 1978 railroads had been charging a higher rate for hauling export coal than for hauling domestic coal over the same distance. Newly posted rates began to remove some but not all of this surcharge.

The railroads lowered the export rates on coal delivered to the Ohio River from West Virginia coal fields in order to relieve congestion at Baltimore and Hampton Roads. However, the new rates were still two-and-a-half times greater per mile of distance traveled than the rates to Hampton Roads. Not even rail spokesmen could make these rates seem rational. Senator Wendell Ford (D, Ky.) pointed out during hearings on export coal some of the many inconsistencies in railroad services and charges. Coal going the same distance in Kentucky might pay as much as $8 more per ton depending upon what railroad was carrying it. Sometimes coal companies had to provide their own locomotives to retrieve hopper cars from sidings in order to get trains back from ports to mines. Senator Ford accused the railroads of uncooperativeness and suggested that their greed for profits might permanently harm export trade (Senate, Energy Committee, 9/17/80).

*N & W's petition to the ICC.* In March 1981, the Norfolk & Western Railroad petitioned the Interstate Commerce Commission to exempt export traffic from the existing rate and minimum service guidelines for determining fair rail rates on coal. In other words, Norfolk & Western sought permission to set its own rates, based on what it claimed would be the pressure of competitive market demand. If the ICC granted this petition, rail rates would float and cost-to-profit guidelines on all export coal rail rates would be removed. This would leave railroads even more free to juggle freight prices at will.

The Norfolk & Western's petition hinged on the argument that unlike most coal hauled in the nation for domestic use, export coal competed in a national rather than a regional market. Minimum service guidelines for single producers were overcome by the competitiveness among rail lines nationally to haul export coal.

The threat of further relaxing rail rate regulation flashed a warning to many traditional coal industry supporters. The old guard of industry exporters, especially those in the CEA, assumed that eastern railroads wanted permission to raise their charges to eastern ports. Railroads appeared overly anxious to grab for themselves newly appearing profits on export hauls, at the expense of coal producers. The traditional coal exporters (spurred on by warnings from foreign buyers) feared that the railroads would raise rates to the point where they would kill newly developing export business. Railroads were already breaking their own loading records each month of 1980–81 for their export hauls; they also wanted to raise their profit margins.

Actually, it was not clear what would happen to railroad rates nationally if they were exempted from the ICC minimum competition and profit guidelines set by the Staggers Act. Some petitioners argued that all rail rates would go up, as they undoubtedly would to eastern ports. But the confusing part was that the eastern railroads were arguing that deregulated rates would stir competition for coal export deliveries to various ports, including some off the east coast, and that effective overall rates might go down. Both Chessie and Norfolk & Western were involved in potential merger agreements which would extend their ability to serve eastern coastal and midwest river ports, and they argued that if coal had many outlets to foreign markets, rates would be kept down.

The enmity between the coal industry and railroad haulers ran deep and was an obvious explanation of the jealous skepticism that coal officials showed in their initial reactions to Norfolk & Western's request for export rate exemptions. Coal companies were on familiar territory in fighting railroad rate charges. Their legal divisions knew much more about railroad rate setting and the complex legalities of ICC regulations than about how to evaluate port financing proposals.

Foreign buyers encouraged coal producers through the CEA to protest rail rate increases. They considered railroad rates a major drawback to American coal. In fact, Connie Holmes was to say later, "Frankly, the reason we have protested the rates so strongly is because foreign buyers expect us to" (conversation, 4/30/81).

## CEA Acts

The history of acrimonious relationships between coal producers and the railroads set the stage for CEA to make a major protest against Norfolk & Western's rate exemption request. CEA counterpetitioned the ICC to continue to protect export coal shippers by maintaining regulated export freight charges.

The Coal Exporters Association mounted a serious effort to fight coal export rate deregulation, which it saw as threatening to coal export trade. CEA testified against the Norfolk & Western's petition to the ICC. It also filed a second complaint asking the ICC to investigate all current export rail charges, which it argued were already excessive and unreasonable under existing rate-setting criteria. CEA asked the ICC to evaluate current charges in light of the Staggers Rail Act's requirement that revenues should not exceed 160 percent of direct costs. CEA claimed that rates for export coal already exceeded the Staggers Act's criteria and that some rates were returning 200–300 percent above cost to the railroads (*Coal News*, 4/6/81).

CEA acted from its experience with eastern exports in filing its complaint. Active exporters feared that deregulation would invite even higher posted export rates for coal. The two eastern railroads were reporting record profits for 1980 and the first quarter of 1981 largely due to export sales. Eastern coal firms did not want to stand by and see railroads reap excessive profits at the long-term expense of export trade. To traditional exporters in the coal industry the Norfolk & Western's petition looked like an open and shut case that the ICC would quickly deny.

However, in September 1981, instead of announcing a decision, the ICC asked for further time to evaluate the situation. A preliminary ICC report said, "It would be useful to study this issue on a nationwide basis, including West Coast ports" (*Inside Energy*, 9/11/81). The preliminary report implied that whether deregulation ultimately would raise or lower rail rates was not clear cut. Old-line coal exporters considered this a bad sign.

The CEA swung into more intense action. It commissioned a study by National Economic Research Associates on the price elasticity of foreign coal demand and the impact on the export market of rail freight charges. It prepared briefs, solicited congressional friends (including Senator Ford) to testify before the ICC, and it publicly protested what it characterized as blatant profit-grabbing by the railroads. CEA accused the railroads of standing in the way of economic recovery and of thwarting the national interest by placing their own interests above the country's interest in exporting coal (*NCA Coal News* citing testimony, 1/11/82).

Among CEA's arguments were that if the ICC deregulated export rates, railroads could give special rates to shippers wishing to send coal over their own piers. Captive export shippers would receive no protection from excessive rates. Coal prices might become so high that U.S. coal would be unattractive to foreign buyers (*NCA Coal News*, 6/21/82). The study commissioned by National Economic Research Associates estimated that rail rates would rise 30 percent if the exemption Norfolk & Western wanted was granted, and that total U.S. exports would drop from 132 to 100 million tons by 1990 (*NCA Coal News*, 4/19/82; 6/21/82). The ICC's hearings dragged on for over a year. Eventually, CEA presented the ICC with forty letters from foreign buyers and statements from several barge and mining companies and port authorities in support of its position.

The CEA's efforts occupied a considerable amount of its time during 1981–82. During 1981 alone CEA spent $600,000 of NCA funds in high-visibility activities to dissuade the ICC from granting Norfolk & Western's request (CEA memo, 1/30/82). Its usual annual budget had been only $70,000, of which only a small part went to lobbying efforts.

The issue of railroad rates allowed CEA to flex its muscles in a new way. The health of the American coal export business seemed to be of central concern to all CEA-NCA members and to justify a major effort to protect it. CEA acted as the incensed voice of American coal exporters, and it was able to bring a variety of observers to its point of view. For example, an editorial in the *New York Times*, which was not often a supporter of the coal industry, called for moderation in the general policy of deregulating industries when other important national benefits were at stake (1/23/82). Inhibiting the growth of coal trade, which removal of regulations on export coal rates would be likely to do, would weaken the dollar, limit economic recovery, and strengthen OPEC, the *Times* said.

To outward observers CEA attained industry-wide stature for its protest activities. Foreign buyers respected CEA for its stand. Enlarged membership by large steam coal firms seemed to be giving CEA greater supraorganizational strength and scope for decisive action. Its protest apparently showed that the coal industry's supraorganizations would take unprecedented stands to protect export coal trade and to protect foreign consumers from unconscionable price hikes.

However, it was obvious to insiders that the assertion of power by CEA was primarily for the benefit and protection of east coast coal producers. The industry's follow-up on the CEA rail protests showed that new entrants into the export area had a dramatically different viewpoint on rail deregulation than the traditional exporters that had dominated CEA in the past.

## Industry Dissension; Reorganization of CEA

The basis for CEA's objection to deregulating export freight rates was their effect on eastern export sales. However, not all firms in the newly expanded CEA and certainly not all those in NCA agreed that eastern freight rates should continue to set the standard for charges on all exported coal. These firms began quietly to voice their objections to CEA's strategy of protesting rail rates, first within CEA and then to the NCA board. The objecting firms questioned the amount of NCA money that CEA was committing to the protest activities and the discretion it was allowed in fighting export rate charges. Although fighting rail deregulation seemed to fit the coal industry's traditional animosity to the rail industry, and it appeared laudable to a variety of publics, in this particular case it was not a strategy acceptable to all firms.

Western and midwestern coal producers had several reasons for thinking that unregulated freight rates might work to their benefit. First, they thought that domestic freight rates in the west (which currently comprised more than half the final price of western coal) might be lowered if railroads chose to charge more for foreign hauls. Exports had not yet materialized anyway for most western firms. The possibility of an immediate domestic advantage far outweighed fear of damage to future foreign sales. Second, western producers thought that rate deregulation could be an incentive to keep both eastern and western export rail rates reasonably low, as competition for export sales increased. In other words, the western firms felt that Norfolk & Western might be right that the export coal market was becoming national. Third, since there was no single obvious port on the west coast to take coal shipments, western export rates were likely to remain fairly competitive, as several rail lines competed for business to different ports. For example, the proposed merger of Burlington Northern with the Frisco line would give Wyoming coal access to as many as six ports, thus putting pressure on it and on other railroads to keep rates low.

In the midwest producers felt that higher eastern rail rates would push coal onto the inland waterway system, where freight charges were highly competitive. This could increase foreign demand for midwestern coal. Since several midwest firms owned barge companies, deregulation could be a double benefit. Barge and rail rates from the Kentucky-Illinois coal basin to the Gulf might possibly become more favorable than those to Hampton Roads, although three times the distance. The absence of congestion and demurrage in the Gulf area would add to savings if eastern coal export charges went up. The ability to use unit trains would hold down charges in the midwest and west.

In short, the expansion of CEA membership and broadened interest by the whole industry in export coal meant that railroad rate setting and potential deregulation had different implications in different parts of the country. It was no longer accurate to say that coal exporters would oppose a railroad ploy to obtain higher rates on export coal to eastern ports. For that matter it was no longer easy to predict how various issues would affect different geographic areas of the still-emergent export chain. What benefited producers in the east might restrict foreign markets in the midwest and west and vice versa.

The conflict between traditional eastern exporters and aspiring ones in the midwest and west led to a realignment of CEA. A group of NCA board members requested reevaluation of NCA-CEA ties and a redefinition of CEA's policy autonomy. Some NCA members thought that the CEA was out of line in going after rail rates so strongly.

In January 1982, two powerful NCA board members met to consider the issue of NCA-CEA coordination. In a private discussion these leaders considered various options each of which would greatly change NCA/CEA relationships: (1) severing NCA's connection with CEA and letting it reconstitute itself outside of NCA's control as primarily an eastern producers organization; (2) folding CEA into NCA and dissolving it as a separate voice; (3) keeping CEA as a spokesbody for U.S. coal exports but withdrawing any policy-making authority from it. These leaders were not pleased that CEA had so little accountability and so much freedom in spending large sums of NCA's money to fight the Norfolk & Western's deregulation petition. On the other hand, they considered CEA potentially valuable as a focal group for representing U.S. coal to foreigners. They decided not to eliminate it altogether. They agreed, however, that the NCA board should retain more budgetary control and approval authority over future CEA policies and projects. According to this restricted mandate, CEA was not to speak publicly on issues or commit itself to spending funds before obtaining the NCA board's approval. CEA was to continue to act as an official greeter and clearinghouse for foreign buyers, but its political activities would be curbed to make them consistent with NCA board priorities. The NCA board implemented this recommendation. CEA would become, in effect, an NCA Transportation Committee for international trade, and would be dominated by the membership and strategic priorities of large steam coal firms. (This section based in part on conversation with coal executive who prepared recommendations for coal leaders' meeting, 1/27/82.)

By this action NCA, led by large western and midwestern companies, was slapping the wrists of traditional coal exporters, and was forcing CEA back into a more ceremonial and docile role. CEA would, from now on, be less dominated by eastern interests, or it would not be tolerated within NCA.

It would be correct to view this assertion of NCA board authority as an example of big coal companies curbing the smaller companies' export association and putting the eastern exporters on notice that coal industry export policy from now on would have to be cleared through big steam coal firms.

Publicly the change was not dramatic. NCA did not formally renounce the CEA's challenge of the Norfolk & Western's petition. After all, NCA had to protect its image of consistent opposition to railroad freight hikes. But the energy and commitment of Connie Holmes' CEA staff pulled back following the NCA board's decision. For example, perusal of the list of forty supporters of CEA's counterpetition filed in June 1982 reveals a lowered industry commitment (*NCA Coal News*, 6/21/81). CEA filed letters with the ICC from the Mining and Reclamation Council of America (MARC, the small producers association), from several small coal sales companies, and from three minor eastern ports. Not even Hampton Roads or Baltimore sent supporting letters. Just three senators expressed support for CEA's position, although NCA had ready access to an impressive list of potential supporters for just such a purpose.[3] Aspiring coal ports on the west and gulf coasts and individual large firms did not identify themselves with the fight to restrain rail rates. Politicians from major coal states were quiet. At least one large producer (one of the new 1980 members) dropped out of CEA during this time to protest its activities. It seems likely that the petering out of intense opposition to the Norfolk & Western's petition was the result of word getting around that the CEA's position was not very important to the coal industry. It was to be left twisting in the wind.

I do not know whether or not western and midwestern coal firms directly influenced the ICC's eventual ruling on export freight deregulation. The ruling was finally announced in March 1983. However, it is interesting that the ICC granted the Norfolk & Western's request to allow export rail rates to fluctuate with market demand (*Washington Post*, 2/25/83; 3/4/83). What to the outside world appeared to be a defeat for coal exporters and a blow to export trade expansion was, more significantly, a change in the power relationship between CEA and NCA.

Now that more major coal industry actors had export interests, CEA would have to act in harmony with dominant NCA policy. CEA was losing whatever autonomy it had formerly maintained within the larger organization and was losing the uniqueness of its voice for the smaller, eastern firms.

## HOT COAL: A SECOND THREAT TO EXPORT TRADE

A second example of supraorganizational activity had quite different consequences. In this example, NCA increased its status as a supraorganization when it successfully protected individual firms from the threat of external regulation because of a serious safety hazard that developed in coal shipping. Internal struggles were less evidently important in this issue than was the elevation of the U.S. coal industry and its trade association to international prominence. NCA was able to achieve legitimation of the industry's interest in avoiding regulatory intervention by helping to develop self-imposed shipping standards the industry could adopt. Individual firms, on the other hand, wanted to avoid any public affiliation with this issue. They used the industry's main supraorganization as a cloak of anonymity and protection.

### What Was Hot Coal?

In the late summer of 1981 at the height of industry optimism about overseas steam coal demand, news began to circulate of a serious problem in ocean loading and transporting of U.S. steam coal. On its long journeys in bulker holds several steam coal export shipments overheated and began to burn at sea. The news alarmed participants in the coal chain. Spontaneous combustion was a known but rare occurrence in met coal shipments. The news reports indicated that the problem in steam coal shipments was more frequent and widespread. Not only was valuable cargo being lost and the lives of seamen and safety of ships at stake, but the future of U.S. coal trade could also be jeopardized.

Spontaneous combustion was not a new problem in coal storage and transportation. Its causes could be located in many physical characteristics of coal. Coal dust is highly explosive. Stockpiles at utility plants and factories are often sprayed with oil or with water in dry summer weather to reduce the internal temperatures of piles and avoid combustion. Methane gas is frequently found in coal. It must be carefully drained to avoid explosions and fires. Many of the high volatility coals found in the west and all lignites posed dangers of self-ignition if transported very far. Also, the sulfur embedded in coal when combined with water releases caustic sulfuric acid and heat.

Combustion and burning at sea presented a serious technical as well as a public relations problem to the fledgling American steam coal exporters. They were not sure what was causing it or how to solve it. The fact that hot coal was occurring in ships at sea brought several new sets of actors into the issue who did not normally deal with coal, but who had high stakes in preserving maritime safety.

*Opinions and conflicting authorities.* The hot coal situation embarrassed producers with their ignorance about their own product, and it quickly posed the possibility of a need for regulatory intervention to guarantee the security and safety of cargoes. Marine insurance firms which had been enthusiastic about growing coal trade and about insuring coal cargoes because of their low risk of hazards from spoilage or spills became more wary.

By October 1981, eleven coal vessels scheduled for long voyages had been affected by the combustion problem. One was refused berth in Yokahama, Japan, and had to proceed to South Korea while still on fire. Three ships loaded at New Orleans caught fire before completing their voyages through the Panama Canal. They were forced to seek refuge in Los Angeles harbor where they were unloaded until the hot spots in the coal cargo could be cooled.

In the ensuing confusion different groups asserted their authority over the situation. Local pilots in New Orleans placed a temporary moratorium on all coal loading until the cause of hot coal could be found. Pilots refused to board ships with coal cargoes. Shippers, pilots, crews, and consumers began to demand elaborate temperature checks in ports and at sea to guarantee safe temperatures in holds.

The most disturbing part of the hot coal dilemma was that no one seemed to be sure how to avoid it. Paol Sachman, a noted international authority from the Danish utility ELSAM, stated "We have until now found no experts on this subject" (Senate, Energy, 11/10/81: 45).

Theories abounded, and each theory spelled trouble for some part of the coal industry. Some sources claimed the cause of hot coal was summer temperatures during loading. This would hurt the southern and Gulf ports which were hoping to capitalize on their year-round loading possibilities as a marketing plus. Other reports said that oxidation of sulfur embedded in the coal released heat following its contact with moisture. This pointed a finger at high sulfur midwestern coal, which traveled to ports in huge barges open to the weather. Zachariah Allen, the well-known consultant, disputed this claim by noting that low sulfur South African coal had been known to catch fire in European stockpiles (Senate, Energy, 11/10/81: 25). High volatility was perhaps the problem, which pointed to the low BTU, high ash coals of the west. Some experts said that coal dust was causing explosions and fire because coal was not being properly compacted and stabilized during loading to lessen air pockets. Others speculated that large shipments were more subject to heating problems than the smaller loads of the past. This, if it proved true, would pose a threat to dredging and to the impetus for getting large ship economies from diverse ports. Transferring coal from barges into ship holds seemed to increase the danger of fires (presumably through stirring up dust). Would mixing coals to obtain lower sulfur contents—a technology necessary to make midwest coal attractive overseas—also pose a danger? Each theory impacted elements in the coal chain that would benefit or lose if it proved true.

Some felt the problem was a simple matter of dishonesty or incompetence. Gerald Patrick, president of Arch Minerals, located the problem in low quality shipments and poor business practices. There have been shipments of mud, rock, "a lot of crap coal" which never should have been sold, he told the Senate Energy Committee (12/3/81: 180). Such shippers will not get repeat business, he said. At the same series of hearings William Daniels, head of the French utility purchasing agency ATIC, turned Patrick's criticism into a veiled warning. He noted what experts already knew, that bad deliveries had "tarnished the reputation of [your] industry" (Senate, Energy, 11/10/81: 123).

*Hot coal as a threat to export trade.* Regardless of its cause, "hot coal" represented an important threat. U.S. coal export shipments could be permanently jeopardized by an inadequate response. The new coal exporting industry could not afford problems of liability, physical safety, technical competence, and business integrity if it were to maximize confidence among foreign consumers about long-term coal sales.

Regulatory groups were alert to the situation but were willing to reserve judgment for a while. "We are trying to see that this doesn't turn into an epidemic," said Captain Keith Schumacher of the Coast Guard's Washington Bureau (*Los Angeles Times*, reprinted in Senate Energy testimony, 11/10/81: 610–11). Furthermore, the Coast Guard—like all the other groups involved in hot coal—had little knowledge about shipping coal overseas and had no special rules for handling it. The Coast Guard was cautiously optimistic that "the industry will be able to resolve the problem itself without government orders being necessary" (*Journal of Commerce*, 10/2/81, reprinted in Senate Energy testimony, 11/10/81: 609).

Connie Holmes confided to me in September 1981 that the hot coal issue was putting her at her wit's end (conversation, 9/23/81). The main fear privately articulated among industry leaders was that "hot coal" would provide an opening wedge for government oversight and standards-setting which would permanently regulate export coal sales (conversation with planning executive, 6/81). This fear was even greater than the threat (so far abstract) of lawsuits and insurance liability claims against individual exporters.

No firm felt that it could afford to be associated with this issue, which promised to have serious ramifications and to which no immediate solution seemed at hand. No individual firm wanted to initiate studies or even to serve on committees investigating the problem. Individually, each firm had a stake in distancing itself as much as possible from the problem of hot coal. The names of firms which had supplied hot coal shipments were not reported in the press. Most individual firms either remained silent or tried to transfer culpability for hot coal to other elements in the coal chain, such as shippers, transloaders, or even the climates at particular ports.

Industry officials downplayed both the prevalence and the danger posed by hot coal. *International Coal Report* quoted the understated responses of unnamed officials. "Industry sources claim that the problem has always existed but with the increase in U.S. exports has become more pronounced" (*ICR*, 3/10/81). The response belied serious concerns. At least one large firm refused to participate in a group gathering information about the causes and issues involved in hot coal for fear of "being out front saying that a problem exists, when it hasn't happened to us" (third party report of conversation with a top executive, 11/18/81).

## Supraorganizational Action

Hot coal problems could not be aired without the cloak of supraorganizational unity and authority to protect individual firms. Hot coal looked too dangerous for any individual firm to confront alone. Hot coal was a perfect issue for NCA to exercise its impersonal, protective function. It was to NCA that the industry turned for guidance. Without ready initiatives from the coal industry, national or international regulatory groups might try to impose a patchwork of standards of inspection, coal quality, handling, liability coverage, or a myriad of other specifications and conditions on coal sales which could prove burdensome, counterproductive, or even fatal to the export market. The coal industry wanted to avoid external interventions into its business if at all possible. It wanted to keep standards for coal shipments within its own control.

The coal industry, through NCA, chose a strategy combining self-examination, fact-finding, setting of voluntary standards, and if necessary, acceptance of self-regulatory controls to avoid government (or even private professionial) intervention in its business. An NCA-CEA task force was formed to study the hot coal problem. It met (somewhat frantically, according to Connie Holmes' account) to pool what little was known about the causes of hot coal, but no quick solution of the technical problem appeared. Colonel Herbert Haar, the assistant director of the Port of New Orleans, who was an advisor to the panel, admitted that no one even knew how to go about finding out what was causing hot coal problems (conversation, c. 9/18/81).

Conflicting studies (some of them old and not related to steam coal) were brought out. They implicated pyritic crystalized sulfur in coal which when exposed to moisture released corrosive acid and heat. The author of one study recommended coating the inside of all coal barges with noncorrosive material, but this explanation of hot coal was not convincing to all industry members. Apart from the factual question, an explanation that pointed a finger at sulfur would be a public relations threat to midwest coal.

In the meantime, groups beyond the coal industry were, as expected, asserting their interest and jurisdiction over the issue. Some kind of guidelines had to be set. The U.S. Coast Guard, local pilots' associations, international marine cargo insurance companies, and coal buyers all wanted to be a part of the discussion of hot coal and of any new procedures. Safety was not the sole concern. Standards inevitably meant greater expenses in shipping and handling coal, and both buyers and sellers wanted to protect themselves. The Coast Guard and pilots urged that international safe shipping standards must be set.

To mollify all groups, and because the issue was obviously becoming bigger than NCA could handle alone, an international panel was formed under sponsorship of the Intergovernmental Maritime Consultive Organization (IMCO) and the American Society for Testing and Materials (ASTM). IMCO is a loosely associated United Nations organization which facilitates cooperation among governments on matters of international shipping. The Maritime Safety Committee recommends measures to IMCO to promote safety. ASTM is a professional, technical society of scientists and engineers which is skilled in considering the problems of hazardous cargoes. ASTM has issued voluntary standards for materials handling since 1898. NCA served as a major advisor to this group, which also included major shippers and receivers of steam coal.

The problem of hot coal was quickly raised to a level of international concern because of the inevitable complexity of export trade. NCA was the most logical body to represent the American coal industry. International cooperation and coordination such as the U.S. coal industry had not been involved in before now seemed to be an expected part of its daily business.

In April 1982 this international group reported its findings and recommendations. Admitting that "technology and knowledge are still 'primitive' " about the causes of hot coal, the report set the probable blame on methane as the combustible property which was causing fires in coal ships (*ICR*, 3/26/82). IMCO recommended periodic temperature checks of coal piles and of cargo holds, thorough compacting of cargoes, and extreme caution in conducting mid-stream loading of coal from barges to ships. It set criteria on which rising temperatures of coal cargoes could be assessed and the consequences avoided before combustion occurred. These standards would be voluntarily implemented through the cooperation of the coal industry and local pilots' groups.

NCA succeeded in protecting American producers in two ways with these standards. First, laying the blame for combustion on methane (which is commonly found in all varieties of coal) did not place the onus on coal of any particular type, quality, or geographic location. Compacting was recommended, but the blending of different ranks was not identified as a causal factor. Also, and most importantly, the standards to be applied would be voluntary. NCA had shown its good faith in participating in negotiations to set new interindustry standards, and partially through these efforts there was no move to legislate these standards into legal restrictions with penalties for noncompliance. NCA influence and cooperation had created an effective protective shield around the emerging U.S. coal export business. Whether nontraditional exporters had any influence on the diplomatically stated standards which IMCO adopted is not possible to say from the public record. NCA was certainly well aware of the concerns of different geographic groups, that placing the blame for hot coal on certain coal properties could be ruinous for southern, western, and/or midwestern export trade. Apparently NCA did its best to avoid these implications in the final standards.

Fewer problems with hot coal shipments were reported during the winter months of 1981–82. The IMCO report was accepted by the safety committee of the International Pilots Association. For the present, at least, it seemed that collaborative problem solving by NCA leadership had successfully staved off a possible threat of intervention and regulation of the export business. NCA had accomplished all of this in a way that was acceptable to all of its members.

## THE EMBEDDED INTERESTS OF LARGE COMPANIES IN SUPRAORGANIZATIONS

Behind the unity and unanimity presented by strong supraorganizations individualized strategic activities and differences of opinion can and do take place. Supraorganizations are in effect fronts for dominant industry coalitions, and their leadership role may become the more ceremonial and bland or innovative and aggressive depending upon how much their activities are approved by the dominant coalition at any particular time. Thus, in supraorganizations, the interests of dominant firms are embedded in the ostensibly consensual statements of broad associations.

In both examples used in this chapter, supraorganizations acted on behalf of the interests of large steam coal producers. As further confirmation, we can examine the views of some large firms about their participation in trade associations.

The firm where I worked had a distinctly proprietary view of trade associations. Executives expected NCA and CEA to act as direct extensions of their strategic political interests, or they did not wish to participate in them. A member of the NCA Harbor Dredging Task Force explained his decision to pull back from active coalition involvement in port development legislation in early 1982 with an explanation of his expectations about NCA: "There are other issues I've got to attend to. We've gotten them up to speed. Let NCA pick up the ball now. That's what we're paying them for" (conversation, 2/26/82).

In another example I was told, "Connie [Holmes] has to listen to us because we pay a large part of her salary" (conversation, 6/4/81).

The attitude that the supraorganization should simply echo the individual lobbying efforts of a single major firm belies to some extent the principle of majority-rule decision making in supraorganizations. Yet even the most powerful large firms had less control over association positions than over the strategic positions of their own firms. The price of supraorganizational solidarity is that a certain amount of autonomy is yielded up to the supraorganization by its member firms. To achieve strength in numbers some genuine collaboration must take place. But in most supraorganizations, including those involved with export coal, the positions deemed consequential by large, dominant firms are not far below the surface of the positions articulated by trade associations.

The relative ease of manipulating associations and the tendency to seek strength and legitimacy through collaboration no doubt explains the multiplicity of supraorganizations which occur.

Coal export issues changed the relationships among coal industry members and their supraorganizations. The power of large coal companies was influential but embedded within these associations. Export issues became the occasion for coal companies to work together in new ways to improve their industry's clout and public image. The big companies wanted to speak for and to control the industry as much as possible through these associations, and they asserted their influence behind the scenes.

## SUMMARY OF SUPRAORGANIZATIONAL REALIGNMENTS

Supraorganizational realignments were prompted by the perception that the environment posed a threat of intervention in the industry's internal affairs which old supraorganizational routines might not be equipped to handle. Supraorganizational strategies emphasized collaboration among firms to preserve the unity and autonomy of the industry and to preserve individual firms from harmful effects. By acting together industry members were successfully able to hold off unwanted intervention and to maintain or even to enhance the industry's reputation for cooperation, reliability, and consumer protection. In relying on supraorganizational strategies the industry was invoking old methods and updating them for new problems it now perceived. Federative strategies had successfully protected the industry in the past.

The scope of activities of the two coal industry trade organizations involved with export issues increased during 1980–82, as they became involved in new duties and issues and as they represented industry members in new settings. NCA and CEA drew influential publics to their points of view and they attained visibility and enhanced status for their growing expertise.

Yet, both of the examples also indicated that to varying degrees supraorganizational activities are an expression of the dominant power coalition in an industry. The importance of this recognition is that supraorganizational activity—although formally a representative expression of an industry's positions—is rarely noncontroversial among the members of a federation. Supraorganizations do not

remain for long out of synchrony with the strongest voices compos-
ing them. Thus, when the domains of concern between NCA and
CEA began to overlap and conflicts developed, the larger organization required CEA to conform to a policy desired by its strongest
members. This fundamentally altered the organizational integrity
of the CEA. In the formulation of standards to protect the industry
from hot coal, the issue of a dominant industry coalition was not
evident in the public record. However, IMCO's extreme care in issuing final recommendations that were not "biased" against any kind
of coal argues that it may have been influenced by the impact that
various less carefully balanced recommendations would have on
nontraditional steam coal exporters who were also major U.S. coal
firms.

CEA's actions on the rail rate issue and NCA's on the hot coal
problem represented distinct types of supraorganizational activity.
CEA's ultimate comeuppance, administered by the dominant forces
within NCA, illustrated supraorganizational activity as a front for a
dominant coalition's strategic ends. CEA was free to act
autonomously, without the specific endorsement of the entire industry, as long as its actions were of little consequence to the dominant firms in the NCA. Once CEA's actions became controversial, its
strategies were curtailed to fit the strategies of the dominant firms.

CEA continued to protest the deregulation of rail rates after the
March 1982 NCA board decision in the interest of retaining the industry's reputation for consistency, but the urgency had gone out of its
arguments. In the future, CEA policy stands would have to be cleared
with the larger organization, and they were unlikely to include rail rate
deregulation. A centrifugal force for consistency was forcing out the
varied outlying perspectives among association members that had
previously been allowed to express themselves. CEA policy was becoming more explicitly the single-minded policy of the powerful, major,
steam coal producers who were now joining CEA.

Hot coal presented a different problem. NCA took on the role
of officially representing the U.S. industry amid international
negotiations on a tension-packed issue. NCA became the deputized
spokesman and protector of U.S. coal export interests. The
industry's presumed willingness to cooperate voluntarily to solve a
difficult problem elevated its international reputation for integrity
and professionalism, enhanced its public image, and legitimated its
public stands. NCA's supraorganizational action was also able to
protect individual firms from the glare of public identification with
this issue.

Supraorganizational activity is but one layer of interorganizational network strategies being used during 1980–82. It neither

supplanted nor suppressed other kinds of interrelationships. This type of strategy proceeded from a particular and unique view of the kind of environment the developing U.S. coal exporters were confronting.

Supraorganizations take important and decisive stands which commit their members to political and social positions. They bring industry interests together and coordinate them for mutual protection. This makes supraorganizational strategies different from other interorganizational relationships. In the impersonal stands taken by supraorganizations individual firms' strategies are indistinct. But, as the chapter has shown the policies and positions of supraorganizations are not far from the strategic goals of its most dominant members. In the case of the coal industry during 1980–82, the dominant coalition in its trade associations concerned with export trade was changing. This placed new strains on old supraorganizational relationships. The shift was similar to the entrance during the 1970s of newly-created or newly-purchased oil-owned coal companies into the coal industry's midst and into places of prominence in its policy councils. Such a change is relatively rare. It is likely to have ramifications throughout the industry's structure of which supraorganizational activities are only one—though a major—example.

## NOTES

1. Other coal industry associations were not active in speaking out about exports. The Mining and Reclamation Council of America (MARC) has about 300 members, including many small firms. Its president Ben Lusk spoke at the AAPA convention about exports, but otherwise MARC was not active in debates on port development and other coal exports issues.
2. The Bituminous Coal Operators Association (BCOA) is the management-labor negotiating group for the coal industry.
3. For example, NCA distributed a 24-page analysis of Senate voting records to its members in January 1982 called "What Senators Are in a Position to Help the Coal Industry" (NCA memo, 1/11/81).

# 9 *Macrocooperation in National and International Policy-making*

## WHAT WAS MACROCOOPERATION?

The coal export situation brought a broad array of social and political goals into contact with business ends. Nationally, the opportunity to export coal became linked with national security, and economic recovery. Internationally, it was an occasion for the western community to assert independence of OPEC and the Soviet bloc. The overlapping of concerns created a new pattern of realignments in the coal industry.

The most obvious example of the interfusion of international, national, and commercial goals was the political commitment by western nations, following the 1979 oil crisis, that they would increase world coal trade (with a large portion from the United States) as the most acceptable solution to world energy problems. This commitment, which was announced in the "Principles for IEA Action on Coal" signed in 1979, was an important influence on U.S. coal export sales during 1980–82. U.S. coal companies, especially the largest and most powerful firms, had much to gain if they could harness this favorable attitude toward coal to their strategic ends. The largest American steam coal firms (and their owners) began to act to insure that they would have some say in this macropolicy-making.

Chapter 5 discussed the U.S. government's role in providing new sources of information to coal firms. The government's activity was a partial indication of newly overlapping national political and business concerns. This chapter concentrates on the rhetorically and institutionally shared assumptions that were beginning to influence U.S. coal industry activities during 1980–82. The chapter speculates from the small amount of evidence available on how these macrocooperative activities have come about and how they may alter the U.S. coal industry.

Some export-related activities in 1980–82 showed that the interests of government and industry were commingling. These were a departure from most of the coal industry's history of acrimonious relationships with the federal government. Yet, the activities and the environmental perception supporting them had developed gradually. Their origins stretched back at least to the 1973 oil crisis.

The need to reach back in time to explain the origins of macrocooperative relationships suggests that there may be more to them than simply another type of strategic interorganizational realignment like entrepreneurial or coalitional realignments. Macrocooperation may be analogous to a paradigm shift or to a structural change in basic industrial-governmental relationships similar to Stinchcombe's (1965) identification of economic eras, or Karpik's (1977) descriptions of generic types of capitalism. Both Stinchcombe and Karpik trace the origins of overarching structural-economic and institutional change to shifts in the widely-shared institutional rules according to which diverse organizations act. These broad rules can contain many types of realignments. Nevertheless, no matter how widely-shared the assumptions about growing interconnections between the interests of business and of government, implementation of organizational structures to facilitate joint planning and cooperation are not inevitable; nor will access to such structures be accessible to all. This discussion points out specific macrocooperative relationships that related to exports of coal in 1980–82 and traces these relationships to gradually emerging assumptions about interdependency. The assumptions—implemented as interorganizational strategies— are modifying and may continue to modify the traditional laissez-faire and regulatory roles of government with respect to the coal industry toward a role more oriented toward conjoined business-government policy-making and planning.

As a result of exports, coal was no longer so self-contained an industry as previously. The very task of selling coal abroad brought U.S. coal executives into new relationships with their own and with foreign goverments. Secondly, the *owners* of U.S. coal companies emerged as important stakeholders in coal export trade. Coal leaders were less apt to act or to think of themselves acting alone. Most importantly, macrocooperative activities showed that the historical antagonism between government officials and U.S. coal leaders was being replaced by organizationally-sanctioned commitments to cooperative planning and mutual support. Although some of these activities were in themselves of small consequence and were just beginning to be seen during 1980–82, they showed that the U.S. coal industry was having to think about itself and to act in new ways. In previous chapters I described how export trade brought changes in four separate layers of interorganizational network relationships, creating different patterns of interaction among network participants, and how these strategies were based on particular views about environmental problems. The patterns discussed so for were entrepreneurial, affiliative, coalitional, and federative. This chapter concentrates on a fifth pattern of interaction based on a different environmental view. This pattern overlays the others. The chapter describes the increasingly intertwined relationships of coal business leaders with national and international macroplanning institutions. The primary view implied by this sort of interorganizational activity was that the environment was highly interconnected and thus it created multiple vulnerabilities as well as multiple opportunities for coal sales.[1]

In this chapter our focus on the U.S. coal industry widens. The lens moves back to consider how realignments in the industry reflected the economic and political goals of the United States and other western nations. This was an important layer of network realignments during 1980–82, but it is not always readily attributable to incidents that I was able to observe directly. My vantage point inside the industry offered many insights into the emergence of macrocooperative activities; however, the relevant actors quickly leaped beyond my ability to observe them at close range. For this reason the evidence in this chapter is more general and speculative, and it must rely on more remote sources than that in previous chapters.

## Macrocooperation Defined

Macrocooperation means that the goals of normally distinct groups were converging. Dissimilar organizations found themselves working and planning together and jointly advising each other. The ends that groups were pursuing overlapped, making the assumptions supporting them noncontroversial. Assumptions were incorporated into national rhetoric and into international institutions.

The most obvious example of this, as I have mentioned, was that increased world coal trade (with a large portion from the United States) was accepted as the most viable solution to world energy problems. Once this political commitment was made, public policy and private aggrandizement were woven into a single tapestry involving trade development, international political negotiations, and sales. During 1980–82, I observed no opposition to increasing coal exports as a *goal*, because coal exports by that time had became tied to assumptions taken for granted in American society, such as the value of industrial expansion, the importance of internationl stability, and the efficacy of mercantilism in world trade. American world leadership had become an important national value underlying U.S. export sales.

The blending of national and international priorities with commercial goals drew members of the U.S. coal industry into cooperative involvements and new relationships with the federal government and with international political groups, many of which have already been described. These involvements were quite different from the wary adversarial relationships that the U.S. coal industry had often had with government leaders (see Chapter 3).

Goal transference thus bolstered the cause of U.S. coal exports and transformed a business opportunity from a relatively simple question of commercial expansion to one involving a major shift in global interactions. Coal leaders and public officials were equally apt to view exports in this way.

U.S. coal leaders even began to sound more like politicians and world statesmen. Whereas in the past they had often scolded government officials for restrictive policies on strip-mining, clean air, synfuels research, or coal slurry pipelines; or for the government's failure to recognize that "electricity does not come from kite strings";[2] their statements now sounded more like diplomatic pronouncements. R.E. Samples, chairman of NCA in 1981, noted positively that the U.S. industry stood ready to fulfill the world's needs. "It is obvious from the events of the last two years that the United States and indeed the world community is serious about making the transition from oil to coal as expeditiously as possible" (*World Coal*, Nov./Dec., 1981:86). Coal leaders were recognized as custodians of a resource which could reorganize the fuel dependencies of major nations. Their leaders were invited to step forward into new roles. Although in still a very minor way, coal showed signs that it might become a cherished national and international resource.

## Perception of the Environment as Interconnected

In many public and private statements political leaders and coal producers revealed their belief that the export situation was qualitatively different from their experiences in domestic commerce. They saw that unprecedented cooperation from many diverse participants would be required to pursue foreign trade successfully. The prevalent view was that the coal exports issue was intricately connected with U.S. goals of national economic policy and foreign relations as well as with the purely commercial goal of selling more coal. This view was well expressed by Senator Mathias (R, Md.) in his opening statement at the Foreign Relations Committee hearing in April 1981.

I think that the fact that we are holding this hearing in Baltimore today underscores two facts. First, the fact that foreign relations today revolve around economic factors and depend upon economic factors. The Committee on Foreign Relations is fully cognizant of this very great change in the nature of the world itself. Secretary Haig in his confirmation hearings placed great emphasis upon the economics of the world as being a determinant factor in foreign policy. Second, the fact that this hearing is being held out of Washington today I think underscores the determination of the Foreign Relations Committee to fully restore the economy of this country, and to see that foreign relations are conducted in a manner which is consistent with the health of the domestic economy. To that extent foreign relations have become domestic. . . .

An effective, coherent U.S. policy to encourage coal exports is imperative if we are going to capture a large part of the world coal export market. But the magnitude and complexity of the enterprise will require sustained coordination between all levels of government and industry. Dredging harbors, developing new terminals, arranging long-term contracts, and improving the necessary transportation network will require sustained coordination and cooperation among all elements of the economy. But whatever the effort is that's required, it will be worth it because success translates into jobs for American workers.

OPEC has thrown down a challenge to American inventive genius and I think our boldness in responding to this challenge has immense long-term implications for our own energy independence and ultimately for the price of OPEC oil. We must act aggressively to get those ships out of the bay and onto the oceans, putting our coal into the furnaces of the world. (Senate, Foreign Relations, 4/28/81: 1–3)

Mathias was one of many political and business leaders who were expressing these views.

Why did coal leaders begin to involve themselves in macrocooperative activities? There are many reasons—including prestige, good public relations, business contacts, and genuine commitment to relieving western nations from their dangerous reliance on unstable energy supplies. However, one explanation can unite all of these proximate causes. Coal companies devoted precious time and resources to macrocooperative activities as a strategy in order that they could influence the national and world institutions which promulgate policy and reflect the social values on which energy decisions are made. Through macrocooperative activities coal leaders could get closer to influencing these political agendas and social values personally and directly. The main problem implied by an interconnected environmental view is the multiple subjectivity of actors to events and groups far beyond themselves. Many U.S. coal producers had personally experienced the effects of social values changes on coal sales during the 1950s, when coal's image as dirty, inconvenient, and unsafe had caused domestic sales to plummet. Macrocooperative activity offered the possibility of intervening to help promote political decisions and assumptions favorable to coal expansion.

Widespread agreement about the goals being pursued by helping to export American coal created a supportive national and international climate in which U.S. coal exports could grow. It also greatly influenced the kinds of interorganizational relationships in which industry members became involved. But most importantly, the parties involved in coal exports could see that they would achieve mutually enhancing ends by adopting coordinated strategies to reach economic and political goals.

## MACROCOOPERATION IN NATIONAL POLITICS

### Supportive Rhetoric

U.S. coal industry leaders found that a variety of official and unofficial public voices were willing to support their interests in coal exports. Commentators as diverse as Milton R. Copulos of the conservative Heritage Foundation, Russell Train of the World Wildlife Fund, Eliot Cutler, a Carter appointee in the Office of Management and Budget, *The New York Times*, and a spectrum of powerful politicians (including Kissinger, Haig, and Senators Hatfield, Jackson, Johnston, Mathias, Moynihan, Percy, Randolph, Thurmond, Warner, and others) were on record in their support.

Hearings by the Senate Foreign Relations Committee were themselves an indication of conjoined government-industry interests in U.S. foreign coal trade. It was unusual for the committee to hold hearings on a commercial issue. Senator Mathias opened the hearings in Baltimore by reminding listeners that "Foreign relations today revolve around economic factors." Coal exports, Mathias said, whether from Baltimore or elsewhere, were a matter of the national security of U.S. allies. Senator Percy, chairman of the Foreign Relations Committee, emphasized similar points in a hearing held in Carbondale, Illinois, which was attended by coal buying representatives from eight countries (Senate, Government Affairs, 6/1/81). Percy promised to apply his energy to both the business promotion and strategic issues in coal export trade. "The

Foreign Relations Committee is going to be very deeply involved in seeing that we move this along. I guarantee that," he said (55).

This interest by two powerful majority-party senators, both of whom were from coal producing states and were influential in foreign affairs, was not lost on either the domestic producers or foreign buyers of coal. Both Mathias and Percy were mindful, of course, of the jobs and economic benefits which coal exports would bring to their constituents, and their statements about the important link between U.S. security and coal trade should be seen partially in this light. Nevertheless, their influence in areas important to foreign governments outside coal sales (such as the sale of fighter planes to Taiwan) introduced into coal sales an element of interlinked business-government complexity and subtlety that had not existed before. This combination of factors heightened the awareness of the coal industry about participants in macropolitics and placed the coal industry in a new kind of interorganizational climate.

No one who spoke about coal exports in these (or later) hearings predicted the number of jobs or the specific foreign policy goals to be attained. What was important was that a rhetorical connection between these issues was joining them in the minds of policymakers, coal producers, and the public. The goal of U.S. exports was not just commercial expansion; but also a matter of national security and public pride.

## The Carter Administration's Coal Export Policy

Promotion of coal exports became a matter of explicit U.S. policy when the United States pledged to double coal use and production by 1990 in the "Principles for IEA Action on Coal" signed in May 1979. This agreement was reconfirmed by President Carter at two subsequent Economic Summit meetings, at Tokyo (1979) and at Venice (1980). As part of this pledge the United States also agreed to work to expand world coal trade.

Secretary of Energy James Schlesinger had advised President Carter in June 1979 of the critical need to expand coal production and use. "If this nation is to cope effectively with economic and national security problems during the rest of this century the obstacles to increased coal production and use must be removed by an effective national commitment to coal" (Report to Carter quoted by *World Coal*, Nov. 1979: 47). The energy secretary made the connection between coal use and national security that would accompany virtually all public discussions of coal exports during 1980–82.

Carter assigned coal exports a privileged place in his administration, under the aegis of Ambassador-at-large Henry Owen of his cabinet. After the 1979 oil crisis Carter considered coal exports to have strategic significance. Coal exports were discussed several times by the National Security Council. Coal leaders praised Carter for giving coal export issues high priority. They judged that the personal attention of the president would be needed to address the complicated infrastructure and policy problems that coal exports raised (Bagge, Senate, Foreign Relations, 4/28/81: 140–42).

Carter appointed the Interagency Coal Export Task Force (discussed in Chapter 6) to develop recommendations for how the United States could meet its pledge to increase coal use and trade. When it was appointed in May 1980, Carter expected to be starting a second term and developing new legislative initiatives on energy at the time the report was due, in January 1981. Instead, Ronald Reagan was elected, and the ICE report was passed on to his administration. Coal export policy, though, remained consistent under Reagan.

The ICE report amassed a huge amount of technical information and market forecasting for domestic industry use. It amounted to a detailed marketing survey conducted at government expense. The ICE report was hailed by industry as "a very unusual document because it makes sense" (Bagge, AAPA, 2/17/81). It placed government on record in a supportive but limited role. Coal companies had recommended and preferred this policy stance. Thus, the ICE report was an important first step for communication and cooperation among government and private interests. Fourteen executive departments participated in the ICE task force. This was another indication of the extensive breadth of issues and the remarkable degree of consensus which the report represented.

Through the ICE Task Force the federal government extended its prestige and its services to the coal industry in support of export trade. It acknowledged that coal exports were an important policy consideration worthy of national concern. The typical adversarial relationship between government and the coal industry was set aside and a new basis of partnership and mutual benefit was being established. This mood was a significant departure from their animus on other policy issues.[3] Government and industry were working together toward mutually enhancing ends.

President Carter scheduled a White House Conference on Coal Exports held in December 1980 over which he personally presided. Invitees were about 200 representatives from the coal industry, environmental groups, labor, transportation, ICE Task Force member agencies, ports, and representatives of twelve foreign countries. The purpose of the conference was to reassure foreign buyers of American commitment to stand behind coal exports. Coal producers and foreign buyers had been worried about the sanctity of export contracts since the start of the coal boom. They wanted to know that the United States would not use political embargoes against coal, such as those placed on soybeans and grain to the Soviet Union in the 1970s.

At the conference President Carter emphasized the seriousness of American contractual obligations. He cited many laws upholding contracts, and he said that only a "national emergency" would interrupt coal exports. If not all observers were completely satisfied with these reassurances, it was primarily because by the time of the conference Carter was a lame duck president. Invitees might have preferred a conference sponsored by the new administration.

However, the conference itself showed that the White House was supportive of coal trade and the president had personally articulated a policy that coal industry executives had been urging him to take. The ambiguity raised by Carter's caveat that a national emergency could interrupt coal shipments concerned some foreign buyers—it was of course during a time of emergency that they wanted to be protected from fuel supply interruptions. But it was hard to see how Carter could have broached this topic and still allowed adequate leeway for unforeseen eventuality.

The White House Conference was a formal policy gesture. Carter wanted to get coal exports pointed in the right direction and to reinforce American commitments to them. The conference brought industry, government, and foreign representatives together and gave them the same charge. In a complex, divisive, competitive business with a long history of distrust of government the conference set a new tone of mutual support and government approval.

## Reagan Administration Coal Export Policy

Coal export policy moved smoothly from the Carter to the Reagan administration. Coal leaders were prominent members of President Reagan's energy campaign advisory committee and of the task forces preparing the new administration's priorities. In these roles they were able to keep coal industry interests including exports high on Reagan's list of priorities. Since the industry was relatively pleased with coal export policy under Carter, and since the demand for steam coal was booming at ports, they did not request changes. Coal leaders only asked that coal exports be kept as an important item on the new administration's agenda (conversation with government representative, 12/16/80). Except for insisting that user fees be applied to port development projects (see Chapter 7), the Reagan administration continued the policy of supportive nonintervention and cooperation with the coal industry that Carter had followed.

Requiring user fees was of course a big difference. OMB's oversight of expenditures and of budget deficits held a much bigger role in Reagan's than in Carter's administration. It might be argued that by insisting on port fees, the Reagan administration was actually downplaying coal development policies, although still giving them verbal support. In some ways Reagan was downgrading coal export issues. He omitted them from the agenda at both the Ottowa (1981) and the Versailles (1982) Economic Summit meetings when more pressing matters intervened.[4] He transferred authority over export issues from visionary planners at the Department of Energy to more mundane implementers at the Department of Commerce.

But if these actions were meant to lower the priority of coal exports in his administration, they were not interpreted in this way by major members of the coal industry. Industry leaders were generally pleased with Reagan's policy. In each case countervailing circumstances could justify the president's decisions.[5] What the leaders saw was that Reagan was institutionalizing and implementing coal export goals merely outlined by Carter. This would give them a place to take problems about coal exports within the administration.

President Reagan issued a national coal export policy statement in July 1981 shortly after the Economic Summit Conference at Ottawa. It was virtually identical with Carter's policy, and it paralleled the requests coal industry leaders had made of the administration in their May 1981 meeting (see Chapter 7). Asked what he thought of Reagan's coal export policy, Carl Bagge said "We love it" (*St. Louis Post Dispatch,* 7/19/81: 14A).

*The Coal Interagency Working Group.* President Reagan organizationally established coal exports within his government by appointing a subcabinet-level Coal Interagency Working Group (CIWG) to carry out coordination and daily administration of coal export activities. This new interagency group was to continue on an ongoing basis the work of Carter's ICE Task Force. It would serve as the focal point within government for coal export issues.

Secretary of Commerce Malcolm Baldridge in announcing the official coal export policy said that the administration's intent was to remove "government impediments" to coal export trade, while "helping the nation's trading partners lessen their dependence on oil supplies" (Department of Commerce Press Release, 7/21/81). This joining of commercial and public policy goals would be accomplished primarily through low-profile nonintervention activities and official trade promotion. Relaxation of certain rules on strip-mining and administrative hastening of licensing of coal terminal facilities were expected through Vice-President Bush's Task Force on Regulatory Relief. Otherwise the CIWG would be a touchstone for information on coal trade policy and for promotion.

The promotional activities of the CIWG overlapped closely those already being pursued by individual coal firms and by NCA. In many ways they therefore seemed somewhat redundant and expendable to industry officials. Rather than the specific activities, it was what these government activities represented that was important. They were manifest evidence of the fundamental agreement between government and industry about the role that the government would play in encouraging coal export trade.

## Trade Promotion

Assistant Secretary of Commerce William Morris, who was helpful to the coal industry on port dredging, headed the CIWG. In addition to his activities on the port deepening bill, Morris began a low-key but nevertheless significant—because it had never been done before—official promotion of U.S. coal trade. Morris described his job to the Senate as "vice-president for sales and marketing" for U.S. coal sales abroad (Senate, Foreign Relations, 4/28/81:35).

In December 1981, Morris went abroad to promote U.S. coal. He toured four European capitals and met with members of the European Common Market's energy division to discuss future U.S. coal sales. (*ICR*, 12/4/81). Europeans were apprehensive that U.S. exports would rob the EEC of jobs in European mines. But Morris emphasized that the tremendous growth projected for steam coal use was well beyond Europe's full-output capacity.

Morris' trip was followed in May 1982, by a thirty-one member official U.S. delegation which visited Spain, Italy, France, and Belgium. The trip was a media event. The group departed amid banners and hoopla. Secretary of Commerce Baldridge (standing in front of a prominent sign proclaiming "Exports Mean Jobs") reiterated the strategic significance of increased coal trade and announced the trade mission's goal: to demonstrate the capacity, reliability, and commitment of U.S. industry to supply any projected level of demand for coal (*NCA Coal News*, 5/24/81). The ten-day mission included five members of Congress, administration leaders, and eleven coal industry representatives (most from large steam coal firms).

A trade mission is a public relations gesture of minimal policy significance, but as an organizational indicator of how far the coal industry had come in interfusing its interests with those of official Washington, this was a significant event. This trade mission was a first for coal. It again illustrated the partnership between the interests of government policymakers and the coal industry.

## Export Trading Companies

Most foreign countries allow firms in the same industry to combine their sales strength when they conduct foreign sales. This was the basis of the British West Indian Tea and Sugar companies of the eighteenth century. By contrast, the United States does not give its exporting companies this freedom. Strict antitrust restrictions on interfirm collusion have limited U.S. firms in their ability to market goods jointly abroad. In many settings this prohibition has been a hardship on them, particularly for small American firms. It has put American companies at a competitive disadvantage. The coal export situation heightened the fact that U.S. coal businesses were disadvantaged compared to the well-coordinated and efficient sales organizations (and buying cartels) that typically handle energy in foreign countries.

In 1981–82 Congress considered a bill altering U.S. antitrust restrictions on foreign sales and authorizing U.S. export trading companies. The bill would allow American companies to form cooperative sales forces through bank holding companies. These holding companies could promote and negotiate sales abroad in the name of all members. Unlike the port development bills the Export Trading Companies Act sailed through Congress. It passed in August 1982. Supporters came forward from a wide variety of industries. With the act, coal companies had won a new tool with which to conduct export business. The Export Trading Companies Act was a concrete indication of government's willingness to relax conventional rules in areas that would help coal export trade. Although coal companies took no part in the public testimony presented to Congress on this bill, coal firms watched its progress with interest (legislative meetings, 1/16/81; 3/9/81; 4/23/81).

The coal industry did not actively support the Export Trading Companies Act. Large coal firms considered it to be of greatest benefit to smaller producers. Small producers could pool their sales forces and make more efficient use of small staffs to sell coal abroad. The use of export trading companies might allow small coal firms to participate in foreign business which would otherwise be closed to them. However, the act was not restricted to use by small companies. Once the bill was passed, large coal firms realized that, although it would keep many American competitors in foreign coal trade, large firms could make good use of export trading companies to develop joint ventures and to set a favorable price on exported coal.

Passage of the Export Trading Companies Act was another small indication that the U.S. was following a national policy supportive of export trade. U.S. policy invited coal firms to join forces and plan together for offshore sales in a way forbidden to them in their domestic business.

## New Chip in Foreign Policy

Interest in coal exports lapped over from the more instrumental departments of government (Commerce, Transportation, Energy, and Army Corps of Engineers) to the Department of State, the Department of Defense, and the National Security Council, because of what coal exports represented as a potential way to wean the world away from dependency on OPEC oil and Soviet natural gas. The federal government became a partner in the development of coal exports because a case was made that coal was a commodity critical to the security of western allies (and to a lesser extent to the hopes for industrialization in less-developed countries).[6] The nations and companies which controlled world coal trade would be in a position to affect U.S. national security interests. Coal was becoming a new chip in the foreign policy game.

During 1980–82, coal exports were sometimes invoked—even if vaguely—in diplomatic and strategic negotiations to obtain support for other U.S. policies. Reagan officials (and prominent others) believed that the Soviet gas pipeline would make western European nations much more vulnerable to Soviet political pressures, because they would be dependent upon the pipeline as an essential source of fuel. Among the offers made to western nations to encourage them to break off pipeline negotiations was a promise of secure U.S. coal supplies at reasonable prices (*Inside Energy*, 9/11/81). Secretary of State Alexander Haig, and later Secretary of State George Schulz, explicitly referred to coal exports as one way to wean the west away from *both* OPEC and Soviet energy domination (*New York Times*, 7/29/81: IV 1: 6). In these contexts, coal exports had become a tool in U.S. foreign relations. What did this mean to the U.S. coal industry?

## Changes in Outlook of Coal Leaders

Interpenetration of coal industry business concerns with diplomatic and strategic political goals is less advanced in the

United States than in any country abroad. In most countries decisions about energy are as organizationally centralized and politically sensitive as decisions about purchases of advanced technology or weapons. Political and industrial interests are, in fact, the same. They are handled by parallel ministries of government. Coal leaders are often revered and diplomatically trained government officials.

The fact that energy policy is handled in high circles of foreign national governments meant that American coal producers came into close contact with high government officials overseas and political and foreign policy issues, as soon as they began to seek foreign coal sales. A coal executive on a selling trip might easily sit down with the top energy minister of a foreign country. In addition to learning the technical needs and physical capabilities of these new customers, coal officials for the first time needed to keep themselves informed about the foreign policy issues in their own and other countries which might influence negotiations. At the same time, these sales contacts held significance for U.S. foreign policy, and important deals were of concern to U.S. officials. Business and government were developing new kinds of interests in one another. Coal leaders were being asked to display new skills—sometimes to their consternation.

I was told that one U.S. delegation to China was surprised to be confronted with questions from a Chinese Deputy Premier of Energy about a recent U.S. decision to sell jet fighters to Taiwan. The delegation had come, it thought, merely to "sell coal" (third party conversation, 10/81). In another incident, a trip to France was postponed partly because of the election of the Socialist Francois Mitterrand and the thought that this might alter France's policy toward buying a foreign energy resource. Such considerations were new for coal leaders. They added complexity and new areas of uncertainty to sales. Coal officials on sales trips were sometimes perceived as spokesmen of official U.S. diplomatic policies by their foreign sales partners. They were treated abroad as semidiplomats. These new relationships made it important (to both American businesspeople and government) that strong partnership be maintained. Coal officials began to request—and to obtain—State Department and National Security Council briefings. Coal executives were growing into better informed and more sophisticated world leaders.

## MACROCOOPERATION THROUGH INTERNATIONAL AGENCIES

The conjoined interests between business and national political leaders were also reflected in international organizations.

The basis for this cooperation stretched back to 1973. As I have noted, the assumptions supportive of macrocooperation in world coal industry network relationships emerged gradually over a period of years. Some patterns of interaction and recognitions of mutual interest began as early as 1973, after the first oil crisis. In 1979, international joint coal planning was more explicitly institutionalized. Macrocooperation seemed to accelerate and become an accepted part of international interorganizational relationships after 1980. Although this chapter mostly concerns post-1979 developments, it is important to remember that the basis for this cooperation stretched back at least to 1973, and that it may represent a far-reaching shifting of the background in which the coal industry is set; the full implications of which still may not be fully evident.

## The International Energy Agency

The major organizational response by western countries to the 1973 oil crisis was the formation of the International Energy Agency (IEA) organized in November 1974. Twenty-one of twenty-four countries in the Organization for Economic Cooperation and Development (OECD) joined the IEA.

The IEA has not become a powerful counterforce to OPEC. Nevertheless, it has provided a joint forum for economic discussions, analysis, and planning of energy issues. IEA nations pool information and have, to some extent, coordinated their energy and environmental policies.

The second oil disruption, in 1979, sent another shock wave through the world community. For the second time in six years oil supplies to western Europe and Japan were jeopardized and prices were out of control. To protect fragile economies heavily dependent on imported fuels, fuel diversification looked like the only practical guard against future uncertainties. This recognition enhanced the international importance of coal.

In May 1979, just two months after the outbreak of the Iran-Iraq War, and as fuel shortages and price rises were pressing on Europe and Japan, IEA nations adopted formally their fuel diversification policy statement, "Principles of IEA Action on Coal." Through this agreement the IEA member states announced their intention to work toward increased coal use. They pledged also to increase steam coal trade. The Principles of IEA Action were reconfirmed in statements signed at the Tokyo (1979) and Venice (1980) Economic Summit Conferences.

Political commitments need technical implementation to be acted upon. The IEA needed to enlist the cooperation of the world's coal industries. World coal leaders from IEA countries were now thrust into prominence.

## The Coal Industry Advisory Board

The Coal Industry Advisory Board (CIAB) was organized under the IEA's intergovernmental umbrella in direct response to the 1979 oil crisis. The CIAB established a role for a group of coal producers and supporting industry representatives from thirteen nations in IEA policy-making. The CIAB facilitates commercial relations between countries and helps the IEA gather information and report the progress of nations in meeting their goals to expand coal use. Most importantly, the CIAB has brought coal producers, particularly those from the United States, into new roles with respect to other international energy leaders.

The CIAB's thirty-four officially appointed members represent coal industries, transportation, and coal burning utilities throughout the world. Eight are U.S. representatives. The United States has the largest delegation. They are appointed by the White House from private industry. This sets U.S. representatives apart from the coal representatives of most countries, who often have some official relationship with their national government. In addition to the eight U.S. delegates several multinational firms which own major U.S. coal resources are also members of the CIAB, and they increase the influence of the U.S. coal industry.

As representatives of the world's largest coal industry, and one of the few industries privately controlled, U.S. producers stood to gain more than most CIAB members in personal prestige and profits from their participation in macrocooperative policy-making. U.S. producers who were members of the CIAB justified the time spent in these sessions as a responsibility to assert proactively the value of increased coal use for the entire U.S. industry's benefit. When sessions became more technical than policy-setting they began to lose interest (conversation with CIAB technical associate).

The CIAB met for the first time in June 1980. It reviewed the coal policies of IEA member nations and drafted a report on how IEA countries could meet their pledges to expand coal use and trade by 1990–2000. The CIAB's findings were accepted by IEA ministers at their December 1980 meeting. Thus CIAB policy recommendations became the codified policies of the IEA states.

Meeting as a group at least twice a year, the CIAB has now become an established part of international intergovernmental structure. Through it, U.S. coal leaders, as businesspeople with expertise about their normal areas of operation, advise and, in effect, set policies and recommendations for western governments. This gives the firms which have representation on the CIAB wide exposure and greatly increased influence in national and international affairs. It also reconfirms that the goals of the coal industry and the governments it advises are intertwined.

The influence of large U.S. firms is underlined when one realizes that reports of the IEA are often used as high status evidence in Congress or at the White House to influence national policy debates. Hence, the 1980 CIAB report to the IEA ministers was composed by the technical associates of CIAB members, many of whom were executives of U.S. coal firms. The report was adopted by the IEA as submitted. Later this same report was presented by the U.S. coal leaders who had helped author it to President Reagan's staff (Counselor Meese and Transition Team Chairman Halbouty) as evidence that international opinion supported both increased coal trade and port dredging. Economic and governmental interests were truly becoming intermeshed in this situation.

The CIAB intends to plan continuously for energy needs on a world level. This is shown in a small way by its recent shift from a Working Group to a Standing Group on Long-Term Cooperation (IEA memo, 8/25/81). This small indicator implies that major coal leaders will continue to have direct input into the political recommendations and official policies adopted by the IEA.

## The World Coal Study

The same unity of purpose between governments and coal leaders could be seen in embryo in the most ambitious macrocooperative effort prior to the CIAB, the World Coal Study (see Chapter 6). Although this two-year project, begun in 1978, was not intended to be an ongoing institutional advisory board, the World Coal Study brought together leaders in industry, research, and environmental studies from sixteen countries to provide information and to advise world leaders about the prospects of future coal use.

WOCOL had no official intergovernmental status, but its report and recommendations carried the weight of prestigious and knowledgeable participants. WOCOL was an important example of international macroplanning and the solidification of coal industry values into the social fabric of world energy awareness. It also elevated coal leaders to new roles.

WOCOL had a much larger overall membership than the CIAB, including large delegations from each of sixteen participating nations. In the U.S. delegation Atlantic Richfield, Bechtel, Inc., and a large coal firm—AMAX Coal—were representatives. British Petroleum Co. and Shell Coal International, major owners of U.S. coal firms, were included on the rosters of other countries.

WOCOL created the foundation for macrocooperation and information sharing among the coal industries and the governments of various nations. It even included delegations from nonwestern countries, such as Poland and China.

## INFLUENCE OF LARGE U.S. FIRMS IN MACROCOOPERATIVE ACTIVITIES

Large coal companies or NCA were the most apt to participate in macrocooperative activities. MCA represented the interests of large companies (see Chapter 8). Only very prominent leaders of large U.S. coal firms were appointed to national panels or to international groups such as WOCOL and the CIAB. Such appointments were subject to rank and protocol considerations within the industry as well as to political clout with government leaders. Four of the five largest U.S. firms were represented in the two main international macrocooperative efforts: Peabody, Consolidation, Amax, and Pittston.[7] (See Table 9.1.)

Nicholas Camicia, the CIAB chairman, was from Pittston Co. A vice-chairman Thornton Bradshaw, was president of Atlantic Richfield Co. Other U.S. members were top executives of Conoco, Inc., New England Electric, Peabody Coal, Bechtel International, R.S. Industries, and Joy Manufacturing. This was similar to the composition of the U.S. WOCOL delegation. The U.S. retained chairmanship of the CIAB in 1983, when Nicholas Camicia resigned and R.H. Quenon of Peabody Coal took his place.

**TABLE 9.1. Companies with U.S. Coal Interests Which Had Representatives on WOCOL and CIAB**

| *WOCOL* | *CIAB* |
| --- | --- |
| AMAX, Co. (AMAX Coal) | Atlantic Richfield (Arco Coal) |
| Atlantic Richfield (Arco Coal) | Bechtel, Inc. (Peabody Coal) |
| Bechtel, Inc. (Peabody Coal) | Conoco, Inc. (Consolidation Coal) |
|  | Peabody Coal |
|  | Pittston Coal |
| British Petroleum (Old Ben Coal) |  |
| Shell Coal International | British Petroleum (Old Ben Coal) |
|    (Massey Coal) | Shell International Petroleum |
|  |    (Massey Coal) |

Participation in these groups conferred status on members. Appointments to the CIAB and WOCOL were coveted. Political influence was invoked to obtain and to maintain appointments. Coal leaders often alluded among their peers to their positions on these international groups (Jackson, The Energy Bureau, 12/6/80; Major, AAPA, 2/17/81).

Macrocooperative activities broadened the normal experiences and contacts of large coal firms. Leaders grew into roles in which evenhandedness and diplomacy were more important than aggressively competing with their sister firms. While maintaining an interest in their own firm's sales, leaders were forced to consider the welfare of the entire U.S. industry, and sometimes the objectives of American foreign policy as well. Coal leaders were placed in situations where their competitiveness and their experience protecting the industry from outside interference were less applicable than skills of conciliation and tact.

Appointments to macrocooperative leadership have the potential to create a small, internationally knowledgeable, U.S. coal industry elite. As the export market continues, this elite may effectively utilize its international contacts and expertise to capture foreign coal sales. But in the meantime, conferred status, if not contracts, became more concentrated among these firms. Status brought with it a sense of noblesse oblige by the large toward the smaller U.S. firms.

Formation of the American Coal Federation in mid-1982 may be an example of this new spirit within the industry. The American Coal Federation was formed to provide the entire coal industry with a comprehensive image-building and promotional organization that will consolidate the activities of several of the industry's most jealous supraorganizations (NCA, MARC, BCOA, and UMWA). Its guiding hand was Robert H. Quenon, CEO of Peabody Coal, who helped bring about the Federation after noticing on a European trip the impressive public relations and sales efforts mounted by European coal industries (*NCA Coal News*, 7/7/82). Although exports were not to be the only concern of the American Coal Federation, they were an important impetus in making coal companies realize that the U.S. coal industry needed to get its act together. This new organization was not explicitly needed by large coal firms. They could obtain good public relations on their own. Coordinating this kind of industry-wide effort was bound to involve time and aggravation with only problematic payoff. Pride in presenting a better image of U.S. coal to the public seemed to be Quenon's major rationale. The effort required reaching out to different groups and interests and coordinating them around a common goal. Although this example does not show explicit blending of U.S. coal industry interests with foreign policy goals, it does indicate a broader spirit of shared concern among industry members for each other than had been typical. In this way it was a kind of macrocooperative realignment.

The realignments of network power coming about because of international involvement and joint planning among government and business leaders might be compared to a benevolent aristocracy. Appointed leaders were acting on their own behalfs as well as on behalf of less powerful members of the industry to promote coal. An elite was beginning to speak for all industry members in hopes of institutionalizing values that would encourage a "return to coal," and "American" fuel.

## The Influence of Coal's Owners

It is now necessary to look more closely at just which firms were gaining prominence in macrocooperative planning activities. The three largest steam coal firms (Peabody, Consolidation, and Amax) had representatives on WOCOL or the CIAB. Arco and Massey—large steam coal firms that had shown interest in exports—were also represented on these bodies through their oil-parent firms. However, among these coal firms only Peabody Coal Company, the nation's largest firm, was represented by its own CEO. Consolidation and AMAX were represented by the heads of their parent corporations. Even Peabody had its influence extended by the extra input of Bechtel Corporation representatives. What, if anything, does this upping of the ante among the executives engaged in international coal policy-making mean? Why didn't the leaders of U.S. coal firms participate directly in these international groups? Since the parent firms of many coal companies were oil companies, wasn't there a conflict between the interests of oil and the policy of promoting coal in international forums?

Full answers to these questions are beyond the scope of the study that has occupied us here. The answers would require a different look at the U.S. coal industry. But the traces of an answer are implied in much that has already been said.

The potential for U.S. steam coal exports expanded the relevant scope of operations of U.S. steam coal firms into an area in which they had little knowledge. Fusion of national and international goals with the goal of expanding coal exports brought diverse groups together because of their common concerns. However, the U.S. industry's lack of experience in these areas and the high relevancy of the political and resource decisions being made to other energy fuels drew the owners of coal firms—who typically had more experience with complex international negotiations than their coal subsidiaries—into open participation in macrocooperative activities. This made the U.S. coal industry's activities less independent and self-contained. Owners and suppliers, as well as political leaders, became active parts of the U.S. coal industry's interorganizational network. The boundaries of the coal industry's network were expanding outward. The coal industry was operating more fully as an indistinguishable element in the vast energy fuels industry.

U.S. steam coal companies lacked familiarity and experience with world affairs. Although the large U.S. firms showed the greatest interest in international macrocooperation, even executives from the largest U.S. coal firms had been uninvolved with world politics and international trade before 1980. Large U.S. coal firms were being introduced to international affairs in part *through* their associations with macrocooperative groups. They were not included in such groups for their international expertise, but for their technical knowledge. To the extent that coal firms had direct input to these international groups only the very largest firms were called upon. But even among the largest U.S. coal firms, their parent firms were much more likely to be experienced about *both* world affairs and coal than they were.

Macrocooperation indicates movement in the direction of blending the interests of government officials and industry representatives. In this instance, the interests of different energy-related industries also began to blend together. Philip Selznick (1957) said that when the values of an enterprise become institutionalized in a society. its leaders will become "statesmen." Coal leaders were showing signs of becoming more statesmanlike. But their parent firms were already pros. The representatives of these companies were literally statesmen of the first rank.[8]

Governments were turning for advice to coal. A major difference between this situation and previous reliance on oil officials for advice (Blair, 1976) was that the ownership of energy industries was now intermingled. Large U.S. coal companies are predominantly owned by large multinational corporations, many of which are in energy resource industries. Roughly 25 percent of U.S. production in 1980 was owned by oil and gas firms. In 1982 almost 60 percent of U.S. coal output was from coal firms owned entirely or in part by companies which were not themselves primarily coal producers (based on 1984 Keystone Coal Information Service data). This figure was only 25 percent in 1966. When multinational corporate owners stepped in to exercise their interests in fuels planning in international circles, they could draw on huge staffs and resources which dwarfed even the largest U.S. coal firms.[9]

The multinational owners of coal recognized its strategic and international importance before coal firms themselves. They had bought into reserves and production capabilities (in the American west and Australia) in the 1960s and 1970s. By 1980, multinational parent corporations controlled six of the U.S.'s fifteen largest coal firms. Only two of the forty largest U.S. coal firms remained financially independent. In the export boom of 1980–82, every firm which showed serious promise in U.S. export trade, especially at the macrocooperative level, had some connection with a multinational investor. By the same token, multinational owners often took the places of coal industry representatives in macrocooperative activities. These parent companies assigned top-ranked executives to macroplanning forums. They kept their coal subsidiaries informed but partially in the background as they shaped international energy policy.

The owners of U.S. coal firms are multinational corporations with knowledge of international affairs and enormous access to resources. These owners encouraged and supported their coal subsidiaries in pursuing an active role in world coal trade. Ownership of the largest coal firms by energy and technical engineering multinational corporations pulled these firms into the international arena and eased their entry into world coal trade by making available to them investment capital for entrepreneurial ventures, sharing with them management expertise and analyses, and agreeing to go along with coalition strategies on port development. Multinational firms offered their coal subsidiaries support through their familiarity with international legal and financial arrangements, and they shared their political judgments and contacts with them. Sometimes equipment or contracts held by owners, such as ships, land, or coal export backhauls, gave their subsidiaries an advantage in export sales. The owners of major coal companies also served prominently on multinational planning organizations. The arrangements between coal subsidiaries and their owners were not always collegial and mutually supporting. Coal companies operated with a great deal of autonomy from their owners. The traditional jealousy between coal and oil persisted, even though ownership of the two industries was intertwined. For example, the interests of the large coal firms and those of oil companies conflicted over proposed user fees for deepening ports. Oil companies, which could undoubtedly overcome any coal policy they felt was threatening, tolerated this opposition.

Nevertheless, the power of multinational ownership was latent in most export activities during 1980–82. Oil, gas, engineering, and other multinational interests have bought so heavily into energy fuels that whatever balance among energy feedstocks is settled upon, it will benefit these huge firms. Price-fixing may not occur, but economic control is firmly entrenched. This fact pervaded coal export expansion issues. It enlarged the implications of coal export activities beyond the immediate coal industry. Through diversification into various sources of energy the multinational owners of coal firms have successfully tied their business goals to the social aspirations of both industrialized and developing nations for economic growth, industrial development, political stability, and national strength. Coal is but one contributor to these goals.

To this extent, the explanation behind large coal firms in the United States taking over the export market from small ones lies institutionally outside the immediate group of large U.S. coal producers and rests with the strategies and interests of the owners of the largest steam coal firms. Coal's owners are relying on the largest U.S. coal companies (which are mere ants by comparison with these multinational corporate giants) to carry forward their aspirations to control all major sources of energy. Until a few more years of U.S. coal export experience have passed it will be hard to tell how much the largest U.S. coal firms have enhanced their status or consolidated their power within the U.S. coal industry from macrocooperative international exposure. It already appears that very large firms are affected more favorably than small U.S. firms by macrocooperation as by the other types of industry realignments which have emerged because of export trade. It seems apparent that these realignments have the potential to restructure the U.S. coal industry into a narrower pyramid with a few large multinationally owned firms at the top.

## Summary of Macrocooperative Realignments

In this chapter I have shown that government and U.S. coal companies developed conjoined interests in promoting U.S. export trade. The coalescence of interests led some of the largest U.S. companies into macrocooperative relationships with government policymakers at both national and international levels. These activities conferred on them added status and afforded them opportunities to develop their leadership and expertise within their industry and in world policy-making settings. The coal firms which participated in macrocooperative efforts used them as ways to secure the social acceptability of coal and of increased international coal trade in ways that would inure to the benefit of their own firms and to the benefit of the U.S. coal industry as a whole.

By participating in national and international cooperative groups, these companies were acting on a view that the environment is multiply interconnected with many cross-ties among economic and political factors. Normally competing groups—such as those from different countries, or different firms in the same business, or buyers and sellers of one commodity—can have congruent goals and reasons to work together. Large firms pursued strategies of macrocooperation in order to exert statesmanlike influence over the policies and social values which they considered problematic in the long-run expansion of world coal use and trade.

Macrocooperative activities gave U.S. coal industry leaders unprecedented access to policymakers and to their international colleagues. It increased their status as elite leaders within the U.S. coal industry, although it remains to be seen whether this status will be translated into market power. Through macrocooperative activities U.S. coal leaders developed a greater sense of noblesse oblige and responsibility for their whole industry's welfare.

The atmosphere surrounding macrocooperative realignments was one of increasing congruence between the business goals of individual coal firms and the goals of the U.S. government. Business leaders exhibited statesmanlike behavior in international forums. They were accorded new respect by their peers. Their interests were favorably pressed by diverse commentators. In conducting their normal business of selling coal they increased their familiarity with political conditions outside of their normal expertise, and they found that they needed to attune their negotiations to politically-charged settings. They developed increasing reliance on services of the federal government (as discussed in Chapter 6), as did the government on them, for intelligence and support. In all, these leaders increased their sophistication and their knowledge of world politics through their involvement in export sales. This had the effect of realigning the U.S. coal industry. The U.S. government and the coal industry were no longer as adversarial as historically they had been, and the coal industry was no longer so self-contained. The image which macrocooperative network realignment brings to mind is a multiply-bonded molecule or a geodesic dome in which stability and tension are created simultaneously through multiply-linked, structurally interacting forces.

The key U.S. coal industry actors in international macrocooperative activities were the largest U.S. coal firms. But even more significant was the involvement of the multinational corporations that owned U.S. coal companies. Multinational corporations that owned coal and other energy assets seemed to be trying to use international forums to consolidate a global social values agenda which would favor them no matter what political decisions are made about uses of particular energy fuels. The activities of multinational owners of U.S. coal firms affected the U.S. coal industry by explicitly expanding the coal industry's interorganizational network. The U.S. coal industry could not remain isolated from its owners or from other major interests in energy where export sales were involved.

The precise effects of the involvement of coal owners and of other industrial interests in coal export trade is beyond the scope of this study. The shadows already being cast by these outside groups during 1980–82 indicate, however, that this may be an important area of future influence on U.S. coal industry realignments.

## NOTES

1. R.H. Quenon quoted this remark in an article he wrote for *World Coal*, Nov. 1979. It was originally made by Carl Bagge in a report to the president on coal use.
2. Carl Bagge referred to Ambassador Owen as one of the few friends the coal industry had in the Carter administration (Senate, Foreign Relations, 4/28/81: 142).
3. An internal memo where I worked described dissatisfaction with the conference and with the vagueness of the president's reassurances. It expressed regret that the conference had been held (memo, 12/16/80). However, I attributed this dissatisfaction primarily to the fact that the assurances were not being given by the new administration.
4. Consideration of the Soviet gas pipeline predominated at the Ottawa Summit Conference in 1981. Although coal exports were not discussed directly, they were proposed later as an inducement to get western nations to drop their commitments to purchase Soviet gas—to no avail.

    President Reagan did not discuss coal exports at the Economic Summit of 1982 at Versailles, although he received a letter urging him to do so from sixteen House and six Senate members (*NCA Coal News*, 6/7/82). By then, falling world oil prices had taken some of the initial sheen off coal export prospects. Apparently, Reagan and his advisors did not consider coal export issues crucial enough for the summit talks.
5. Transferring oversight of the nation's coal export policy from Energy to Commerce made sense if the president intended to carry out his promise to dismantle the Department of Energy. Reagan removed coal export issues from the purview of the National Security Council, but they were still discussed in the White House by the Cabinet Council on Commerce and Trade, a principals-only group of cabinet officers led by the secretary of commerce. Reportedly coal exports was the only coal issue this group discussed (Ferritor, Borre, and Morris testimony, Senate, Foreign Relations, 4/28/81).
6. See State Department testimony about bilateral and multilateral technical assistance programs to promote coal use in less developed nations (Senate, Foreign Relations, 4/28/81: 49–54).

7. I cannot explain the absence of Island Creek Coal, the fourth largest U.S. firm, from macrocooperative panels. Lawrence and Dyer (1983) suggest that parental profits-skimming may be an explanation for Island Creek's erratic behavior.

8. For example, George Shultz who served as the Bechtel Corporation representative on the CIAB from 1980 to 1981, later became U.S. secretary of state.

9. The largest U.S. coal firm, Peabody Coal, had total revenues of $1.2 billion in 1980. In contrast with this the owners of coal firms are much larger. For example, Continental Oil Company (Consolidation Coal's owner) even without considering the resources of its parent company, Dupont, is an $18.8 billion firm; Shell Oil Company had sales of $22.3 billion in the United States in 1980; Bechtel, one of four owners of Peabody Coal is a $7 billion per year corporation (*Million Dollar Directory*, Vol. 1, 1983).

# 10    Conclusion

## FIVE LAYERS OF NETWORK REALIGNMENTS

During 1980–82 the coal industry awoke to new possibilities for international involvement in export trade. Heightened activity to capture and expand sales brought about network realignments which showed that six to ten major firms were gaining power with respect to smaller coal firms in the export market. Consolidation of power occurred in five separate layers of interorganizational activity: autonomous competition for profitable participation in the market, clustering around new sources of information for technical knowledge, bargaining by coalitions to obtain better positioning for market control, dominance by supraorganizations to protect and legitimate the industry, and elite influence in macro-organizations. These realignments have the potential to narrow control over U.S. steam coal export sales to a narrow pyramid of large multinationally-owned coal firms.

I found five types of perceived uncertainty and views of the environment in the coal industry during 1980–82. They are analogous to Karpik's "logics of action" and to the strategic assumptions about uncertainty that Crozier and Friedberg define as rules of a game. These nonobservable rationales linked the strategies organizations adopted to the problematic concerns that actors (and by extrapolation firms) believed the environment presented. These relationships were displayed analytically in Table 2.1.

The environment viewed as a *simple economic market* brought forth *entrepreneurial* strategies of autonomous, one-on-one competitions to insure a firm's participation in the market. Network stress and realignment were revealed in the tensions between innovations and standard operating procedures. This network pattern was individualistic, relatively democratic, chaotic, and random. Success seemed tied to luck as much as to any other factor.

Uncertainty perceived as *technical complexity* elicited establishment of *new sources and vendors of information* and the clustering of firms around specialized providers of information services. The structure of this network pattern was still moblike, but affiliational clusters, consisting of firms and their supporting groups tried to direct and control the environment through their mastery of information. Organizations involved in this pattern of realignment were striving for specialization through information mastery and to achieve rewards based on differentiated merit.

*Political coalitions* emerged in response to a *restricted environmental view*. Infrastructure and resource restrictions were considered limiting factors to attaining adequate market share and growth. Temporary ad hoc groups formed alliances and bargained with each other to insure their members the best possible access to limited rewards. These realignments resembled transitory webs which bound interests temporarily together and then were abandoned. The goal of this interorganizational pattern was zero-sub bargaining and oligopolistic control over limited shares of available resources.

Firms joined and supported federative *supraorganizational groups* to protect themselves from the perceived *threat of external regulation*. Industry members sought conjoined action in order to obtain with the least risk to themselves common protection against intervention into their affairs. The network organizational structure of supraorganizations was like a shield or umbrella, with the organization of power resembling both a federation and an oligarchy.

*Macrocooperative activities* were the most tentative and difficult both to identify and to portray. They emerged from culturally pervasive assumptions about the *congruent and highly interconnected goals* of business and government in promoting coal use. Business and government participated in joint activities to institutionalize, promote, and legitimate their mutually desired social values. This form of network organization was like a complex molecule or a geodesic dome with all parts related to each other in dynamic tension. The predominant characteristic of power exercised by firms in macrocooperative activities appeared to be the noblesse oblige of an aristocratic elite.

These layers of network realignment, which I likened to design overlays or theatrical lighting gels, are depicted schematically in Figures 10.1 and 10.2. Figure 10.2 shows how each schema was

**FIGURE 10.1. Simple Schematic Depiction of Interorganizational Network Patterns Showing Characteristic Arrangements**

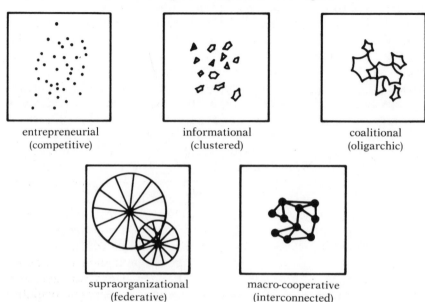

entrepreneurial
(competitive)

informational
(clustered)

coalitional
(oligarchic)

supraorganizational
(federative)

macro-cooperative
(interconnected)

changing during the course of my study. It is likely that these patterns could be found in other networks and could be used to analyze them.

## HOW DOES THIS STUDY RELATE TO GENERAL UNDERSTANDING OF NETWORK ANALYSIS?

Uncertainty is the usual explanation provided by management literature for why executives formulate strategies and for why organizations adapt to their environments in particular ways. Well-known theorists, such as Aldrich; Burns and Stalker; Chandler; Child; Emery and Trist, Hannan and Freedman; Lawrence and Lorsch; Pfiffer; and recently Lawrence and Dyer (1983), disagree over whether individual cognitive decisions or resource constraints and functionalities are stronger influences on organizational behavior; but their overall message is that organizations adjust themselves to external influences or they do not stay in business. The literature on organizational adaptation—borrowed from evolutionary biological systems—argues that environments select those organizations that will survive, placing them in specieslike niches, according to the effectiveness of relationships they establish with hostile outside forces.

**FIGURE 10.2.  Depiction of Dynamics
of Network Realignments**

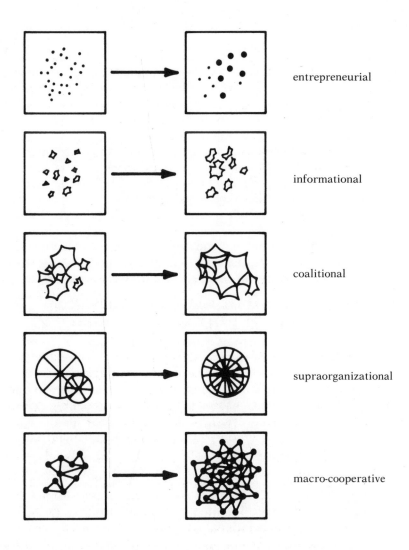

entrepreneurial

informational

coalitional

supraorganizational

macro-cooperative

Many of these theorists try to identify typological environmental characteristics that would help organizations identify how they should act most effectively. This is to stare into the wrong end of the telescope. Regardless of what environmental factors we are able to identify at a macrolevel, it is only after an industry or a firm has taken some strategic action that its environment is operationally defined. Then it places itself with respect to historical and economic situational contingencies *it* defines as important. Organizational actors make various parts of their environments germane through their acknowledgment and recognition of external conditions and the strategies they undertake to control them. Other parts they suppress or ignore. Analysts who place organizations in certain environments ultimately do so according to those organizations' current and past actions. They would place them elsewhere if different actions had been taken, and then a different environment would be defined. This is post hoc methodology. In fact, an environment that appears turbulent to one industry or firm may seem the reverse to another. Turbulence and uncertainty do not have known continuums. As metaphorically persuasive as these concepts are they are not adequate predictive explanations for what organizations actually do.

It is possible to get beyond the circularity of environment-organization causality by asking what specific factors business executives see as uncertain in concrete situations. New situations can be especially helpful for examining whether different kinds of uncertainties elicit different kinds of organizational and interorganizational responses. This study provides data about the variability of network responses in a specific case.

The study divides the vague, baggy concept of uncertainty into five specific problematic concerns. Each realignment pattern is distinctive and structurally unique. Each pattern shows organizations in interactive relationships where decision-making power is distributed in different ways. I have shown that strategic actions, network relationships, and the uncertainties from which they arise are more varied than previously acknowledged. My study illustrates a systematic method for disentangling complex network interactions based on simple schematics and presents a clearer vision of interorganizational power. Adaptation mechanisms in an evolving network are shown to be "neither automatic, nor uniform, nor unilateral" (Crozier and Friedberg, 1980: 96).

At the beginning of this study I portrayed general systems theory and management science as abstract and limited in their ability to convey and predict the complexities of interorganizational relationships. It now seems to me that I have not so much thrown out general systems theory as amplified it by emphasizing the need for contextual concreteness much previous literature has lacked.

This revision of network theory does not replace the important physical processes and material linkages that operate in a functional system, but it places information processing strategies in controlling positions as important drivers of social interactions.

Information flows and the interpretations of human actors are missing in conventional organization/environment theory. It is easy to forget that roles, functions, and even abstract processes like selection and retention are carried out by real people. Inclusion of the social action perspective as a modification of general systems theory acknowledges explicitly the instrumentality of human actors as shaping mechanisms in all organizational and social systems. Human actors with various levels of knowledge, goals, and interpretive capacities should be the basic units in organizational network analysis.

This focus links my work with a modification of general systems theory of which I was unaware while writing this study. Living systems theory as articulated by James Grier Miller (1978) is an attempt to map the basic processes of all living systems in terms of their exchanges of matter, energy, and information. Miller recognizes similarities among all living systems from the cell to the supranational system. Through coordinated study of these systems it may be possible to derive characteristics of health or pathology across levels. The two basic processes of all living systems according to living systems theory—matter/energy transfers and information transfers—seem to me to reconcile the general systems perspective and the criticisms of it outlined by Crozier and Friedberg. Conventional systems theory can give us good insight into matter/energy transfers; living systems theory adds to this the importance of a central information process that Miller calls "the decider." Although Miller explicitly rejects consciousness as necessary to the decider process, I find his emphasis on decoding, associating, encoding, and channeling information through networks compatible with my emphasis on personal interpretations and power as central to network structure. Living systems theory may be a parallel approach to that presented here for systematically mapping and measuring the structure of networks and accounting for interpretive nuances in them.

Like living systems theory, this study provides a set of concrete analytic categories for examining network relationships at different levels, and it suggests the kinds of behavior that accompany each type. Layers of interorganizational relationships can be separated or superimposed, systems and subsystems can be modeled or studied individually, and various single or cross-level hypotheses and explanations can be identified for further study. The structural-functional network of industry interactions that was portrayed in Figure 2.1 is amplified by building in dynamic, idiosyncratic, and multilayered information flows in the network that alter its arrangements and contextual meaning.

## ARE THE ANALYSES AND EXPLANATIONS IN THIS CASE STUDY GENERALIZABLE TO OTHER INDUSTRIES?

The main thrust of this research was to lay out the various styles of network interaction coal companies engaged in rather than to provide integrative interpretations of them. However, it is appropriate here to suggest several explanations that might bring these activities together and provide insight about other settings.

At its simplest level the study can be seen as confirmation of Michels' (1949) "iron law of oligarchy." Power flowed toward the largest firms with the greatest clout and control of social and material resources. Differentiation, democracy, aberrant opinions, and nonmodal practice showed signs of being pushed out of favorable positions in the network. Oligarchy and elitism were growing.

On the other hand, group interests were powerful and successful in articulating their needs and in bargaining effectively for what they wanted in a fluid situation. While the emerging situation was chaotic and institutionalization of routines was low, the field was relatively open for new participants, creative planning, and enactment of favorable influence positions both for new and old participants. The strongly opportunistic flavor of events was reminiscent of March and Olsen's (1979) garbage can model of organizational behavior. Solutions were looking for problems, and problems were redefined, ignored,or highlighted to fit the current strategic goals or operational systems participants had most readily at hand.

Coal people exercised a great deal of pragmatic, hit and miss, "satisficing" behavior in the absence of reliable factual data, as they attempted to exploit benefits from the anarchic situation. They exercised selective attention to problems and very soon were distracted to other concerns. In this setting the opportunities for bombast, hype, and unsupported promises were great, but so were the possibilities for emerging with new-found influence, technical mastery, and increased market share. One hypothesis might be: Because the systems of interaction were new, they proceeded more on strategic/situational or even personal criteria than on the basis of routines and established "accounts" for organizing intersubjective knowledge. As the network matures more stable patterns with less time spent on searches may emerge. This would follow from Zucker's (1977) work, which has shown that in an experimental situation persistence of a decision-making system depended upon the availability of institutionalized criteria ("shared accounts") for determining what a rational decision would be.

This insight suggests possibilities for follow-up in at least two directions. The criteria for choosing a particular interorganizational strategy in an evolving network could be explored through the economic notion of transactions costs. Calculation of the cost and benefit of obtaining information by applying resources oneself or through delegation or affiliation with another agency may lie behind choice of a particular interorganizational relationship. A hypothesis might be that interorganizational network patterns involving more members, more diffuse goals, and more complex internal decision structures will form as the expense and individual risk of desired information increase. This hypothesis could be tested in a variety of settings where, for example, deregulation of markets, new legislative requirements, or new product technologies have changed the basic rules of conduct in an interorganizational setting. Obvious industries for such analysis would be those with dynamic technologies and political vulnerabilities such as aerospace, chemicals, electronics, and communications or expanding service industries such as banking, airlines, hospitals, and processed foods.

The second direction for research would be to focus on longitudinal stages or interactive types of interorganizational networks. Types of patterns and their persistence, routinization, institutionalization, and innovation may vary significantly over time. This study already provides some evidence to suggest that each network pattern had a distinctive lifespan based on its interactive complexity and goals. This observation is consistent with the predictions of living systems theory. But it needs to be tested more thoroughly in measurement studies. The complexity and lifespans of network patterns could provide insights into organizational health, renewal, decline, and the mode of reproduction of complex networks. Perrow (1984) recently suggested that there may be pathologies or unrecognized complexities in certain systems that make them prone to error and to unanticipated breakdowns. Identifying these pathologies in interorganizational networks in advance of disastrous accidents would be a great benefit to industrial efficiency as well as to societal well-being.

Both these lines of research and other implications yet to be drawn show that the end of my study is a new beginning. It may be possible to unite functional studies of network interactions with concrete measures of the interpretive processs human actors use to decode and process information in a wide variety of comparable studies. Ideally, a body of knowledge will be developed that management scientists, sociologists, policymakers, and working managers can use as a reliable and persuasive system to address and integrate their common concerns.

# Theoretical Appendix

## A New Approach to Organizations and Their Environments

## THEORETICAL APPENDIX

This appendix discusses the theoretical paradigms on which most work on organizations and environments is based. Second, it describes the methods and assumptions of the emerging "social action perspective." In the last section I discuss my contribution to the social action perspective in this study.

## MAJOR PARADIGMS OF ORGANIZATION-ENVIRONMENT STUDIES

Organization-environment studies have drawn contributors from a wide variety of scholarly fields, including management studies, sociology, political science, social psychology, and to a lesser extent economics. In general, studies can be divided into two major strains: (1) the search for formal organizational theories (most heavily promoted by management faculties); and (2) the study of institutional (or industrial) sociology. Formal organizational theory is by far the predominant paradigm.[1]

Most *organization-environment theorists*, including both management scientists and structural-contingency sociologists, have proceeded from assumptions based on general systems theory. They have conceived of the organization-environment relationship as analogous to that of a living organism. They have sought to uncover laws of organization-environment interactions, whether in order to prescribe how to manage better, or to advance a "basic mechanics" of organizational behavior. In general, these systems theorists conceive of the organization nonpolitically—as neutral or passively responsive to a formative environmental medium which surrounds it. The model of living organisms they adopt is at a simple biological level: that of an amoeba, a human fetus, or a plant (Terreberry, 1968). Abstract dimensions borrowed from von Bertalanffy's (1950) general transport equation (equifinality, growth, self-regulation, constancy of direction) or Darwinian descriptors (variation, selection, retention; Aldrich, 1979) are used to describe organization-environment interactions, rather than the messier intentions, goals, and decisions of people. Descriptive categories attempt to identify whole-system characteristics.

The *institutional school of sociology*, had its heyday in the 1950s, though it is now making a slight comeback. This school emphasizes understanding organizational behavior in relation to the structure of the larger society. It relies on detailed case study research to draw out how larger social relations are writ small in contemporary institutions. This strain of work, at least among American sociologists, has been profoundly influenced by structural-functionalism (the intellectual precursor of general systems theory).

The two major strains of organization-environment studies have therefore approached the study of organizations and their environments differently. However, both of these traditions are alike in that each views the environment as an array of external, objective forces or events which exert causal force on a focal organization. Analytically they are traceable to the same intellectual roots.

## Approach 1: The Search for Formal Theory

The predominant strain of organization-environment studies has been deeply imbued with general and later open systems theory. Hence, concentration has been on contingency, interdependence, exchange, and adaptation of the system to the environment.[2] Whether studies have focused on linking the environment to changes in internal management and performance (as most have) or have studied external environments explicitly, they have proceeded from two basic assumptions inherent in systems theory: that the environment is, in principle, a reality of objective factors. In addition, many studies have proceeded as though the environment were empty uninhabited space outside the organization. (Network theory, which I will discuss later, is an advance over the latter approach, but it does not usually set aside systems theory's two basic assumptions.)

Aldrich and other population theorists argue that the environment acts pervasively on organizations. The organization essentially has no control over environmental variables (see Aldrich and Pfeffer, 1976). The search is for taxonomic categories to describe the environmental field and for universal laws to explain the regularity of environment-to organization adaptations. This approach does not place the organization in an interacting set of other organizations whose interactions with it and with each other *constitute* the environment.

Emery and Trist (1965) suggested that environments could be categorized according to characteristic interorganizational patterns of exchange, which they called "causal textures." They proposed a two-by-two matrix to categorize environmental textures on a continuum according to their degrees of motion and of predictability. Causal textures, they said, are the "determining conditions of the exchanges" among organizations in a particular environmental setting (30). In other words, environments—as a whole—can be classified, and their type determines the predominant type of interorganizational exchange that will take place. Emery and Trist identified four main causal textures of environments: placid-randomized, placid-clustered, disturbed-reactive, and turbulent. These basic categories have been elaborated and extended by many later theorists (for example, Jurkovitch, 1974; Shortell, 1977; Astley and Fombrun, 1983).

Emery and Trist explicitly embraced the systems paradigm of organization-environmental studies. Their analysis shifted attention usefully from research which had focused almost exclusively on the effects of the environment on internal management to consideration of the interactions in the field itself. However, by assuming that organizations are systems that must adapt themselves to a distinctive causal field in order to survive, Emery and Trist ushered in a period of more and more abstract explanations for organization-environment interactions: a development that was, interestingly, at odds with the very explicit case data that they presented in their seminal article.

In addition, Emery and Trist were infected with the notion that the environments of all organizations in the modern day are becoming more unpredictable and increasingly complex. Thus, they clouded from the outset whether their matrix was a taxonomy of environments that develops historically and sequentially or whether it was merely a classification scheme.

Work following Emery and Trist considered the "field" (Rogers, 1974), "social space" (Molnar, 1978), and "external perspective" (Breuer, 1978) that they emphasized. However, most researchers did not rethink the systems theory assumptions of organization-environment interactions. The contingency relationship between the environment and the organization was assumed to originate in the environment's characteristics, which it was also assumed could be homogeneously defined. Environmental characteristics were thought to exert formative control over interorganizational behavior. This image is explicit in the natural selection theorists such as Aldrich and Hannan and Freeman. It is less obvious but inherent in the assumptions of resource dependence theorists such as Pfeffer and Salancik, Benson, and Tushman. Much work in this tradition thus continues to search for convincing environmental classification schemes and ideal types of interaction. Robert Miles (1982) study of the tobacco industry is the most promising rethinking of the organization environment paradigm by an organizational theorist to be published lately.

## APPROACH 2: THE INSTITUTIONAL SCHOOL OF ORGANIZATIONAL SOCIOLOGY

Organizational sociology (as opposed to management-oriented formal organizational theory), has taken a slightly different approach. Organization-environment studies have included historical, institutional, and cultural (and a few economic and political) studies. These studies provide descriptive explanations of organization-environment interactions and have avoided systems theory's abstractions. For example, the works of Selznick, Gouldner, Touraine, Goldthorpe, Stinchcombe, Bell, Galbraith, and Lowi all dwell on descriptive organization-environment relationships. Researchers in this tradition insist on the importance of economic and political conditions and cultural values in shaping organizations and environments. Organizations, for them, reproduce the social relations of the world outside themselves. They reflect society, rather than exert control over it. The environment is not a vague outer realm. It is a set of organizations, ideas, and power struggles that impinge closely on a focal organization.

This "institutional" school and the Marxists (such as Heydebrand, Zeitz, and in his later years Gouldner) have adopted sweeping generalizations to describe the historical and cultural processes of which organizations are exemplifications. Organizations being embedded in society means that they are stamped with historical and developmental necessity which determine their form and future direction. Causal explanations by these writers often seem overdetermined by structural settings. Their explanations are constrained by the circular formalism of the structural-functionalist paradigm, in which structures are defined as "necessary" simply because they support tasks in a system. At their most extreme, the idiosyncratic perspectives of individuals are considered dysfunctional to the rationally ordered abstract roles by which the system works.

That environmental determinism remains alive and well in the institutional school can be seen in the recent work of DiMaggio and Powell (1983). They identify the environment as an "iron cage" containing three homeostatic network arrangements among organizations. My main objection to this approach is that it underestimates the complexity and variability of interorganizational relationships and the distinctiveness of human perception as influences on action. A mark of this is that virtually none of the interorganizational relationships identified by DiMaggio and Powell are network relationships important in my study.

Both the formal theorists and the institutional sociologists operate at very high levels of abstraction to draw their models and historical conclusions about interorganizational behavior. They tend to obscure the extent to which individual, often idiosyncratic, decisions and concrete interactions create important features of environmental settings.

## Network Theory

Network theory is an elaboration of organization-environment theory and has followed the same paradigms. As usually practiced, it is an application of open systems theory, although there are occasional uses of it which derive from the institutional (or "strategic") approach. The network of an organization is assumed to be all of the relevant actors with which an organization comes into contact and all of the relevant relationships in which it becomes involved. The systems researcher maps and measures network relationships, and searches the resulting data for general rules of interaction. Centrality (Levine, 1972), exchange (Cook, 1977), and interdependence (Litwak and Hylton, 1962; Aiken and Hage, 1968) are among the explanatory factors that systems researchers have identified as important in accounting for interorganizational network relationships. Although the approach has yielded some breakthroughs in use of sophisticated computer methodology and interesting descriptive statistics about interorganizational information flows, interlocked directorates, elite power, and patterns of communication; it has proven limited in its ability to capture the multiple layers that make up dynamic network interactions. Studies often seem far from the concerns of real-life interorganizational settings. So far, traditional systems models (even those employing complex path analysis) have not adequately portrayed the complex dynamics of network change or found a way to predict it.[3]

Very little research has been done in this tradition which focuses on how interorganizational networks change, although many writers call for more work in this area. Conceptual suggestions put forth (such as Metcalfe, 1981; Mitroff, Emshoff, and Kilman, 1979; Terreberry, 1968; Tichy, 1981) have been hard to operationalize in positivistically-driven measurement studies.

Relying on predefined boundaries and types of interactions and using cross-sectional data may be partial explanations for why network change has been difficult to study in the traditional paradigm, and for why explanatory factors found by systems-oriented network theorists have been extremely abstract and non-contextual. This research does not build up an empirical network from records and observations, but posits the network based on what is available to be measured.

Alba (1982) reflected recently that the promise seemingly posed by network theory in the early 1970s to illuminate the workings of interorganizational relationships has not been fulfilled. Too often sophisticated mathematical models have not been applied to important substantive questions, he says. The resulting studies have been disappointingly narrow and sometimes trivial, he says.

A few sociologists of the institutional school saw in the network concept an opportunity to revitalize study of organizations and environments in the context of cultural and historical influences on organizations. The relevant task environment (the network) could be studied as it interacted with strategic decision making and organizational goals. This notion was brought to the attention of institutional sociologists through the work of Warren (1967). Warren identified a variety of interactions engaged in by community decision agencies which had different decisional rules: all operating in one environment. Warren and like-minded researchers examine ongoing institutions contextually and build up a picture of network relationships. (See Hirsch, 1972; 1975b; Warren, Rose and Bergunder, 1974; Metcalf, 1976; Stern, 1979; Leblebici and Salancik, 1982; Perrow, 1984). For the institutional sociologists networks are concrete and process-oriented. They involve ongoing, politically-negotiated interactions brought about by resource constraints and task interdependencies but also by the goals and preferences and strategic decisions of organizational actors. Charles Perrow, Hirsch, Silverman, Scott, Benson, and Zeitz are among those who have urged that interorganizational networks be studied in political, historical, economic, and even social-psychological or linguistic terms. This study falls in that tradition. This approach is promising because it attempts to identify specific types or patterns of interaction in the interorganizational field from direct evidence and to examine their processes before we attempt to measure or infer predictors of change.

Yet, when trying to account for institutional change in interorganizational relationships, even the institutional sociologists rarely push their explanations to the point that would allow them to attribute the form interorganizational relationships are taking to perceptions organizational actors have about the environment. Thus, they typically stop short of proposing an alternative model for explaining organization-to-environment relationships that accounts for both historical circumstances and individual perceptual variability.

## Contribution of Phenomenology to Organization-Environment Studies

One departure from the systems-oriented and functionalist paradigms discussed above is the phenomenological approach to organizational network theory. This approach originated in social psychology, popularized by Weick (1979). It was applied to organization-environment studies by Evan (1966), but to my knowledge has not been the basis for empirical organization-environment research. Most studies have emphasized internal self-perceptions and ethnography rather than internal-to-external relationships (for example, see Manning, 1979).

The approach draws on philosophical phenomenology (Schutz; Cicourell; Berger and Luckmann), role theory (Merton), and perception theory (Goffman; Homans; Mead) to emphasize a perspective inside the individual actor, who projects, enacts, or chooses his own environment. Applying this orientation to organizational environments, Evan argues that the organization chooses the set of relevant organizations with which it will interact: its organization set. Phenomenologists have tried to insert into organization-environment study the crucial role played by human judgment, motivation, and interpretation in determining "reality." They challenge traditional formal theorists by arguing that the environment is not singular, not separated by definite boundaries from the people who observe it.

This approach identified a new direction for organization-environment studies, but in their theories the phenomenologists have essentially found no place for the influence of historical and economic factors and for the machinations of organized power. They have trouble accounting for how enactments become integrated into cooperative behavior which exhibits itself as institutional strategy or rules of operation. The phenomenologists proceed from such a subjectivist philosophy that they do not show us how coordinated judgments can come about and can become focused on larger political goals. Hence, their otherwise powerful suggestions have limited applicability for explaining macro-organizational behavior.

## THE SOCIAL ACTION PERSPECTIVE

An emerging "social action perspective" which is being developed as a practical sociology by the European sociologists Michael Crozier, Erhard Friedberg, and Lucien Karpik is directing researchers to unite individual perspectives with macrostructural issues. Although the social action perspective lays aside the search for general organizational theory of the formal, systems-theory variety, it attempts to unite the historico-structural and phenomenological approaches to organization-environment studies.

The premises of the social action perspective are that all organizational behavior is socially constructed. Any analysis of relationships must be traceable ultimately to the decisions, perspectives, and assumptions of people. How close we can get to individual assumptions, i.e., whether we must generalize from firms, coalitions, groups, or departments is a practical matter of the available data and the placement and resources of the particular researcher. Theoretically macrorelationships can be reduced to a series of individual perceptions and decisions which are integrated into larger and larger decisional units through hierarchical or cooperative organizational structures and routines.

Organizations and their environments are intercausal, not because of historical and economic necessity or inevitability, or some inherent rationality operating in history, but because decisions about action are the results of individual strategies and depend upon how participants interpret their power positions with respect to historical circumstances and physical resources in a particular "game" that they are playing. The environment, therefore, is both a physical setting and a sum of enactments about it. External conditions do not impose themselves directly on organizations or on organizational actors. They must be mediated by human interpretations of events. This intermediate interpolation and selection of historical factors designates them "the environment" for organizational actors. The interorganizational network is the sum total of these strategic relationships. History and economics are important structural influences, but they must be formulated into strategic actions to become meaningful to an organization.

*Origins.* The indirect origins of the social action perspective can be found in the comparative historical and inductive methods used by Max Weber (1949) and Charles Perrow (1961).[4] These writers considered human goals and perspectives essential to understanding the relationships between institutions and their settings. For example, Perrow (1961; 1968) asks us to observe a distinction between official and "operative" goals as observed through actual behavior. Selznick makes us vitally aware of the idiosyncratic way organizational leaders shaped the environment of TVA. The social action perspective revives a stance similar to that taken by early writers on organizational history, strategy, and decision making, such as Barnard, Chandler, Child, and Simon. A characteristic of this research was that organizational decisions and strategies were shown to be multiply-influenced and based upon incomplete perceptions and "satisficing" renditions of reality. The researcher had to pay particular attention to sources of information, because the way actors behaved, what they said, and the documents they prepared were the results of the goals they were trying to achieve. Documents—and sometimes the lack of documents—are important sources of interpretative information. (One impressive use of this approach, although not by an organizational theorist, was Allison's (1971) interpretations of the Cuban missile crisis.)

*Methods.* The implications of the "social action perspective" as stated by Crozier, Friedberg, and Karpik are that organizational studies should be conducted in institutional context, with rich descriptions, and explanations unique to the particular setting. Generalizations and conclusions, too, should not be overdrawn. The formulation of universal laws is put aside. Definitions of settings should not be assumed, but become the subjects of critical empirical inquiry.

*Crozier and Friedberg.* According to Crozier and Friedberg (1980) the rules of the "game" being played must be analytically reconstructed from observable events, formal statements of actors, documents, and interpretive interviews or observations, getting as close to individual actors as possible. The goal, however, is not merely to describe subjective reality as actors experience it as in the phenomenological approach but to derive the institutional rule of action (what Karpik has called the "logic of action") operable in a given situation. In the social action perspective, therefore, attitudes expressed by organizational participants are not primarily seen as signs of personality but as indicators of that individual's resource position and goals. In other words, statements and documents are valuable tracings for who is winning whatever interorganizational game is being played and for how institutionally a particular game is viewed. Attitudes in hierarchical companies are interpreted as more significantly manifesting the strategies firms have adopted than the personalities of speakers. The question of individual motivation in the psychological sense is less important than the strategic goals and positioning that individuals and firms seek, because the research question focuses on how organizational constraints and resource positions influence action rather than on whether or not individuals are actualizing themselves. Attitudes are redefined by Crozier and Friedberg from being insights into a subject's past experience to being signs of the strategic assessments actors hold about the opportunities offered in present time for strategic action in the future (see Crozier and Friedberg, 1980: 264–72). By analyzing contextual data in this way, the researcher reconstructs interorganizational situations and can see the kinds of power relationships which are occurring.

Crozier and Friedberg (1980) set aside the distinction between the organization and the environment. What kind of environment exists outside an organization is much less important than the specific types of relationships actors establish inside and outside of the organization to convey resources and establish mutual strategies or routines. According to Crozier and Friedberg there are no objective sources of uncertainty. Sources of uncertainty become significant only when invested in by actors pursuing particular ends.

The social action perspective tends to emphasize relative autonomy and freedom of strategic decisions as opposed to the determinative causality of resource constraints and historical factors. Organization-environment relations are conceived of as in a continuous process of realignment among internal and external actors. According to Crozier and Friedberg,

> Our model is clearly quite different from one in which changes within the environment bring about corresponding changes within the organization. If adaptation takes place, it is neither automatic, nor uniform, nor unilateral. (p. 96)

Still, human action is not wholly free.

> The problem is to . . . elaborate a *research methodology* that will reveal the material, structural, and human conditions of the context which limit and define the actor's freedom and rationality. Then the meaning of his empirically observable behavior can be determined. (p. 24)

*Karpik's approach.* Lucien Karpik espouses the same general social action perspective as Crozier and Friedberg. The organization and the environment are considered interpermeable (1972, 1977, 1978; Weiss, 1981). Karpik, however, is more concerned than Crozier and Friedberg to apply the social action perspective to inductive generalizations about macrosociological issues, particularly the place of important industries in contemporary society. (In some ways he shares this goal for social research with the important French sociologist, Alain Touraine.)

Karpik is interested in focusing on the strategies of top leaders within interacting organizations and in reconstructing from their statements and from observations of their actions the underlying perspectives and rules of operation of large-scale, important industries. In this way, he feels, we can obtain a believable rationale and explanation for macrosociological events. This rationale may not totally supplant intermediate explanations such as those based on resource dependence, organizational stress, or organizational climates and routines, but it provides an overarching explanation which contains them.

Karpik says that the characteristic approaches of organizational leaders embody unique institutional rationalities, their "logics of action" (1972). From the actions and statements of leaders we can reliably induce their perspectives and, more importantly, the operational assumptions of their institutions. Thus, from the actions and statements of leaders one can extrapolate to the "logics of action" of the organizational units for which they speak, such as entire firms or perhaps even industries. There is a problem of extrapolating too quickly from individual to group goals using this approach. Carefully used it can get us much closer to the operative assumptions behind organized action than a method that predefines organizational goals and interorganizational boundaries. By reconstructing logics of action we come to understand why organizations establish various relationships with each other, how they view their options in the interorganizational field, and what various interorganizational relationships mean. Karpik also reminds us that the analysts should not stop there. The actions of organizations should be examined for their linkages to new arrangements of social power.

The form of interorganization power becoming prevalent Karpik calls "technological capitalism." It bears some resemblance to the complex interconnected environment Emery and Trist and Metcalfe have identified as "turbulent," and to the pervasive assumptions of interconnectedness that I found accompanied macrocooperation.

Karpik is greatly interested in the economic relationships that occur in technological capitalism. He calls the capacity both to produce goods and to create (or impose) the market for their consumption the characteristic feature of multinational organizations in advanced technological industries. "What characterizes large enterprise is the political capacity for omnipresent intervention and extension of the field of strategic interdependence" (1977: 52).

The examples Karpik gives of technological industries are international arms and information technology, in which the interests of nation-states, business enterprise, and consumers become inseparable through reliance on science. The nation-state's position as a client for a unique and highly desired product overwhelms its interest as a regulator and effectively places it in a position of collaboration with the expansionist values of private industry.

Karpik's insight is important to this study because the coal industry is just entering a time when exercise of control over macrosocial values might become feasible for it. Although coal is a crucial element for electricity production, it is so abundant, so widely distributed, and so easy to extract that nation-states have maintained easy dominance over their national industries. However, as electricity demand grows, coal resources become depleted in industrialized nations other than the United States, and as problems like acid rain become global, the U.S. coal industry will gain in world strategic importance and the interests of these energy producers and nation states may merge.

## USE OF THE SOCIAL ACTION PERSPECTIVE
## IN THIS STUDY

I have shown that a methodology based on the social action perspective can be applied successfully to study the network of a large, internationally important industry. The method provides insights about the dynamics and information of interorganizational networks that help us refine theoretical explanations of them, particularly when they are undergoing fundamental change.

I identified five views of the environment that formed separate "logics of action" for distinctive interorganizational network patterns. Attitudes about the specific kind of uncertainty the coal industry faced led organizations to engage in specific realignments of their network to address that uncertainty.

The interorganizational network was in continuous process of realignment, with different flows of information, search procedures, and strategies operating simultaneously. The types or realignments I identified constituted separate layers of interaction and provide an analytic model for systematic network analysis. Each layer needs to be disassembled and reassembled to understand the network. Each layer was individually provocative, but in itself was incomplete.

1. *Entrepreneurial activities* led to increased one-on-one competitiveness; autonomous network behavior; a relatively chaotic but democratic free market.

2. *New sources of information* and expertise led to specialization and more clustered associations with providers of expertise; new affiliational relationships developed.

3. *Coalitional activities* led to temporary alliances and bargaining among oligarchically striving ad hoc groups; market control was a network objective.

4. *Supraorganizational activities* protected and shielded the industry, through federative associations, from external interference; federative-style decision making was often controlled behind the scenes by powerful groups.

5. *Macrocooperative activities* led to institutionalizing political values supportive of coal use and trade; some evidence indicated that elitism and aristocratic leadership for the entire industry was emerging.

No single or predominant style of interorganizational interaction characterized the interorganizational field. The various chapters of the case study showed that in the coal industry a multiplicity of styles of network interaction occurred simultaneously. This layered analytic approach, that brings individual perceptions and network structural relationships into close proximity, provides a method that can be applied in diverse interorganizational situations.

## NOTES TO THEORETICAL APPENDIX

1. Until the past five years the institutional school of sociology had been considered by many organizational scholars a moribund tradition. Its qualitative case studies were thought to have little to offer modern researchers with their sophisticated quantitative analysis techniques. References to these studies are omitted in many important literature reviews on organizations and environments such as Aldrich and Pfeffer, 1976; Aldrich and Whetten, 1981; Starbuck in Dunnette, 1976.

2. Some well-known systems theories of organization-environment interaction include: Burns and Stalker, 1961; Levine and White, 1961; Lawrence and Lorsch, 1967; Haas and Drabek, 1973; Cook, 1977; and Katz and Kahn, 1978.

3. A partial exception may be the cybernetic models based on operations research and rational decision theory. However, these do not predict and describe change in real networks as much as they model the relationships which *ought* to exist in an economically rational world (see Wollmer, 1980). Such models are most helpful for making decisions involving concrete variables such as investments, production scheduling, and military logistics. They are less powerful in predicting information flows and degrees of interdependence which can be politically deflected.

4. Discussion of the origins of the social action perspective is indebted to Weiss, in Zey-Ferrell and Aiken, 1981, and to lecture presentations by Michael Aiken at Washington University, fall 1982.

# Bibliography

References to specific sources (both primary and secondary) are noted in brief form in parentheses in the text. Except for personal conversations, they refer to documents listed in the Bibliography. References cite a document in the way that will make it most easily and quickly locatable in the Bibliography. For example, hearings of the U.S. Senate Committee on Energy and Natural Resources are cited "Senate, Energy" with the date and relevant page number. The full reference can be found in the Bibliography section "Public Documents" under U.S. Senate, Committee on Energy and Natural Resources.

Also, in the interest of both brevity and clarification, magazine and newspaper articles are cited in both the text and Bibliography according to their corporate origins rather than by their particular author or title (i.e., *Business Week*, not Petzinger, and not "Coal—Strike Bound"). This format, although unconventional, seemed more accurate, since it was often more important to know that a particular source was publishing articles on coal trade than who wrote the particular piece or how it was headlined.

## ORGANIZATIONAL THEORY

Aiken, M., & Hage, J. (1968). Organizational interdependence and interorganizational structure. *American Sociological Review, 33,* 912–30.

Alba, R. D. (1982). Taking stock of network analysis: A decade's results. In S. B. Bacharach (Ed.), *Research in the sociology of organizations: Vol. 1* (pp. 39–74). Greenwich, Conn.: JAI Press.

Aldrich, H. E. (1979). *Organizations and environments.* Englewood Cliffs, N.J.: Prentice-Hall.

Aldrich, H.E., & Pfeffer, J. (1976). Environments of organizations. In A. Inkeles, J. Coleman, & N. Smelser (Eds.), *Annual review of sociology: Vol. 2* (pp. 79–105). Palo Alto, Calif.: Annual Reviews, Inc.

Aldrich, H., & Whetten, D.A. (1981). Organization sets, action sets, and networks: Making the most of simplicity. In P.C. Nystrom and W.H. Starbuck (Eds.), *Handbook of organizational design: Vol. 1* (pp. 385–408). London: Oxford University Press.

Allison, G.T. (1971). *Essence of decision: Explaining the Cuban missile crisis.* Boston: Little, Brown.

Astley, W.G., & Fombrun, C.J. (1983). Collective strategy: The social ecology of organizational environments. *Academy of Management Review, 8,* 576–87.

Barnard, C.I. (1983). *The functions of the executive.* Cambridge, Mass: Harvard University Press.

Barnet, R.J. & Muller, R.E. (1974). *Global reach: The power of the multinational corporation*. New York: Simon & Schuster.

Bell, D. (1973). *The coming of post industrial society: A venture in social forecasting*. New York: Basic Books.

Benson, J.D. (1975). The interorganizational network as a political economy. *Administrative Science Quarterly, 20*, 229–49.

Benson, J.K. (1977). Innovation and crisis in organizational analysis. *Sociological Quarterly, 18*, 3–16.

Berger, P.S., & Luckmann, T. (1967). *The social construction of reality*. Garden City, N.Y.: Doubleday/Anchor.

Breurer, F. (1978). De Interorganisationele Analyse [Interorganizational Analysis]. *Mens en Onderneming, 32*, 32–44 (Dutch).

Burns, T., & Stalker, G.M. (1961). *The management of innovation*. London: Tavistock.

Chandler, A.D., Jr. (1962). *Strategy and structure: Chapters in the history of the industrial enterprise*. Cambridge, Mass.: MIT Press.

Child, J. (1972). Organizational structure, environment and performance: The role of strategic choice. *Sociology, 6*, 1–22.

Cicourell, A.V. (1973). Meaning in social interaction. *Cognitive sociology*. Harmondsworth, Eng.: Penguin.

Clark, B.R. (1965). Interorganizational patterns in education. *Administrative Science Quarterly, 10*, 224–37.

Cook, K.S. (1977). Exchange and power in networks of interorganizational relations. *The Sociological Quarterly, 18*, 62–82.

Crozier, M. (1964). *The bureaucratic phenomenon*. Chicago: University of Chicago Press.

Crozier, M.(1972). The relationship between micro and macro sociology. *Human Relations 25*, 239–51.

Crozier, M., & Friedberg, E. (1980). *Actors and systems*. Chicago: University of Chicago Press.

DiMaggio, P.J., & Powell, W.W. (1983). The iron cage revisited: Institutional isomorphism and collective rationality in organizational field. *American Sociological Review, 48*, 147–60.

Emery, F.E., & Trist, E.L. (1965). The causal texture of organizational environments. *Human Relations, 18*, 21–31.

Evan, W.M. (1966). The organization-set: Toward a theory of interorganizational relations. In J.D. Thompson (Ed.), *Approaches to organizational design*, (pp. 174–91). Pittsburgh: University of Pittsburgh Press.

Galbraith, J.K. (1967). *The new industrial state*. Boston: Houghton-Mifflin.

Goffman, E. (1958). *Presentation of self in everyday life*. Edinburgh: University of Edinburgh.

Goldthorpe, J.H. (1968). *The affluent worker: Industrial attitudes and behavior*. Cambridge: Cambridge University Press.

Gouldner, A.W. (1954). *Patterns of industrial bureaucracy*. New York: The Free Press.

Gouldner, A.W. (1979). *The future of intellectuals and the rise of the new class*. New York: Seabury.

Haas, J.E., & Drabeck, T.E. (1973). *Complex organizations: A sociological perspective*. New York: Macmillan.

Hannan, M., & Freeman, J. (1977). The population ecology of organizations. *American Journal of Sociology, 82,* 929–64.

Heydebrand, W.V. (Ed.). (1973). *Complex organizations: The results of empirical research.* Englewood Cliffs, N.J.: Prentice-Hall.

Hirsch, P.M. (1972). Processing fads and fashions by cultural industry systems: An organization-set analysis. *American Journal of Sociology, 77,* 639–59.

Hirsch, P. [M.] (1975). Organizational analysis and industrial sociology. *American Sociologist, 10,* 3–10. a.

Hirsch P.M. (1975). Organizational effectiveness and the institutional environment. *Administrative Science Quarterly, 20,* 327–44. b.

Homans, G. (1950). *The human group.* New York: Harcourt Brace.

Jurkovich, R. (1974). A core typology of organizational environments. *Administrative Science Quarterly, 19,* 380–94.

Karpik, L. (1977). Technological capitalism. In S. Clegg & D. Dunkerley (Eds.), *Critical issues in organizations* (pp. 41–71). London: Routledge & Kegan Paul.

Karpik, L. (1978). Organizations, institutions, and history. In L. Karpik (Ed.), *Organization and environment: Theory, issues, and reality.* (pp. 15–68). Beverly Hills, Calif.: Sage.

Katz, D., & Kahn, R.L. (1978). *The social psychology of organizations.* (2nd ed.). New York: Wiley.

Lawrence, P.R., & Dyer, D. (1983). *Renewing American industry.* New York: The Free Press.

Lawrence, R.R., & Lorsch, J.W. (1967). *Organization and environment.* Boston: Harvard Business School.

Leblebici, H., & Salancik, G.R. (1982). Stability in interorganizational exchanges: Rulemaking processes of the Chicago Board of Trade. *Administrative Science Quarterly, 27,* 227-42.

Levine, J.H. (1972). The sphere of influence. *American Sociological Review, 37,* 14–27.

Levine, S., & White, P.E. (1961). Exchange as a conceptual framework for the study of interorganizational relationships. *Administrative Science Quarterly, 5,* 583–601.

Litwak, E., & Hylton, L.F. (1962). Interorganizational analysis: A hypothesis on coordinating agencies. *Administrative Science Quarterly, 6,* 395–420.

Lowi, T.J. (1979). *The end of liberalism: The second republic of the United States* (2nd ed.). New York: Norton.

Manning, P.K. (1979). *Police work.* Cambridge, Mass: MIT Press.

March, J.G., & Olsen, J.P. (1979). *Ambiguity and choice in organizations* (2nd ed.). Bergen, Norway: Universitetsforlaget.

Mead, G.H. (1967). *Mind self and society.* Chicago: University of Chicago Press. Original work published 1934.

Merton, R.K. (1968). *Social theory and social structures.* New York: The Free Press. Original work published 1949.

Metcalfe, J.L. (1974). Systems models, economic models, and the causal texture of organizational environments: An approach to macro-organization theory. *Human Relations, 27,* 639–63.

Metcalfe, J.L. (1976). Organizational strategies and interorganizational networks. *Human Relations, 29,* 327–43.

Metcalfe, [J.] L. (1978). Policy-making in turbulent environments. In K. Hanf & F.W. Scharpf (Eds), *Interorganizational policy-making: Limits to coordination and central control.* London: Sage.

Metcalfe, [J.] L. (1981), Designing precarious partnerships. In P.C. Nystrom & W.H. Starbuck (Eds.), *Handbook of organizational design: Vol. 1 (pp. 503–530).* London: Oxford University Press.

Michels, R. (1949). *Political parties: A sociological study of the oligarchiel tendencies of modern democracy.* New York: The Free Press.

Miles, R. [H.] (1982). *Coffin nails and corporate strategies.* Englewood Cliffs, N.J.: Prentice-Hall.

Miller, J.G. (1978). *Living systems.* New York: McGraw-Hill.

Mitroff, I., Emshoff, J.R., & Kilman, R.H. (1979). Assumptional analysis: A methodology for strategic problem solving. *Management Science, 25,* 583–93.

Molnar, J.J. (1978). Comparative organizational properties and interorganizational interdependence. *Sociology and Socal Research, 63,* 24–48.

Pearce, D.W. (Ed.). (1981). *The dictionary of modern economics.* Cambridge, Mass.: The MIT Press.

Perrow, C. (1961). Goals in complex organizations. *American Sociological Review, 26,* 854–65.

Perrow, C. (1979). *Complex organizations: A critical essay* (2nd ed.). Glenville, Ill.: Scott Foresman.

Perrow, C. (1984). *Normal Accidents.* New York: Basic Books.

Pfeffer, J., & Salancik, G.R. (1978). *The external control of organizations: A resource dependence perspective.* New York: Harper & Row.

Rogers, D.L. (1974). Sociometric analysis of interorganizational relations: Application of theory and measurement. *Rural Sociology, 39,* 487–503.

Samuelson, P.A. (1973). *Economics* (9th ed.). New York: McGraw-Hill.

Schutz, A. (1967). *A phenomenology of the social world* (G. Walsh & F. Lehnert, Trans.). Evanston, Ill.: Northwestern University Press.

Scott, B. (1979). The organizational network: A strategy perspective for development. *Dissertation Abstracts International.* 40–9, 5114–A. *(University Microfilms No. 8006513).*

Selznick, P. (1949). *TVA and the grassroots.* Berkeley: University of Calif. Press.

Selznick, P. (1959). *Leadership in administration.* New York: Harper & Row.

Shortell, S.M. (1977). The role of environment in a configurational theory of organization. *Human Relations, 30,* 275–302.

Silverman, D. (1968). Formal organizations or industrial sociology: Towards a social action analysis of organizations. *Sociology, 2,* 221–38.

Silverman, D. (1970). *The theory of organizations.* London: Heinemann.

Simon, H.A. (1957). *Administrative behavior.* New York: Macmillan.

Starbuck, W. (1976). Organizations and their environments. In M.D. Dunnette (Ed.), *Handbook of industrial and organizational psychology* (pp. 1069–123). Chicago: Rand McNally.

Stern, R.N. (1979). The development of an interorganizational control network: The case of intercollegiate athletics. *Administrative Science Quarterly, 24,* 242–266.

Stinchcombe, A.L. (1965). Social structure and organizations. In J.G. March (Ed.), *Handbook of organizations* (pp. 142–93). Chicago: Rand McNally.

Terreberry, S. (1968). The evolution of organizational environments. *Administrative Science Quarterly, 12,* 590–613.

Tichy, N.M. (1981). Networks in organizations. In P.C. Nystrom & W.H. Starbuck, *Handbook of organizational design: Vol. 2.* (pp. 225–49). London: Oxford University Press.

Touraine, A. (1971). The firm: Power, institution, and organization. In A. Touraine, *The post-industrial society.* New York: Random House.

Turk, H. (1977). *Organizations in modern life: Cities and other large networks.* San Francisco: Jossey-Bass.

Tushman, M.L. (1977). A political approach to organizations: A review and rationale. *Academy of Management Review, 2,* 206–216.

Van de Ven, A.H.,Walker, C., & Liston, J. (1979). Coordination patterns within an interorganizational network. *Human Relations, 32,* 19–36.

von Bertalanffy, L. (1950). The theory of open systems in physics and biology. *Science, 111,* 23–28.

Warren, R.L. (1967). The interorganizational field as a focus for investigation. *Administrative Science Quarterly, 12,* 396–419.

Warren, R., Rose, S., & Bergunder, A. (1974). *The structure of urban reform.* Lexington, Mass.: Lexington Press.

Weber, M. (1947). *The theory of social and economic organization.* (T.Parsons, Ed, A.M. Henderson & T Parsons, Trans.). New York: The Free Press. Original work published c. 1919.

Weick, K.E. (1979). *The social psychology of organizing* (2nd ed.). Reading, Mass.: Addison-Wesley.

Weiss, J.W. (1981). The historical and political perspective on organizations of Lucien Karpik. In M. Zey-Ferrell & M. Aiken (Eds.), *Complex organizations: Critical perspectives* (pp. 392–95). Glenview, Ill.: Scott Foresman.

Wollmer, R.D. (1980). Investment in stochastic minimum cost generalized multicommodity networks with application to coal transport. *Networks, 10,* 351–62.

Zald, M.N. (1981). Political economy: A framework for comparative analysis. In M.Zev-Ferrell & M. Aiken (Eds.)., *Complex organizations: Critical perspectives* (pp. 237–62). Glenview, Ill.: Scott Foresman. (Originally published in M.N. Zald, *Power in organizations,* 1970).

Zeitz, G. (1980). Interorganizational dialectics. *Administrative Sciences Quarterly, 25,* 72–88.

Zucker, L.G. (1977). The role of institutionalization in cultural persistence. *American Sociological Review, 42,* 726–43.

## SECONDARY WORKS ON COAL, ENERGY, AND RELATED INDUSTRIES

Ackerman, B.A., & W.T. Hassler, (1981). *Clean coal/dirty air: Or how the Clean Air Act became a multibillion dollar bail-out for high sulfur coal producers and what should be done about it.* New Haven: Yale University Press.

Barnett, R.J. (1980). *The lean years: World resources and the politics of scarcity.* New York: Simon & Schuster.

Bartlett, A.A. (1979, Sept.). Forgotten fundamentals of the energy crisis. *Mineral and energy resources: A review of developments.* Publication of Colorado School of Mines, 22, 5, entire issue.

Binkley, J., & Shabman, L. (1980, Dec.) Implications of recent user charge legislation for barge transportation of agricultural commodities. *Southern Journal of Agricultural Economics,* pp. 117–23.

Blair, J.M. (1976). *The control of oil.* New York: Vintage.

Chakravarthy, B.S. (1981). *Managing coal: A challenge in adaptation.* Albany: State University of N.Y. Press.

Charles River Associates, Inc. (1976). *Cartelization in the world energy market: A draft report.* Unpublished manuscript.

Congressional Quarterly, Inc. (1981, March). *Energy policy* (2nd ed.). Washington, D.C.: Congressional Quarterly.

Duchesneau, T.D. (1975). *Competition in the U.S. energy industry.* Report to the Energy Policy Project of the Ford Foundation. Cambridge, Mass.: Ballinger.

Gordon, R.L. (1970). *Evolution of energy policy in Western Europe: The reluctant retreat from coal.* New York: Praeger.

Gordon, R.L. (1975). *U.S. coal and the electric power industry.* Prepared for Resources for the Future, Inc. Baltimore: The Johns Hopkins University Press.

Horwitch, M. (1979). Coal: Constrained abundance. In R. Stobaugh & D. Yergin (Eds.), *Energy future: Report of the Energy Project of the Harvard Business School.* New York: Random House.

Johnson, J.P. (1979). *The politics of soft coal: The bituminous industry from World War I through the New Deal.* Urbana, Ill.: University of Illinois Press.

Kohl, W.L. (1982). *After the second oil crisis: Energy politics in Europe, America, and Japan.* Lexington, Mass.: Lexington Books.

Lapedes, D.N. (Ed.). (1976). *Encyclopedia of energy.* New York: McGraw-Hill.

*The million dollar directory.* (1983). Vol. 1. Parsippany, New Jersey: Dun's Marketing Services.

Morgan, D. (1980). *Merchants of grain.* New York: Penguin.

Moyer, R. (1964). Competition in the midwestern coal industry. Cambridge, Mass.: Harvard University Press.

Moyer, R. (1975). Price-output behavior in the coal industry. In T.D. Duchesneau (Ed.), *Competition in the U.S. energy industry.* Cambridge, Mass.: Ballinger.

*National Trade and Professional Associations of the U.S.* (1983). Washington, D.C.: Columbia Books.

Newcomb, R. (1978). The American coal industry. *Current History,* 74, 206–9.

Reid, T.R. (1980). *Congressional odyssey: The saga of a senate bill.* San Francisco: W.H. Freeman.

Risser, H.E. (1958). *The economics of the coal industry.* Lawrence, Kan.: Bureau of Business Research, School of Business, University of Kansas.

Sampson, A. (1975). *The seven sisters: The great oil companies and the world they made.* London: Hodder & Stoughton.

Schenker, E., & Brockel, H.C. (1974). *Port planning and development as related to problems of U.S. ports and the U.S. coastal environment.* Cambridge, Md.: Cornell Maritime Press, Inc.

*Ulrich's international periodical directory.* (1982). New York: Bowker.

Vietor, R.H.K. (1980). *Environmental politics and the coal coalition.* College Station, Tex.: Texas A & M University Press.

Wadleigh, F.R. (1926). International trade in coal. *Annals of the American Academy, 127,* 102–111.

*World Coal Study.* (1980). (Vols. 1 and 2). Cambridge, Mass.: Ballinger. (Cited in text WOCOL).

## PUBLIC DOCUMENTS

I.C.F., Inc. (1980, Aug.). *The prospects for world coal trade: An analysis and review of the literature.* Prepared for the Interagency Coal Export Task Force. Washington, D.C. Available through U.S. Department of Energy Public Information Reading Room.

International Energy Agency. (1980, Dec.). *Report of the IEA Coal Advisory Board.* Paris: Organisation for Economic Cooperation and Development.

International Energy Agency. (1981, Aug. 25). *Coal prospects and policies in IEA countries.* Working paper. Paris: OECD.

U.S. Congress. (1981). *Proposed bills: Port and Navigation Improvement Act of 1981 and sundry titles.* 97th Congress, 1st sess. S 68, S 202, S 576, S 809, S 828, S 1389, S 1692, HR 55, HR 636, HR 4627. Committee prints.

U.S. Congress. *Congressional Record.* (1980, Dec. 5). 96th Congress, 2nd sess., Senate. Coal port crisis: A crucial federal initiative, *126* (171), pp. 1–6.

U.S. Congress. Congressional Research Service. The Library of Congress. (1980, Sept. 12). *Background on coal export problems.* Prepared at request of Senate Committee on Energy and Natural Resources. Xerox.

U.S. Congress. Congressional Research Service. The Library of Congress. (1981, June 26). *Port user fee—based on the turnover of vessel-carried U.S. foreign trade.* Xerox.

U.S. Congress. Congressional Research Service. The Library of Congress. (1981, Sept.). *A Congressional handbook on U.S. materials import dependency/vulnerability.* Report to Subcommittee on Economic stabilization, House Committee on Banking, Finance and Urban Affairs. 97th Congress, 1st sess. Committee print 97-6. (Cited CRS, *A Congressional Handbook*).

U.S. Congress. House. Committee on Government Operations. (1980, Aug.). *Twentieth report: Adequacy of the federal response to foreign investment in the United States.* 96th Congress, 2nd sess. Hearing record.

U.S. Congress. House. Committee on Interstate and Foreign Commerce. (1980, May 20). *Final report of the World Coal Study, "Coal—bridge to the future."* 96th Congress, 2nd sess., Serial No. 96-149. Hearing record.

U.S. Congress. House. Committee on Interstate and Foreign Commerce. (1980, Dec. 17). *Coal transportation problems in the midwest.* 96th Congress, 2nd sess. Serial No. 96-238. Hearing record.

U.S. Congress. House. Committee on Interior and Insular Affairs. (1981, May 7, July 16). *Foreign takeovers of U.S. mining firms.* 97th Congress, 1st sess., on HR 2826. Hearing record.

U.S. Congress. House. Committee on Merchant Marine and Fisheries. (1981, April 24; May 22, 26; July 16, 22, 28; Sept. 10). *Port development: Parts 1–2.* 97th Congress, 1st sess. Serial Nos. 97-23, 97-25. Hearing record.

U.S. Congress. House. Committee on Merchant Marine and Fisheries. (1982, Mar. 9). *Committee Report 97-454 Part 1: Port development.* 97th Congress, 2nd sess. Committee report.

U.S. Congress. House. Committee on Public Works and Transportation. (1981, June 16, 17; July 14, 15). *Port development.* 97th Congress, 1st sess. Serial No. 97-26. Hearing record.

U.S. Congress. House. Committee on Public Works and Transportation. (1982, Mar. 2, 3, 9–11, 16–18, 23, 24). *Improved operation, maintenance, and finance of the nation's water transportation.* 97th Congress, 1st sess. Serial No. 97-74. Hearing record.

U.S. Congress. Joint Hearing before the Subcommittee on Antitrust and Monopoly of the Committee on Judiciary, U.S. Senate, and the Subcommittee on Energy and the Environment of the Committee on the Interior, U.S. House of Representatives. (1978, June 28). *Hearing record.* 95th Congress, 2nd sess. Committee print. (Cited Horizontal Divestiture Joint hearing).

U.S. Congress. Office of Technology Assessment. (1981, Apr. 1). *Coal exports and port development: A technical memorandum.* Washington, D.C.: Government Printing Office. (Cited OTA Report).

U.S. Congress. Senate. Committee on Energy and Natural Resources. (1980, Sept. 16, 18, 19). *Coal exports.* 96th Congress, 2nd sess. Serial No. 96-159. Hearing record.

U.S. Congress. Senate. Committee on Energy and Natural Resources. (1981, Nov. 10, Dec. 1, 3; 1982, Sept. 16). *America's role in the world coal export market: Parts 1–4.* 97th Congress, 1st and 2nd sess. Serial No. 97-104. Hearing record.

U.S. Congress. Senate. Committee on Environment and Public Works. (1981, Apr. 21–23; June 8, 12, 16, 18; July 16, 24). *Water resources policy issues: Parts 1–2.* 97th Congress, 1st sess. Serial No. 97-H 14. Hearing record.

U.S. Congress. Senate. Committee on Environment and Public Works. (1981, Nov. 20). *S 1962: Figures on the local impact of harbor maintenance costs.* 97th Congress, 1st sess. Committee print.

U.S. Congress. Senate. Committee on Environment and Public Works. (1981, Dec. 15). *National harbors improvement and maintenance act of 1981: Report of the Committee on S 1692.* 97th Congress, 1st sess. Committee report.

U.S. Congress. Senate. Committee on Foreign Relations. (1981, Apr. 28). *U.S. competitiveness in international coal trade.* 97th Congress, 1st sess. Hearing record.

U.S. Congress. Senate. Committee on Governmental Affairs. (1981, June 8). *Factors affecting the export of high-sulfur coal from the eastern interior basin.* 97th Congress, 1st sess. Hearing record.

U.S. Department of Army. Corps of Engineers. (1978). *Waterborne commerce of the United States: Parts 1–5.* Washington, D.C. Government Printing Office.

U.S. Department of Army. Corps of Engineers, et al. (1980, June). *Moving U.S. coal to export markets: An assessment of the transportation system's capability to handle future coal traffic.* Prepared by the Army Corps of Engineers, Department of Commerce, Maritime Administration, Department of Energy, Department of Transportation. Washington, D.C.: Government Printing Office.

U.S. Department of Army. Corps of Engineers. District of Atlanta, Ga. (1980, Oct.) *Survey report on Mobile harbor.* (Available from USCOE-Atlanta).

U.S. Department of Army. Corps of Engineers. New Orleans District. (1980, Dec.). *Deep draft access to the ports of New Orleans and Baton Rouge, La.: Vols. 1–2.* (Available from USCOE-New Orleans).

U.S. Department of Army. Corps of Engineers. New York District. (1980, July). *Norfolk harbor and channels, Virginia, deepening and disposal: Vols. 1–2.* (Available from USCOE-New York).

U.S. Department of Commerce. Bureau of the Census. (1980, Aug.). *U.S. waterborne exports and general imports.* Annual 1979. FT 985-17-13.

U.S. Department of Commerce. International Trade Administration. (1980–81). *Foreign direct investment in the United States: Transactions 1980; 1981* Washington, D.C.: Government Printing Office.

U.S. Department of Energy. (1979, Dec.). *Coal exports study.* Reprinted in U.S. Senate Energy Committee Hearing: *Coal Exports,* 96th Congress, 2nd sess., Sept. 16–19, 1980, pp. 137–237.

U.S. Department of Energy. Assistant Secretary for International Affairs. (1980, Sept.). *Overview of U.S. coal export terminals.* Prepared by Soros Associates. DOE/IA/10066-01.

U.S. Department of Energy. (1981, Mar.). *Final report of the interagency coal export task force.* DOE-FE-0012. (Cited *ICE report.*)

U.S. Department of Interior. Bureau of Mines. (n.d. c. 1978). *U.S. bituminous coal exports used for metallurgical purposes, 1971–1978.* Prepared by G. Markon. Unpublished. (Received from National Coal Association.)

U.S. Department of Interior. Bureau of Mines (1982). *Minerals Yearbook, 1980; Area reports: International.* Washington, D.C.: Government Printing Office.

U.S. Federal Trade Commission. Bureau of Economics and Bureau of Competition, (1978, Nov.). Staff report on the structure of the nation's coal industry. FT 1.2: C63/3/964-79-7814. (Cited *FTC report.*)


## MAGAZINES AND NEWSPAPER ARTICLES

*Business Week.* (1979, Aug. 20). Coal: The global market boom forced by OPEC. No. 2599, p. 36.

*Business Week.* (1979, Sept. 24). The oil majors bet on coal. No. 2604, pp. 104–7.

*Business Week.* (1979, Oct. 29). The new international strategy for U.S. coal. No. 2609, pp. 91; 95.

*Business Week.* (1981, Sept. 21). BP's drive for a share of U.S. coal exports. No. 2706, p. 35.

*Coal Industry News.* 1980–82. [Weekly newspaper.] Special issues on coal exports June 19, 1981; July 13, 1981.

*Forbes.* (1980, Aug. 18). Hughey, A. The growing boom in coal exports, *126* (4), 46, 48.

*Fortune.* (1962, Dec.). Tugendhat, G. A billion-dollar coal market? pp. 102–5.

*Fortune.* (1977, May). Loomis, C.J. Down the chute with Peabody coal, pp. 228–33.

*Fortune.* (1981, Dec. 14). White, D.F. The coal-export gamble, pp. 122–29.

*Harvard Business Review.* (1983, July).

*Industry Week.* (1981, May 18). Coal exporters may be a bit too eager, pp. 42, 44–45.

*Inside DOE* [Previously *Inside Energy,* weekly newsletter of the Department of Energy].

*International Coal Report.* [News digest published by *Financial Times,* London]. 1980–82. Cited *ICR.*

*Journal of Commerce.* (1980, Nov. 5). Mantrop, S. Coal industry plans to invest in export port facilities.

*Journal of Commerce.* (1981, Feb. 17). Coal transportation: Mine to market. [Special issue.]

*Journal of Commerce.* (1981, Oct. 2). Mongelluzzo, B. Task force to probe New Orleans hot coal.

*Journal of Commerce.* (1981, Dec. 3). Morison, R.F. Senate panel clears port development bill.

*Los Angeles Times.* (1981, Nov. 10). Trounson, R. & LaRiviere, A. Stubborn ship fires linked to low-grade coal. Reprinted in Senate, Energy Hearing record, Nov. 10, 1981, pp. 610–11.

*National Journal.* (1980, May 24). Madison, C. The coal industry remains uneasy but an export boom may be on the way, pp. 848–50.

*National Journal.* (1981, Feb. 7). Madison, C. Money for deeper U.S. coal ports—Needed or just more pork barrel? pp. 225–28.

*New York Times.* (1980, May 18). Looking for the catch in coal [Editorial].

*New York Times.* (1981, Dec. 23). Making coal pay for itself [Editorial].

*New York Times.* (1982, Jan. 13). Trent, P.C. (Chairman Public Securities Association). How to finance port dredging. [Letter to the editor], p. 22.

*New York Times.* (1982, Jan. 23). Whose gravy train of coal? [Editorial on rail rate regulation].

*Richmond Times Advocate.* (1980, June 13). Brydges, M. Coal confusion clarified before solons.

*St. Louis Post Dispatch.* (1981, July 19). Reagan will stress coal sales abroad, 14A.

*Wall Street Journal.* (1980, July 18). Petzinger, T. Jr. Coal exchange at Hampton roads being pushed by businessmen's group.

*Wall Street Journal.* (1980, Aug. 29). Petzinger T., Jr. Inadequate U.S. port facilities threaten potentially huge export market for coal.

*Wall Street Journal.* (1980, Dec. 22). Petzinger, T., Jr. Digging deeper: Major oil companies increase their share of U.S. coal output, p. 1, 13.

*Wall Street Journal.* (1981, Feb. 27). Petzinger, T., Jr. Inadequacy of U.S. coal export terminals sparks oil-money push to expand capacity.

*Wall Street Journal.* (1981, Mar. 18). Cutler, E.R. The U.S. role in world coal [Letter to the editor], p. 28.

*Wall Street Journal.* (1981, Mr. 26). CFTC accuses firm and others of selling illegal coal futures, p. 44.

*Wall Street Journal.* (1982, Mar. 30). Carey, S. Planned expansion in coal loading ports is scaled back as the export boom wanes, p. 29.

*Washington Post.* (1981, May 29). Behr, P. Baldridge suggests ways to increase coal export.

*Washington Post.* (1981, Nov. 18). Head of North American Coal Exchange indicted.

*Washington Post.* (1983, Feb. 25). ICC proposes major changes in railroads' coal hauling monopolies, p. C9.

*Washington Post.* (1983, Mar. 4). Feaver, D.V. ICC deregulates coal box car railroad rates, p. C8.

*World Coal.* (1978-1981, Nov. issues), Markon, G. World coal trade. Nov. 1978, pp. 20–23; Nov. 1979, pp. 28–33; Nov. 1980, pp. 36–41; Nov.-Dec. 1981, pp. 43–49. (Cited Markon, *World Coal*).

*World Coal.* (1979, Nov.). Bennett, O., Jr. USA coal industry: Demand-limited, pp. 46–47.

*World Coal.* (1979, Dec.) Doerell, P. U.N. symposium stresses bright coal future, pp. 20–21.

*World Coal.* (1980, April). No. 4.

*World Coal.* (1980, Nov.). Quenon, R.H. United States: Coal's renaissance may be at hand, pp. 50–52.

*World Coal.* (1981, Feb.). Doerell, P. Seaborne steam coal trade may quadruple in 1980, pp. 27–28.

*World Coal.* (1981, May-June). Doerell, P. Coal prices surge upward, p. 74.

*World Coal.* (1981, Sept.-Oct.). Schneiderman, S.J. Coal buyers and sellers talk key issues at "coal summit," pp. 68–69.

*World Coal.* (1981, Nov.-Dec.). Samples, R.E. United States moving to realize a golden opportunity, pp. 84–86.

## COAL INDUSTRY PUBLICATIONS

*Coal Daily* 6/5/80. [Newsletter, Pasha Publications].

*Coal Now.* (1980–82). [Newsletter of the Mining and Reclamation Council of America].

*Coal Outlook* 8/11/80. [Magazine, McGraw-Hill].

*Keystone Coal Industry Manual.* (1979–81). Prepared by Mining Information Services of the McGraw-Hill Mining Publications. New York: Charles H. Daly, McGraw-Hill.

Keystone Coal Industry Manual. *U.S. coal production by company, 1982.* (1983). New York: McGraw-Hill.

*Keystone News Bulletin: Coal Industry Activity Report.* (Occasional issues 1982–84). New York: McGraw-Hill.

National Coal Association. (1980–82). *International Coal Review.* [Statistical summary of exports and newsletter.]

National Coal Association. (1980, May 7). *Report to the President (Carter).* Washington, D.C. National Coal Assocation.

*NCA Coal News.* (1980–82). [Weekly newsletter of the National Coal Association].


## PRIVATE TECHNICAL REPORTS

Bentz, E.J. & Associates, Inc. (1981, July). *Economic study of the impact of a 55-foot channel on various cargo movements in the port of New Orleans.* Prepared for the Board of Commissioners of the Port of New Orleans. Unpublished paper. (Available from the Port of New Orleans).

Board of Commissioners of the Port of New Orleans. (1980, 1981). *U.S. coal export opportunities and the critical need for deepening the lower Mississippi River channel.* [Brochure and report].

Consolidation Coal Company. (1981). *Report on coal exports.* (Available from Consolidation Coal Company).

Data Resources, Inc. (1980, July 25). *Oceanborne coal export facilities in the 1980's.* Prepared by Ruth S. Carey, DRI Coal Service, pp. 61–63.

Illinois Central Gulf Railroad. (1980, Oct. 10). *The world export coal market.* Prepared by ICG Railroad Marketing Department. (Available from ICG Railroad).

Peabody Coal Co. (1981, Feb. 28). *Impact of increased steam coal exports on the Corps of Engineers proposed project for deep draft access to the ports of New Orleans and Baton Rouge, La.* [Technical report]. (Available from Peabody Coal Co.). Reprinted in Senate, Energy Committee hearing record, Dec. 3, 1981, pp. 140–79.

Western Governors Policy Office. Western Coal Export Task Force. (1981, Dec.). *Western U.S. steam coal exports to the Pacific Basin.* Denver, Col.: Western Governors Policy Office. (Cited WESTPO report). Excerpts reprinted in Senate Energy Committee hearing record, Dec. 1, 1981, pp. 127–491.

## CONFERENCE PROCEEDINGS, ANNOUNCEMENTS, PRESS RELEASES, AND MISCELLANEOUS MATERIALS

American Association of Port Authorities. (1981, Feb. 17-19). *Coal and ports seminar.* [Conference proceedings.]

*Coal Outlook.* (1980, Nov. 10-11). *Mine to Market: Coal transportation today and tomorrow.* [Conference proceedings and papers.]

The Energy Bureau, Inc. (1980, Dec. 6-7). *Coal exports.* [Conference proceedings.]

U.S. Department of Commerce. (1981, July 27). *[Reagan] Administration's coal export policy unveiled.* [Press release.]

# Names Index

# Subject Index

# About the Author

Kathryn Simpson Rogers is a Senior Associate at the Center for the Study of Data Processing, Washington University St. Louis, where she conducts research on organizational information systems and teaches courses in management and enterprise-wide planning for business executives.

She has done a variety of interdisciplinary research and has consulted for business, government, and nonprofit organizations.

Dr. Rogers holds a B.A. *magna cum laude* from Smith College, an M.A. from Columbia University, and a Ph.D. from Washington University St. Louis.